CLAIMING THE VIRGIN

CLAIMING THE VIRGIN

The Broken Promise of
Liberation Theology in Brazil

Robin Nagle

ROUTLEDGE: NEW YORK & LONDON
1997

Published in 1997 by
Routledge
29 West 35th Street
New York, NY 10001

Published in Great Britain by
Routledge
New Fetter Lane
London EC4P 4EE

Library of Congress Cataloging-in-Publication Data

Nagle, Robin.
    Claiming the Virgin : the broken promise of liberation theology in Brazil/Robin
Nagle.
       p. cm.
    Includes bibliographical references and index.
    ISBN 0-415-91566-X (alk. paper).—ISBN 0-415-91567-8 (pbk. alk. paper)
    1. Catholic Church–Brazil—Recife—History—20th century. 2. Mary, Blessed
Virgin—Cult–Brazil—Recife. 3. Liberation—religious life and customs. 5. Recife
(Brazil)—Church history—20th Century.
    I. Title.
BX1467.R43N34 1997
282'.8134–dc21   96-48791
                                                  CIP

For Libbet Crandon-Malamud
1948–1995

~ CONTENTS ~

⋙ ACKNOWLEDGMENTS ⋘

This work would not exist without the help of many people, and it is impossible to thank them here in the measure they deserve. Without the aid of the John D. and Catherine T. MacArthur Foundation, the research would not have happened; in 1989 the Foundation supported me in a pre-dissertation research summer in Recife and other parts of Brazil, and then again in 1990 and 1991 for longer fieldwork. Once I returned to the United States, the Roothbert Fund aided with some write-up support. I thank both organizations for their resources and generosity.

Among the individuals who helped bring this to fruition, those to thank first, and to thank most deeply, are the residents of the Morro da Conceição. For no reason except their own graciousness and warmth, they welcomed my into their homes, families, and lives. They were patient with my many questions, seemingly endless curiosity and chronic cultural ineptitudes. Many of them have become lifelong friends. Of those, none is more dear to me than Lina and Dijé, and now Dogival and Elizangela, with whom I lived and to whose home I return whenever I'm in Recife. I would not have lasted, nor have learned as much, without their wisdom, humor, guidance, and trust.

I'm also especially indebted to members of the Morro's Conselho de Moradores, or Residents' Council, as well as members of The Resistance, who took the time to read and comment on a previous draft of this work. Their insights, comments, and corrections were invaluable. They will not necessarily agree with everything I say in this version, but I hope they recognize that I took many of their suggestions to heart.

There were many outside the Morro, in Recife and other parts of Brazil, who deserve great thanks. Sidney Pratt, along with Jucy Barbosa, helped me start and on many occasions kept me going. Bob Singelyn pointed me in the right direction from the very beginning. Virginia Barry gave me balance, the benefit of her profound and quiet wisdom, and her friendship. Cecília Mariz, John and Genene Murphy, Roberto Motta, Marjo de Theijo, and Cecília Sardenberg kept me sane, as did Rosalee Bender, Rachel Prance, and many of the Mennonites living in Recife during the early 1990s. Even more important, all these people were especially helpful when I needed to talk through problems with the research, with my conceptualizations, with my confusion in confronting what often seemed enigmas of life in northeast Brazil.

Many in North America were vital to this project's development. I'm especially grateful to Annette Weiner, who was my most astute and demanding critic. But for her insights, and especially her hard questions and insistent encouragement, I'd still be floundering. I'm indebted to Tom de Zengotita for his patient and penetrating analyses, and owe Claire Cesareo Silva and Elizabeth McAlister more appreciation than I'll ever finish showing them. A bow of appreciation and gratitude to Fred Myers for acting on a hunch and suggesting this to Routledge in the first place. Thanks to those who commented on parts or earlier drafts of this, including Ted Bestor, John Burdick, Eric Canin, Doug Chalmers, Meg Crahan, Carman St. John Hunter, James Kinsella (particularly for his keen editor's eye and flair), Chris Kyle, Cathy Maternowska, George Nagle, Margo Nagle, Daniela Peluso, Barbara Price, Louise Quayle, Paula Rubel, Steven Rubenstein, Irwin Stern, and the anonymous reader at Routledge. Thank you, of course, to Estelle Peisach, and to Monique Guillory and especially to Shalini Shankar for expert library sleuthing and general good will and assistance, and to Mariel Rose for her meticulous work on the index.

Special thanks to some special teachers who marked me for life. Carolyn Dougall and Ellen Schultz taught me much about writing, self-confidence, and teaching with heart and integrity. Alice Carse, who died in 1991, taught me a quieter, deeper way of asking questions and I wish I'd had her guidance in writing this work.

Libbet Crandon-Malamud, my advisor throughout graduate school, died in 1995, and I miss her tremendously — as do all of us lucky enough to have worked with her. Her comments on an earlier draft of this were remarkable for their insight, knowledge, humanity, and thoroughness. She was a scholar of rare intelligence and unassailable integrity, and her warmth touched everyone close to her. Anthropology and academia are much the poorer without her.

Finally, but not least, for their persistent encouragement and faith, blessings on my parents, grandparents, and sisters, and especially on my husband, Jacques Barzaghi.

Whatever merit this work has comes from the contributions of these gifted colleagues, friends, and kin. The flaws are only mine.

This book is about a religious and political movement that originated in Latin America in the 1960s and that tried, in part, to transform the continent's Roman Catholic church across twenty-five years. The movement, called liberation theology — or, as I sometimes refer to it, liberationist Catholicism — taught that genuine Christian faith requires its adherents to work for the transformation of the world, and that such transformation must include social change. Liberation theology ignored the separation traditionally made between secular or especially political arenas, and those more commonly thought to be in the church's purview, like prayer and worship.

This ethnography explores the implications of liberation theology as it was practiced on the Morro da Conceição, a community in the northeastern Brazilian city of Recife. The Morro was profoundly shaped by the teachings and practices of liberationist Catholicism. In fact, the Morro was so deeply influenced by the movement that it became a center for controversy about liberation theology's promises and failures. The controversy transformed into an open conflict, complete with military police, that lasted many months. For a while it put the Morro at the center of international attention as audiences within and outside the church watched to see which of the two primary factions in the conflict would prevail. One faction represented the liberationist church; the other stood for traditional Catholicism.

My goal is to explore the assumptions and practices of liberation theology as they came to life on the Morro, so that the movement itself might be better understood. At the same time, I want to shed light on the struggles of a low-income urban Brazilian community that self-consciously chose a radical form of its traditional religion. There were many utopian predictions about liberationist Catholicism, especially during its height in the late 1970s, but few of those predictions came to pass. The Morro story provides a close-up perspective on why some people found the movement so attractive, why much of the promise about liberationist Catholicism was never realized, why it aroused distrust and even hatred among many in its intended audience, and what now stands in space that had been filled by the liberation movement.

The book starts with an overview of liberation theology in general and its particular place in Recife. This is followed by a brief tour of the region's history. Liberationism did not spring whole from some clever priest's imagination, but rather grew slowly from a blend of influences that can be traced back centuries. Next I investigate the philosophical and political underpinnings of liberationist versus traditional Catholicism, and describe the Morro controversy in some detail. Then narrative and ritual expressions of both are offered as examples of how these underpinnings are made manifest. Finally, I connect the controversy to some of the political consequences and contexts that informed the region and the community, and offer an update on Morro life today.

I lived on the Morro da Conceição for a year between 1990 and 1991, and have been back several times since. The names used in the book are pseudonyms, with five exceptions. The community itself is given its real name, as are the two bishops and two priests who are central to it, because all were in local, national, and international press extensively. Trying to conceal their real identities would have been disingenuous.

While in Recife for my longest fieldwork, I engaged in the messy and sometimes boundary-less task of anthropological fieldwork, in which almost any interaction is a potential source of "data" and relevant written sources are pursued the way clues are ferreted out by a detective in an investigation. I conducted approximately 122 formal interviews and had countless informal, more conversational exchanges. I observed and took part in dozens of masses, meetings, celebrations, and two protest marches. Many fruitful hours were spent in the Pernambuco State Public Archives, the Recife Public Library, the library of the Archdiocese of Olinda and Recife, the library of the Fundação Joaquim Nabuco, CENDHEC (the Centro Dom Hélder Câmara, a documentation service in downtown Recife created to replace the archdiocese's dismantled information center), and the library of ISER (Instituto de Estudos da Religião) in Rio de Janeiro. I co-authored and helped administer a survey that revealed data on nearly 2,500 individuals. Over the course of the year, I accumulated roughly 1,500 pages of handwritten field notes, most of which were put on disk on a friend's computer in once-a-week typing marathons. I give this summary only to show the range of sources and events from which the information in this book was drawn, but it is not an unusual inventory as anthropological fieldwork goes.

There are two caveats that the reader must keep in mind in stepping into this text. First, I am not a theologian and do not pretend to be one. Any statements or claims that sound theological are meant to reflect the views of community residents, or in some cases liberation theologians. Second, I do not believe that liberation theology was "really" a cloaked way to be politically active in a time and place when such activity was dangerous, or that it was "really" all about politics, just dressed up in liturgy. Certainly liberationist Catholics were political in outlook and behavior, as I hope I reveal. But there's a big difference between political engagement inspired by a particular interpretation of faith, and political engagement that is not informed by religiosity. The end results may be the same, but the process of getting to those results and the meanings they evoke are different for liberationist and secular activists. As Mary Douglas notes, "A religious debate goes straight to first principles. . . . A religious debate parades transcendental reasons at the outset" (1992:271). The Roman Catholics represented here were first Roman Catholics; some of them were also grassroots strategists. The religious motives of liberationist Catholics are given great weight because I believe they were central to the movement's strength — and, eventually, to what became its current state of quiescence.

Boa Vista

Macapa

Fonte Boa • Manaus • Santarem

Belem
Sao Luis • Fortaleza

Teresina • Natal

BRAZIL Recife

Porto Velho • Porto Nacional

Aracaju
Salvador

Lake
Titicaca • Cuiaba ■ Brasilia

• Goiania

Belo Horizonte • Vitoria

Sao Paulo • Rio de Janeiro

Curitiba

Florianopolis
Porto Alegre

Yesenia Figueroa

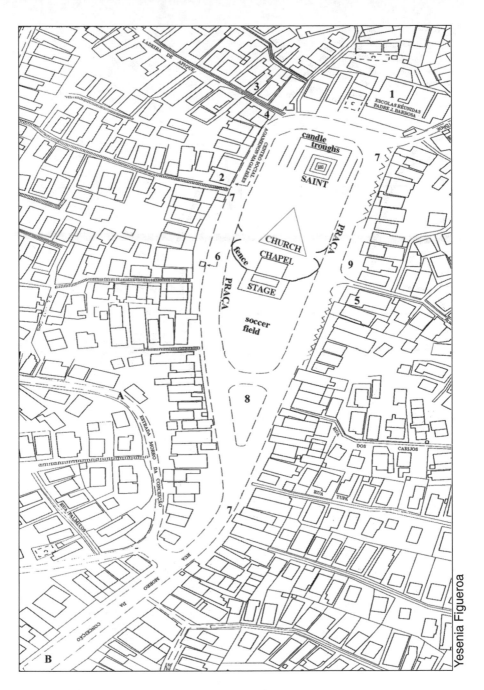

1. Elementary School
2. Health Post
3. Residents' Council
4. Sãn Joias Bar
5. Resistance Chapel

6. Herbalist Stand
7. Bus Stops
8. Children's Playground
9. Resistance Bar

CONSECRATED POLITICS AND ACTIVIST RELIGION

NORTH AMERICA, SOUTH AMERICA

A photograph of a man's face, calm and bright eyed, fills the black-and-white television screen. The picture changes: the same man is in front of many people, his rich voice nearly chanting, "I have a dream!" In a third scene, the man is with a crowd walking down a dusty road.

It is 1968. I am seven years old, sitting on my father's lap as he and my mother and I watch these images. I know four things about the man on TV. He is dead because someone shot him; he was a minister, like my father; he was important and many people loved him, but some also hated him; and his death has upset my parents. My father is very still. My mother weeps.

"This was a great man," my father says quietly. "Remember him. We may never know another leader like him." Years later I learned that he marched with Martin Luther King Jr. in Selma, Alabama. Dad was arrested during the march; a photocopy of his mug shot hangs over my desk.

King's work was my father's most passionate political and pastoral commitment in the early days of the civil rights era. From civil rights work he became involved in antiwar activities and the nascent environmental movement. My mother was similarly engaged, founding an inner-city alternative school and embracing what was then called "women's lib." Throughout our early childhood, my parents took my sister and me to political rallies, antiwar demonstrations, and interfaith worship services complete with folk guitars, felt banners, improvised liturgies, and clerics in sandals.

My parents' activism found its primary outlet through our most important institutional affiliation, the same place King had his start: the church. When I was a child it never occurred to me that anyone would question King, a preacher, extending his pulpit well beyond the confines of a church building. As I understood it, this was a clergyman's job. God was part of everything in the world, I was taught, and depended on His human children to right such wrongs as racism, sexism, and unjust war.

Through the Biblical metaphors of his civil rights struggles, by blending the passion of religious conviction with the clarity of a political goal, King sought nothing less than to reconfigure the ideology of a nation. He was not alone in his work to sanctify a political issue — or to politicize a religious endeavor.[1] He had counterparts all over the world, especially in Latin America. Though they worked from different social, political, and theological contexts, there were Roman Catholics all over South America who shared King's dedication to what became known as "social justice." In 1968, the year King was assassinated, hundreds of Catholic bishops from South and Central American gathered in Medellín, Colombia, for the once-a-decade meeting of CELAM (*Conferência Episcopal Latino Americana*, or Latin American Bishops Conference) to proclaim their church's place on the side of the oppressed. In an unprecedented attempt to realign an ancient transnational institution — the Roman Catholic church — this meeting concluded that the church could only fully know itself as holy if its allegiance were to those whose voices were least heard, whose needs were most often ignored, and whose plight was most desperate.

Many of these bishops and the priests working under them echoed King's cry for political dignity and for economic equity. Several Brazilians in particular had strong voices among their clergy colleagues and, more importantly, among the people whom they believed the church must serve. For instance, Dom Hélder Câmara Pessoa, archbishop of Brazil's northeastern diocese of Olinda and Recife from 1964 to 1985, publicly objected to many measures of repression adopted by the military dictatorship that took over Brazil in 1964. More than once the leaders of the dictatorship proposed Dom Hélder's assassination, though they did not dare kill the Dom, who had international stature as a defender of human rights and critic of the government. The same immunity, however, did not extend to his colleagues. In late May of 1969, a 27-year-old priest named Antônio Henrique, one of Dom Hélder's close associates, was kidnapped, tortured, and murdered. His body, naked and mangled, was found two days later in the meridian of a highway that surrounds Recife.[2] A funeral procession a few days later drew 10,000 participants, though it received scant attention from the local press.

Likewise, Dom Paulo Evaristo Arns, archbishop of São Paulo, faced threats of violent reprisals when he championed the rights of the poorest in his sprawling diocese. In the central Brazilian state of Mato Grosso, Dom Pedro Casaldáliga fought for the rights of indigenous peoples who were being driven from their lands by speculators, developers, and utility companies. He, too, was repeatedly threatened, especially with deportation (he is from Spain). In the north, Dom Antônio Fragoso, archbishop of the diocese of Crateús in the state of Ceará, quietly launched Bible-study communities in the early 1960s, part of an initiative that came to be called ecclesial base communities, or CEBs (for *comunidades eclesiais de base*), and that over the years grew into centers for social activism.

These men were part of a movement meant to promote an understanding of Roman Catholic faith and practice that erased established divisions between social and religious concerns. By 1971, the movement was called the Theology of Liberation.[3] At once fervently religious and overtly political, it advocated a Catholicism that read the Bible as a mandate for social change. Proponents demanded concerted attention for the plight of the poor by organizing demonstrations, creating watchdog groups that monitored human rights abuses, writing articles and books, and using the media creatively. They shaped Scripture interpretation, prayer meetings, and religious celebrations around themes of justice, solidarity, and finding practical solutions to a host of pressing material problems. Like King, liberation theologians questioned the ideologies of nations. They articulated eloquent (though occasionally utopian) challenges to the hegemonies of transnational economic practices, multinational corporate spread, and "development" strategies that promised to bring the best of modernity to the "Third World" but that instead often caused heightened misery.

I don't remember when I first heard of liberation theology, but by the time I was in my early twenties, I was intrigued. The movement sounded like King's work on a continental scale, and men like Hélder Câmara and Paulo Arns sounded like Latin American versions of the civil rights leader.[4] Frustrated by reports that depicted the movement only through theological or social theoretical analyses or through superficial journalistic accounts, I was eager to know what it looked like from the perspective of the people it was intended to serve.[5] I also wondered how the movement used symbols and rituals to attract adherents. Having grown up around churchly rites and tokens, I was sensitive to their powers of attraction. I was curious about how the primary symbols of Roman Catholicism were changed or reinforced in places where liberation theology took hold, how those changes were made, and where liberation theology fit in a larger picture of popular Latin American social movements.

I was in graduate school studying for my doctorate in anthropology when I decided to investigate these questions by making them the center of my dissertation research. After much consideration, I chose to do my fieldwork in Brazil, home to many of South America's most outspoken liberation theologians, with Recife as my base. Recife, a city of three million, sits on the coast of Brazil just below the shoulder of the continent. One of the oldest ports in Latin America, it has struggled under the burden of a depressed economy for nearly four hundred years. Starting in the late 1950s, it was an early home to some of the concepts that eventually informed liberationist Catholicism, and it became one of the movement's centers.

I proposed a straightforward study based on a comparison of two city parishes. The parameters of the research were to be defined by one fairly traditional parish that acknowledged little or no influence of liberation theology, and another that was self-consciously liberationist, preferably with one or two CEBs. I wanted two parishes that were demographically similar, roughly equal in size, and relatively close together so that I could travel between them easily. My central question was straightforward: What were the variables — political, historic, economic, symbolic — that made the movement attractive to members of one parish, while another similar parish did not embrace it?

Much has been written about liberation theology, from several perspectives. Theologians often portrayed it as the best new hope for coaxing Christianity into harmony with its more humane ideals (cf. Boff 1989; Mesters 1985). Some social analysts saw it as a revolutionary initiative poised to create genuine structural change as the poor — inspired, united, and organized — rose up with clear demands for a better world (cf. Berryman 1987; Foroohar 1986; Lernoux 1986). Journalists often showed it as a pitched battle of cynical church and secular powers against righteous, impoverished ghetto dwellers praying and plotting their way to political enfranchisement (cf. Brooke 1989; Hebblethwaite 1989; MacEoin 1980; Ostling 1989; Wirpsa 1990).

While such descriptions were sometimes simplistic, there was no question that liberation theology introduced significant changes to Latin American Catholicism and, in some places, to regional political rhetoric and custom. In Brazil especially, the official institution of the church had been stodgy, quiet, and focused on the upper and middle classes — in other words, directly relevant to a small minority and intent on maintaining the status quo. The majority of the country's population, while claiming to be Roman Catholic, had little contact with priests or other clerics and was left to develop its Catholicism on its own (Bruneau 1974; R. Levine 1995; Mainwaring 1986).

This changed with the agitations of liberation theology, which urged nuns, priests, and seminarians to step outside the faded velvet and chipped gold splendor of church sanctuaries and put themselves into muddy battles for land reform and squatters' rights, into the sweat of factory workers' union struggles, into the tedium of literacy programs and electoral campaigns. It has been suggested that Brazil's clergy "discovered" the nation's people because of liberationist activism (Mainwaring 1989:159), a claim supported by the church's history in that country.

A TRADITION REINVENTED ONCE AGAIN

The institution known as the Roman Catholic church has been around a long time. Depending on who is recounting its history, it started with Jesus, or with his apostle Peter, or with recognition of Christianity as an official religion in the year 313, during Constantine's rule of Rome.[6] Current estimates gauge worldwide membership at 750 million. Starting in the Age of Exploration, when Spanish and Portuguese explorers set off for parts unknown with priests on board, South and Central America became the region in which the church was most thoroughly represented; of those nations, Brazil today claims the largest number of Roman Catholics.

Part of the church's success, both in Latin America and elsewhere, has been its ability to create doctrinal continuity while simultaneously adapting to the popular culture of a given locale.[7] The word "catholic" means universal, and the church intends to present itself the same way wherever it is found. The church's central rituals (baptism, confirmation, communion, ordination, marriage, absolution of sin [now called reconciliation], and anointing the sick [now called Holy Unction, formerly known as Last Rites]) have remained static in their rough outlines across centuries (Shepherd 1965) while taking on particular shapes and tones in various places and times. This blend of stability and malleability is a principal source of the endurance that marks both the rituals themselves and the institution that perpetuates them. It is also a source of continual tension in the church as the forces of tradition and adaptation create competing pressures within the institution. It is part of the reason that the liberation movement became contentious.

Liberation theology represented the continuation of tradition even as it proposed a recalibration of many Catholic practices. The movement was, in part, a response to social upheavals that the postwar/ Cold War era brought to Latin America. Increased industrialization there weakened economic security, which provoked greater mobility of both urban and rural workers. Urbanization intensified, as did the strength of transnational economic forces. In rural northeast Brazil, a corner of the continent already under severe economic stress, these factors put pressure on landowners to increase acreage devoted to salable crops, to mechanize production for increased harvest yields, and to reclaim land that had been set aside for workers' subsistence. Sharecroppers and wage laborers alike found themselves pushed off sugar, cotton, and cacao plantations, and many journeyed to cities for new opportunities. City demographics were altered by the influx of these workers and their families, many of whom arrived without means or shelter. The same pressures that drove people from the countryside, however, were at play in the cities, and jobs were scarce. Migrants swelled the already calamitous *favelas*, or slums founded as squatter settlements that today ring every Brazilian metropolis.[8]

The radical changes that prompted and followed these shifts compelled many within the church — even at the very top of the church hierarchy — to question its established strategies for serving members. Changes in Latin American Catholicism coincided with, and were bolstered by, changes at the Vatican. From one perspective, these changes were decades in the making. Papal edicts like *Rerum novarum*, issued in 1891, addressed questions of workers' rights and urged employers around the world to recognize labor's basic needs and human dignity. But the event that had greatest immediate significance for the liberationist movement was the Second Vatican Council, a conference of the world's cardinals that ran from 1962 to 1965 and that was convened specifically to address the church's need for a clearer global mission and presence.[9] The church also sought a way to stem a growing loss of membership to ever more popular fundamentalist and Pentecostal movements. Vatican II, as the meeting was also called, urged the church to be more relevant by "turning outward toward the world" and by making social problems a central part of its focus (Della Cava 1989).[10]

The Council thus tacitly embraced trends that came to inform liberationist Catholicism unfolding in South and Central America. Clerics with a tendency toward liberation theology interpreted the Council as a call for priests, bishops, and all ordained persons to remember that they were servants, not privileged elites, and to structure their ministries accordingly. Bishops at the 1968 CELAM meeting (the Latin American Bishops' Conference) in Medellín took the Vatican's decisions as outspoken blessings of the church's work at the "base," or on the local level. Base communities, or CEBs, were strongly encouraged as the best way to make real the church's call to confront and ameliorate the needs of the continent's most disenfranchised peoples. Brazilians especially took this to heart; between the late 1960s and early 1980s, there were supposedly between 80,000 and 100,000 CEBs just in that country, involving one million to two million participants.[11] The next CELAM conference, in 1979 in Puebla, Mexico, pushed the church further by proclaiming that it must concretely demonstrate a "preferential option for the poor," an enormously contentious stand.

Negotiations on the institutional level were only as effective as their local implementation. Clergy around the continent who placed themselves at the forefront of liberation theology argued that the social metamorphoses causing confusion in the lives of so many were not adequately addressed by conventional Catholic theology, prayer, or ritual. Though it had long been church practice to serve the poor, this was usually done through charitable works, not by scrutinizing causes of poverty or by asking the poor to tell their own stories. Gradual renovations in various church practices were a necessary part of its survival across time, but many liberationists wanted to move quickly. Their enthusiasm often had an explicitly political tone and thus posed a different kind of challenge — in many regions, an unprecedented one — to both the church hierarchy and to state powers. A brief overview here of the new definitions and practices will give a sense of the movement's ambitions. It will also clarify some of the ways in which liberationists blurred once sharp distinctions between strictly religious matters and those that, according to some, ought to be left to the secular realm.

The concept of hermeneutics has been used for more than a century in studying the Bible (Dilthey 1976; Schleiermacher 1988). In conventional theology, hermeneutics means considering the perspective of those who wrote the Scriptures to better determine meanings hidden in the texts. Liberationists drew on the same notion to remind church leaders that Latin American Catholics understood the Bible and their faith from a unique point of view. They argued that unless the contexts of people's lives were taken into account, church teachings would not be fully meaningful. Furthermore, they claimed that people's own interpretations of the Bible must be recognized and even encouraged, thus allowing the faith to come that much closer to the daily reality of disparate — and often desperate — Catholics.

It was a radical notion. Instead of delivering doctrine to the faithful, this new approach asked the faithful to articulate their experiences so that the church could become relevant to them. It put individuals and communities at the center of the inquiry, rather than putting the church's advancement at the center. In asking that the views of those to whom the church delivered its message be accorded respect, and in urging those audiences to develop their own perspective on Bible stories, liberationist clergy were acting like Protestants, said some critics.

Liberationists drew on an approach called *conscientização*, or conscientization, to encourage Bible study from the perspective of those reading it. The word was coined by Paulo Freire (1970), an educator from northeast Brazil, to mean working within the conditions of people's lives to help them learn the validity and thus the power of their own perspectives, voices, and abilities.[12] He did not originally combine it with Bible study, but it suited liberationist pedagogical goals well.

The problem was that Catholics were unlikely to reach their own interpretations of the Bible if they couldn't read it in the first place. This was especially true in northeast Brazil, where illiteracy rates were as high as 70 percent. The Freirian method became the basis of a regional church-sponsored literacy effort when schools organized through church-owned radio stations broadcast lessons teaching rural workers how to read. Between 1959, when the first schools were launched, and 1964, when the military intervened, more than 6,000 were set up across the northeast.[13] The textbook developed for these programs, called *Viver é Lutar* (*To Live Is To Struggle*), included lessons that questioned salary and land inequities between bosses and workers, and that explained the importance of not selling one's vote.

Theologians and others justified their proactive focus on the poor by proposing a new christology, or theory about the life of Jesus. He was, they noted, a carpenter and fisherman — that is, a worker. Those he tapped as followers were similarly employed, which meant both he and they were poor. Though a common man, theologians said, Jesus advocated the overthrow of Rome's military occupation of Palestine and the creation of a new social order based on communally shared labor and resources. Mary was no longer depicted solely as the pious mother of Jesus, but as a worker's mother who knew poverty, harsh living conditions, and the degradation of losing a son not just to death but through a corrupt political structure. They pointed out that because the poor live in material conditions very like those of Jesus, and because they were the first recipients of Jesus's teachings, they are the Bible's chosen people and thus the proper first priority of the church. Because Jesus himself lobbied against the ruling government of his day, so the poor have the right — indeed, argued some, the responsibility — to agitate for the overthrow of unjust rulers.

Injustice in this new system was equated with sin, an idea basic to Christianity that was also retooled by liberation theologians. It must no longer be limited to the personal, they said, but must acknowledge the sinfulness of political oppression and economic degradation. Many added that capitalism must be recognized as one of the main sources of structural sin.[14] Liberationists argued that capitalism is an inherently unjust and exploitative system requiring the oppression of many for the benefit of a few. Following this, the central idea of salvation could no longer be merely the end result of receiving pardon for one's personal sins. Rather, salvation should mean an end to all forms of sin, especially structural and economic; thus, concluded liberationists, salvation and liberation were synonymous.

To make sense of these new emphases, theologians taught that God plays a role in human history as a contemporary actor in world affairs. Conventionally, God was understood to be outside history, a position that generations of Catholic scholarship found necessary for a deity encompassing both time and the universe. Liberationists said that by sending his son, God demonstrated an active interest in human history that continues today. They further argued that the only way God can be a vital actor in history is by relying on the faithful to carry out his will. In the Lord's Prayer, for example, are the words, "Thy kingdom come, thy will be done, on earth as it is in heaven." The "kingdom" is not an otherworldly haven but a tangible goal; in liberation terms, it is a social system built on justice, not exploitation, and on economies of shared resources, not capitalist hierarchies. "Thy will be done" means people working together to bring about the kingdom now, on earth, as a way of making real the will of God.

To bring about the kingdom, one must engage in orthopraxy, said the liberation theologians. Built on Marx's idea of praxis, it meant practicing one's faith in correct alignment with the teachings of that faith, or putting one's actions in sync with the tradition's orthodoxies. If, as liberationists claimed, church orthodoxy teaches that the poor are God's chosen people, then orthopraxy was the work required of each person of faith to transform the conditions of the poor. Orthopraxy often included activism, rallies, marches, community organizing, lobbying, and even running for office. To those following a liberation vision, activism and politics were not inimical to church teaching but rather a way of expressing one's faith. Jesus himself sought to overthrow a corrupt government, they pointed out, thus signaling God's approval of similar work. "I think that today the Holy Spirit is asking us to attend to the political dimension," explained one lay liberationist. "The Gospel's political dimension is a way of life, it's part of the life of Jesus" (LADOC 1986:3).

These modifications of traditional Catholic teaching were brought from theory into daily practice within ecclesial base communities, designed to be the point at which liberationist teachers and clerics made the movement real. CEBs often started as Bible study groups reflecting on social reality in light of Scripture and blending reflections with practical tactics that addressed specific issues of concern, which ranged from the very local to the most international.[15] Meetings start with a reading from the Bible, often from the day's choices or from Sunday's passages.[16] Then the passage is interpreted in light of what it means for those who are reading it. In a liberationist perspective, readers look for ways to legitimize social struggle, and often they try to see themselves in Bible stories and lessons.

One famous parable is that of the Good Samaritan, and its liberationist analysis demonstrates the movement's emphasis (see Luke 10:25–37 for the original story). The Samaritan comes upon a man who was left for dead after an attack by robbers; the victim had already been ignored by two other passersby who didn't want to get involved. The Samaritan, who did not know the wounded man's status, tribe, or station, rescued him, took him to an inn, and paid for his care before continuing his journey. On his way back through that town, the Samaritan checked to make sure his charge was recovering before returning home. Traditional interpretation suggests that the reader see herself in the Samaritan, willing to help a stranger in need. Sometimes guilty Christians will admit that they see themselves more honestly in the two who failed to help. CEB members, in contrast, see themselves in the man nearly killed and tossed by the wayside. After centuries of various exploitations, they argue, Latin America is like that beleaguered fellow. But the Samaritan is not an outsider who comes to the rescue; rather, Samaritans are individuals who combine their talents to organize a protest rally, to start a school, to found a day-care center, to call a negligent city official to task. The Samaritan is the person contributing to collective and organized strength from the grassroots (Maraschin 1988).

CEB meetings use Bible passages in this way to discuss diverse issues, from the practicalities of confronting the crippling burden of Brazil's foreign debt to plans for rebuilding a neighbor's house destroyed by heavy rains. They address the question of Christian pluralism as an organizing strength, ponder how to teach their fellow Catholics about their God-given responsibility to be agents for social change, and strategize bringing more young people into a crafts project intended to raise money for the parish.

Not surprisingly, given the thoroughness with which it retooled

Catholic theology and teachings, liberation theology became hugely controversial, yet in essence it was based on the simple notion that absolutely nothing is outside God's purview, and that this inclusivity must be acknowledged practically. In the places where the movement took deepest root, even seemingly mundane contests for things like food, shelter, education, and potable water could be — should be, asserted liberationists — consecrated struggles, revelations of faith, and acts of holiness. Not only were the struggles themselves sacred, but questions about why basic material needs required such struggles were also of central importance. This meant that the church's traditional alliances with regional governments could no longer be assumed; as a consequence, the controversies sometimes turned deadly (Arns 1985; Lernoux 1986; Whitefield 1995).

O Dom de Amor: The Bishop of Love

Throughout Latin America, liberation theology attracted dedicated Catholics and disaffected atheists, housewives and university scholars, factory workers and sharecroppers, the elderly and the young. Clerics and lay people determined to realize the promise of the movement in northeast Brazil had no stronger champion than Dom Hélder Câmara. During his twenty-one-year tenure (from 1964 to 1985), the diocese of Olinda and Recife became one of South America's most vibrant centers of liberation theology. To varying degrees, priests under his guidance led their congregations in critical social analysis, community organizing, and literacy classes, among other activities. The movement had vital institutional anchors in the Instituto de Teologia do Recife (ITER, or the Recife Institute for Theology) and the Seminário Regional do Nordeste II (SERENE II, or the Regional Seminary of the Northeast II).[17] Dom Hélder founded ITER and retooled SERENE II around overtly liberationist themes. Seminarians, lay college students, theologians, and clergy from Latin America, Europe, and North America filled the two schools.

The seminaries taught systematic theology, dogmatics, homiletics, and other traditional church curricula, with liberationist spins. The remarkable part of the requirements, however, was the Dom's insistence that students live in low-income and ghetto neighborhoods throughout the diocese — a far-flung jurisdiction that included the inner city and the rural reaches of sugarcane country — and devote a large portion of each week's work to those communities. The Dom believed that neither God nor the church could be understood only through classroom study, but must be comprehended through work with those dearest to God — the poor. This strategy brought the church directly into the lives of people who otherwise might not see a priest (or a priest-in-training) for months or years at a time. It also gave church workers a more intimate understanding of the conditions in which the majority of Recifenses live.

Equally significant to the liberation cause in Recife, the Dom launched a Bible study program. In 1968, after some of his strongest denunciations of government repression, the military forbade him to speak publicly. He argued that he at least needed to be able to reach his flock through a Bible reading, so in 1969 he was allowed one weekly radio broadcast. For fifteen minutes on Sunday evenings, he read and discussed a Bible passage on local radio; this broadcast became the linchpin of an initiative called *Movimento Evangélico Encontro de Irmãos* (Evangelical Meeting of Brothers Movement). Throughout the diocese, Encontro de Irmãos met in small groups in members' homes on Sunday evenings to listen to the Dom, then discussed his reading and their interpretations of the passage. Through increasingly sophisticated exegeses of Bible stories, and aided by an infrastructure based in diocesan headquarters, Encontro de Irmãos became the beginning of CEBs in Recife (do Passo Castro 1987); as of this writing, dozens of groups still meet weekly throughout the region.

"For the Right To Be Church"

I landed at Recife's Guararapes Airport late in the afternoon of October 25, 1990. I had already chosen one Recife parish to study and was confident that I'd find the second within a few weeks, but I arrived at an unusual moment, and it wasn't long before I realized that my best-laid plan to compare and contrast parishes was about to go awry (not an unusual experience in anthropological fieldwork). Six days earlier, on October 19, a neighborhood called the Morro da Conceição (Hill of the Immaculate Conception) had been stormed by military police. The Morro, a low-income community of roughly 20,000 on the northwestern edge of Recife, was famous as a center of liberationist organizing. The

police had been sent by Dom José Cardoso, the bishop who had succeeded Dom Hélder five years before, to cut locks off closed church
doors and supervise the installation of a new parish priest. This was
done over the vehement objections of hundreds of Morro residents,
and it nearly provoked a riot. It was an extraordinary event, even in a
part of the world accustomed to state-sanctioned violence.

The neighborhood raid was the eruption of a long-brewing feud
between Reginaldo Veloso, the priest who had headed the Morro
parish since 1978, and Dom José, his boss. Reginaldo, a soft-spoken, extremely articulate cleric, had an intense commitment to liberation theology and had spent much of his time on the Morro helping build a
savvy, well-organized, effective base for liberationist activism. Dom
José had replaced Dom Hélder when the latter reached the church's
mandatory retirement age in 1985 and had to step down. Reginaldo and
Dom José had become enemies within two years of the new bishop's
arrival, and eventually Dom José suspended the priest for insubordination. Reginaldo refused to leave his parish, allegedly at the insistence
of his congregation, and after months of fruitless negotiation, the
bishop called in the troops to roust the priest and to replace him with
his own man.

Though the decision was dramatic, it was not the first time Dom
José had used military police to achieve his ends (see the Addendum),
and his shaky popularity in the city dropped to a new low. Graffiti on
the Morro and around Recife called him "O Dom de Odio," Bishop of
Hate, a stark contrast to his predecessor's nickname of "O Dom de
Amor," Bishop of Love. Other sprawled messages demanded his removal and accused him of being the devil. Posters pasted on telephone
poles and walls throughout the city announced a protest demonstration at the end of October. The bishop expressly forbade any church
personnel from attending, but many did (though most were careful to
stay out of the eye of television cameras). More than 3,000 people from
neighborhoods all over the city tied up downtown traffic for several
hours, the biggest and most raucous event of its kind in several years.

Within the confusion of the Morro, it seemed to me, I found exactly the question I wanted to explore. The tumult surrounding the
community was rooted in disagreements among members of a single
parish, a place that had simultaneously embraced *and* rejected liberation theology. While media attention was heaped on those who

opposed Dom José and praised Reginaldo, more than a few Morro residents were relieved that the "Red Priest," as they derisively called him, had been officially ousted. Celebrations on the Hill hosted by Reginaldo's loyalists drew hundreds in the first few weeks after the police raid. Many participants wore T-shirts proclaiming *Pelo Direito de Ser Igreja* (For the Right To Be Church), a motto for Recife's liberationists.[18] But at the same time, the priest assigned to replace Reginaldo slowly drew his own followers, and within a few months there were as many people in the church on Sunday mornings as there were in the public school outside the square where Reginaldo led worship services.

Why did some Morro residents find the priest and his liberationism so compelling? Why did others come to hate him and all that he stood for? What did these reactions say about popular activism and its place in contemporary Brazil? What did it mean that the church was a source of such activism? What identities were shaped and what ideologies threatened by liberation theology? Whose power was challenged and how? What was at the core of debates about religiosity, political action, and the course of the community's church and future that excited such intense emotion? These were puzzles I wanted to explore.

The community's extreme reactions to liberation theology, at least as it was taught by Reginaldo, were shaped by a variety of complex, interlocking variables, which in turn point to reasons why the movement itself blossomed and then waned. Some of these variables were unique to the place and included the dynamics of the community. Long before it was a center for politically charged Catholicism, the Morro da Conceição, named for a version of the Virgin Mary called Our Lady of the Immaculate Conception, was a pilgrimage site. A tall statue of Our Lady — also called the Blessed Mother, the Blessed Virgin, the Saint, Holy Mary, Our Mother, and the Mother of God, among other names — dominates the southern end of the *praça*, or square, that levels the top of the hill around which the community is built. The Virgin, erected in 1904, was the Morro's first resident, and she draws more than a million devotées a year. They come especially in the nine days preceding December 8th, her annual *festa*, or celebration; then the Hill is so crowded that it is almost impossible to move up or down the streets and staircases.

Morro residents take great pride in the neighborhood's status.

"Who else gets to live in the shadow of Mary?" smiled Dona Leuza, who has lived almost four decades within a few dozen yards of the statue. She noted that others must travel a long way to be here only once a year, while she can be with the Blessed Mother any time she wants to. "Sometimes in the evening I just go to sit with her," she said contentedly.[19] During the festa, people living on or near the square are continually pestered by pilgrims asking for water, alms, or a bit of food. "It's part of what we give to Our Lady," said Dona Sheila. "We don't walk a long way or do a *promessa* [pledge] like that, so our promessa is to help the pilgrims."[20] The Virgin's presence and her power to draw thousands to the Hill give residents a strong sense of place that not everyone defines in the same way, but that many are willing to defend, particularly if they feel it threatened.

The festa's role in the community, and thus the community's role in the city, was increasingly redefined by Reginaldo. Issues like land reform, union struggles, and Afro-Brazilian empowerment were woven into prayers, songs, and sermons. Many Morro residents were delighted. "The festa made sense in our lives in a way it didn't before," said Dodora, a young woman who was drawn into the church, and into the festa, after Reginaldo changed its tone. She reflected the sentiments of more than a few when she added, "We weren't just praying, we were saying how we would change things."[21] Others were distraught. "It wasn't right," clucked a young man who had grown up on the Hill. "Our Lady doesn't want to hear this nonsense [*bobagem*]. She wants to know that our hearts are pure, not what [political] party we support."[22]

References to the exciting or inappropriate role of politics within church-sponsored events point to yet another variable that shaped the Hill's reaction to liberation theology. Morro residents had starkly divergent understandings of the right way to work the political system for the benefit of the community. Those on the liberationist side advocated community organizing and independence from individual politicians. "We can do it ourselves," argued more than one person. "*We* can determine what the Morro needs, and we don't need to beg for it."[23] They rejected the practice of making relationships with particular politicians whose status was rising and who could thus, perhaps, toss some favors to the Morro.

It was precisely this custom, in place for much of the community's history, that Morro traditionalists wanted to maintain. Residents of the Hill often worked on behalf of individual political candidates who in turn promised resources for that Morro resident and/or for the community, especially if a get-out-the-vote drive made the difference in an election. It reflected an age-old system common throughout the rural northeast called *coronelismo*, in which men with access to various kinds of power bestowed favor in the form of jobs, land, schooling, or pay raises on those beneath them who pledged loyalty. This system, with its echoes of feudalism, was the rule of law in much of the rural northeast until the latter part of this century. Though no longer the force it once was, its vestiges linger. Greater metropolitan Recife is the fourth largest city in Brazil, but a majority of its residents have ties to the rural interior. Many Morro traditionalists felt that patron/client relationships, the contemporary urban legacy of coronelismo, were their best hope for getting attention, and thus services and resources, from local political powers.[24] "We always need the rich," said one exasperated man who lived near the square and who rued Reginaldo's sermons that blasted the wealthy. "They do favors for us. Why should we alienate them? They have been our friends for years."[25]

There were other factors. The conflict on the Morro erupted during a time of significant transition in modern Brazilian history. After a long, slow *abertura*, or opening, during which the dictatorship turned over power to civilian officials between 1974 and 1985, the nation was self-consciously on the edge of a new era. A new constitution had been written and made law in 1988, after five years of debate. A tense presidential race in 1989 came down to two contenders, Fernando Collor de Melo and Luis Inácio (Lula) da Silva. Collor, with an elegant bearing and mellifluous voice, was a relatively unknown aristocrat from the small northeastern state of Alagoas. The less polished, more straightforward Lula was a former union organizer from São Paulo and leader of the PT (*Partido dos Trabalhadores*, or Workers' Party). The PT was a bold young coalition of leftists that had managed surprising victories in several regional elections in the previous four years and that drew heavily on CEB support. Collor won, though not by much, and some analysts felt it was his appeal in the northeast that made the difference.

Ironically, civilian elections deprived liberationists of their clearest enemy. Without the dictatorship to protest, new targets were needed. The floundering economy and runaway inflation seemed good replacements, except that these problems had no individual faces or identities and so were difficult to use. A focus close at hand came in the form of Dom José. More than a few of Reginaldo's followers on the Morro, and liberationists in other parts of the city, had no trouble lobbing harsh criticism at the bishop, but some of Reginaldo's parishioners finally turned away from him when he began publicly criticizing his new boss in the press and on television. It was too great a breach of tradition, structure, habit, and their understanding of the church's tie to holy powers to accept the church's highest regional representative as adversary. After all, according to the structure of the church, the bishop was named by the pope, who was chosen by the cardinals, all of whom worked under the guidance of the Holy Spirit. In this logic, to question the bishop in any substantive, sustained way was to question God's judgment and thus the validity of the entire institution of the church. Many liberationists had no trouble doing exactly that, but for more conservative church members, it was unacceptable.

THE ANTHROPOLOGY OF INSECURITY

Liberation theology provoked a critical assessment of social and political relationships that many people had never before seriously questioned. The festa was a clear example of this. By linking it to political initiatives and causes like women's rights and unionization, its organizers tinkered with its tone, intention, and effect, transforming it into a high-visibility forum for liberationist teachings. This was a bold shift. The uniform rhythms and themes of the festa had given it a predictability that in turn had strengthened its appeal and drew attention, people, and money to the Hill for nearly a century. It expressed a deep and quiescent set of collective beliefs about faith, God, Brazil, community, and one's place in relation to those variables, a function common to pilgrimages and shrines (Bourdieu 1977:167; Bowman 1991; Gross 1971; Mernissi 1983; Sanchis 1983:267; Turner 1978).

These collective beliefs were not identical from one person to another, but their outlines were similar enough to create a common language and set of practices around the festa, and by extension around the Morro community. They included a belief in God and, for most, a close relationship with the Virgin Mary. For many, in fact, the statue of Mary *was* Mary, not merely a painted iron representation of her. There was a fatalistic attitude toward the neighborhood's poverty, and toward poverty in general, as a part of the way the world works. There was a sense of limits that marked the abilities and the futures of Morro residents and of others in a similar class. A common response to the question "How's it going?" (*"Como vai?"*) was "More or less" (*"Mais ou menos"*) or "It's enough to live" (*"Da p'ra viver"*). The world was to be met perhaps with complaint, but without substantial protest of the status quo. These convictions and coping strategies helped make sense of the often chaotic world of northeast Brazil and gave at least a semblance of security. They lent cohesion to the community because they were not questioned; indeed, they worked because many who held them were not entirely conscious of them. The festa in its traditional guise allowed their full expression, with both heavenly and secular sanction; its history reveals its transformation from an elite event to a purely populist gathering.

One of the most radical effects of liberation theology was to question many of those unarticulated beliefs and to challenge their veracity. On the Morro, the festa became an occasion for sophisticated social criticism, thus altering its function as an expression of collectivity. This changed tone was carried throughout the year. Reginaldo, many of his parishioners, seminarians who came to live on the Hill, and community residents who took up political activism through Reginaldo's urgings, questioned much that was previously accepted as given. Topics of criticism included the centuries-old scourge of regional poverty; the roles that God, Mary, and the saints played in the community's dynamics; and the relationship of communities like the Morro with politicians willing to cut deals with individuals and interest groups in exchange for favors. Ties between northeastern landowners and those without plots to cultivate for survival were scrutinized. Liberationists criticized patterns of migration that drew labor from the impoverished northeast to satisfy production needs of the wealthier south. And international bonds of debt and obligation that marked Brazil's (and much of South America's) ties to nations like the United States were cause of special condemnation. The question "How's it going?" (*"Como vai?"*) was often answered, "The struggle continues" (*"A luta continua"*).

Such criticisms provoked heated, often exhilarating debate as individuals began to understand themselves as part of larger processes that they previously had not analyzed but that had clear influences on

their daily lives. "Those reading groups changed my life," remarked Zé
Nildo, a young man on the brink of candidacy for Recife's city council.
He was referring to some of his first contacts with Reginaldo more than
a decade before, in a Center for Reading and Information founded during the priest's early years on the Hill. "I started to see the connections
between the way the world works and the way people on the Morro
live. Once that started, I could never go back to accepting life as it is."[26]
Depending on the place and the time, such analysis was potentially
dangerous. In the eyes of many who did not join the effort, it was plain
stupid. Brazil's military had made amply clear the potential cost of
such questioning; even before the dictatorship came to power and focused especially cruel attention on the northeast, the region's informal
but effective coronelismo system dealt harshly with critics.

One unintended but potent result of the liberationist tendency to
question was to heighten a constant and barely contained insecurity
that marked life in poor neighborhoods. This insecurity took many
forms, though its most common manifestation was violence and death.
Carnival in 1991 was deemed less violent than usual in the Recife/
Olinda region, when only sixty-three deaths were reported in a five-day
period. Murders, muggings, and burglaries happened often enough in
low-income areas to become legendary in more prosperous communities, giving places like the Morro a reputation as havens for drug-
crazed, gun-toting marginais (marginals).[27] I always felt the reputation
was a fierce exaggeration, though it's true that in the first six months I
lived on the Morro, there were ten murders. These, however, were not
random. Six were the work of off-duty police hired to dispatch inconve-
nient individuals, like the 18-year-old who learned the tricks of car theft
while visiting a relative in São Paulo and came back to ply his new skills
in Recife (but not for long). Four of the ten murders happened in one afternoon, when a long-brewing feud between two families met a bloody
end (see Linger 1992 for more about violence in Brazil).

Death from other causes is equally frequent. The Brazilian attitude
toward death differs from that of North Americans. It is more casual
(though not any less wrenching), more intimate, and more public.
Death in North America tends to be segregated from daily life by hospitals, doctors, hospices. In Brazil, people who live in neighborhoods like
the Morro often die at home or from accidents that are not so common

in the United States, like stepping on a live electrical wire that has fallen into a mud puddle during a storm, or from diseases like cholera, Chagas, or general malnutrition — "illnesses of the Middle Ages," noted a former Minister of Social Welfare (quoted in Branford and Kucinski 1995:21). Bodies are not immediately scooped up by ambulances but lie at home or in their crumpled state after a fatal accident. On November 2, the Day of the Dead and a national holiday, cemeteries are not only full of the living remembering departed loved ones, but are also graced by corpses of the recently deceased who await burial, wearing their finest clothes and looking waxy. Babies are especially hard to see this way; their glassy open eyes are deeply chilling. Burial plots are rented, and those who cannot afford one use a casket only to transport the body, not to inter it; once it arrives at the cemetery, the body joins the other dead poor in a common burial area, and the casket goes back to the store.

An unnerving sign of the easy frequency of death, by whatever cause, is seen in the casket stores that proliferate in Recife and in many northeastern cities. They are open twenty-four hours a day, since bodies are not embalmed and by law must be in the ground within twenty-four hours of death. It is eerie to be riding a bus early in the morning, or strolling down a street in the evening, or even traveling home in a cab late at night, and see the cheery coffin sellers lolling in front of their shops awaiting their next customers, the most ornate and decorated examples of their wares leaning against their store fronts. When I first arrived in Recife, I tried never to walk on the same side of the street as these shops, but the criss-crossing I had to do to keep this superstition proved too cumbersome.

Insecurity takes other forms. Health problems diagnosed as "nerves" but more likely rooted in malnutrition are especially common among women. Such a diagnosis gives them responsibility for a problem not of their creation, and demands a solution outside their means (Scheper-Hughes 1989, 1990). Inflation in the early 1990s was a continual punishment, making it impossible to plan even the simplest household finances or to anticipate how far a minimum salary might stretch from one month to the next. Alcoholism and family violence left scars, especially on women and children. Formal employment opportunities were always scarce, leaving many families dependent on the vagaries of informal markets and even illicit activities. Droughts in the region's rural desert sometimes swelled Recife households as desperate family members came to the city in search of work, relief, survival. Illness, always a threat, often ruined the precarious finances of an entire family if it lingered or if it struck a principal wage earner.

The solace offered by the church, and more importantly by the Virgin herself, is for many a significant antidote to the uncertainties of daily life. "I come here [to the church] to forget about everything in the day-to-day (*cotidiano*)," sighed Dona Maria Pequena, a Morro resident for many years. "As soon as I'm in this sanctuary, I can become calm again."[28] Her sentiments were echoed by several other women nearby. Tradition, thought to be natural, anchors the rites and beliefs that mute the anxiety inherent in class and economic degradation, and a shallow but intermittently effective harmony prevails.

Liberation theology evolved directly from the same realities, but proposed a very different response. One cannot escape uncertainties, said members of the movement, even in the sanctuary of the church, so let's learn how to change them. To do that, adherents proposed understanding them more completely. Thus began the liberationist drive to analyze, to penetrate, to question — and thus began its biggest threat to would-be followers who were not interested in knowing the "real" source of their insecurities, nor learning how they were charged with bringing about structural change.

The crisis that erupted on the Morro, and that epitomized much of the tension generated by liberationist Catholicism throughout Latin America, points to "incompatible theories of practice" (Bourdieu 1977:15) found within one supposedly homogeneous community and within one supposedly unified religious tradition. There were stark disagreements about the understanding of how one negotiates a difficult life, what compromises one will or will not make, and what accommodations are necessary to achieve a variety of ends. Such an array of choices in turn pointed to divergent definitions of self, community, history, tradition, politics, and religion; these were particularly contentious points of debate between liberationists and conventional Catholics. Liberation theology stepped into, and heightened, a controversy that touched on the most fundamental elements of life in a deeply insecure part of the world.

IMPLICATIONS, FROM SAINT TO CONTINENT

Both the success and failure of the liberation theology movement in general are clear in the particularities of the Morro da Conceição. People who had not crossed the threshold of a church in years were drawn back by Reginaldo's determination to link the church's message to the daily concerns of his parishioners and by his fearlessness in taking on sensitive political subjects. Many who had attended church all their lives found in the liberationist version of Catholicism a more vital and relevant expression of their faith. This experience was repeated throughout the continent, as liberation-minded laity and clergy gave activist language and shape to their liturgies, Bible studies, and catechisms — and extended their religious faith to political endeavors.

At the same time, however, liberationist changes in the Morro church, and in much of Latin American Roman Catholicism, alienated many who had been important sources of church support. Many faithful, lifelong Catholics did not recognize the rhetoric that they felt had replaced the calmer sermons they were used to from a priest; the new, overtly political tone of the Morro's annual festa was seen as a disturbing example. In Brazil and in other parts of the continent, recent and vividly recalled dictatorships still inspired hesitation among people unwilling to risk their own or their family's security to challenge powerful economic and political forces.

These two tendencies represented much that was right and much that was troubling about liberationist Catholicism, and on the Morro both trends had outspoken representation. One community, deeply divided, held people with an equally strong need for both practical solutions and otherworldly utopias, vision and solace, action and contemplation. In the parochial context of individual dioceses, especially in those countries that had known military rule, the movement questioned assumptions about relationships of power and control that had defined political and religious life for generations. In the larger context of historic Catholicism, these divergent forces represented tensions that the church has felt since its earliest days, when prophetic voices urging change met priestly voices urging caution and guarding the tradition.

Liberation theology never became the continent-sweeping peaceful revolution that many of its advocates had predicted; it is found today more in the remnants of what it tried to become than in an active, vibrant practice of what it promised. Advocates often professed a Catholicism that better reflected the aspirations of those bringing the liberation message than the needs of the people to whom the message was directed. The movement's biggest weaknesses were its inability to recognize the role of crucial historic, political, and economic forces that shaped the choices of "the poor," those meant to be "liberated" by this new Catholicism, and its inability to appreciate that "the poor" cannot be met as an undifferentiated collection of people with the same world view, needs, and desires. Even in a community as demographically homogeneous as the Morro da Conceição, there were vastly different reactions to liberationist teachings.[29] In trying to rearrange a five hundred year old tradition, liberationists did not always recognize the weight of a very old and particular set of constraints that shaped the lives of so many impoverished Catholics. Nor did they appreciate the strength of the institution in either blessing or damning their efforts.

The controversies that preceded and followed the police raid on the Morro throw liberation theology into sharp relief. The situation provides an ideal prism through which to refract the many elements that made up liberation theology in a place where it had clear institutional support, from the archbishop and from many among the laity, for more than two decades. How could a movement so heartening have yielded, finally, such inconclusive results? The story that unfolds here explains at least part of the answer. I move from a local focus to a broader perspective and back again to illustrate why, even in its extremes, the drama on the Morro resonated with incongruities and contradictions that were part of liberationist Catholicism in many parts of Brazil and in the rest of Latin America, and that in turn were tied to divergent strategies necessary for survival in various parts of the continent. I start with the figure who stands at the heart of the Morro da Conceição — its geography, conflict, identity — and at the heart of popular Roman Catholicism: the Virgin Mary.

2

PORTRAIT OF THE NORTHEAST

The Lady Leads the Way

As Nossa Senhora da Conceição (Our Lady of the Immaculate Conception), the Virgin Mary has lived on the Morro since 1904, longer than any other resident. Except for the coats of paint that have slightly rounded her iron form over the years, and a surrounding walkway that hides her original granite base and allows pilgrims to climb to her very feet, she looks like she did at her inauguration so many decades ago. A silver-painted cupola shelters her. A painted blue robe, lined in pink and gold, still drapes from her shoulders and covers her white dress. Her hands are folded in prayer and hold a rosary, her crowned head is tilted slightly forward and to her left, her eyes are soft, and her downward gaze is benevolent, even gently pained, or perhaps puzzled. She balances on a globe while serenely crushing a serpent underfoot. When she was first carted to the top of the hill and placed on her pedestal, she dominated an expanse cleared of the tropical forest native to the region, a space created to accommodate her and a city's worth of dignitaries, church officials, and citizens who celebrated her arrival. The year 1904 was a hard one in Recife, though not novel for the trauma; a dysentery epidemic had claimed more than 3,000 lives, no doubt upping the number of people who trekked to the Morro to pay homage to Our Lady.

Before the 3.5 meter, 1,806 kilo Virgin lived there, the Morro's only visitors were occasional picnickers hardy enough for the steep climb and happy for the views and perpetual breeze that the hill afforded. When the priests, politicians, and devotées of that first festa quit the hill after several days of churchly (and not-so-churchly) celebrations, the land beyond the Virgin's cleared ground remained lush forest, and no one lived nearby. If she had raised her head and looked straight beyond the Hill to the east, she could have seen other forested hills, then lowlands in a similar mosaic of green cut by three rivers winding seaward. The verdant hues of the forest were broken by the darker uniform green of undulating sugar stalks surrounding a few remaining local *engenhos*, or sugar plantations. Among the trees and engenhos was the occasional church spire or belfry tower, beyond which Our Lady could have seen the harbor. In 1904, Recife's approximately 115,000 residents had not yet moved far inland from the port, then crowded with square-riggers, coastal schooners, packet ships, chimney-funneled steam ships, local one-masted sailboats, *jangadas* (masted rafts of fishermen), and the occasional barque. Just north along the same shoreline the Virgin could have seen the older, faded graciousness of Olinda's hills, optimistically dubbed "Little Lisbon" when they were settled in the early 1500s. Beyond all this, on a clear day, she would have seen sea and sky separated by a line so pencil-thin that often it was hard to find.

The Virgin became known simply as the *Santa,* or saint, and her presence altered the place. To prepare her ground, a road had been cut into the Hill, making the Morro accessible, and a train line nearby made it an easy trip from the city. In 1906, a small round chapel with a tall steeple was built about 100 yards directly in front of the Santa to house offerings left for her and to provide clergy a place for small masses and other rites. A former slave named Dona Beatriz appointed herself the Santa's *zeladora*, or protector and caretaker. She was already old when she became the Hill's second resident. She kept her post as zeladora until she died in the 1930s, and some of today's elderly Morro inhabitants remember her with fondness and nostalgia. "Now she was a real zeladora," harumphed Seu Bitu, an old man who grew up near the praça. "She did it for love, and she never let anyone disrespect the Santa. None of this smoking *maconha* (marijuana) or wearing skimpy clothes around Our Lady. Dona Beatriz didn't allow any of that."[1] Dona Beatriz also helped with the annual festa, though this service never earned her the publicity that accrued to local merchants and church dignitaries on the same occasion.

By the end of the 1910s, rumors about a textile mill scheduled to open a few kilometers north of the Morro clinched its appeal as a place to live. The earliest homes on the Hill, made of mud and sticks, were built around the area cleared for the Santa, and she watched the community steadily create itself.[2] The chapel was expanded when a tiled roof was built out from it; with creaky benches inside, it served as a makeshift school run by nuns.

Our Lady in almost any form (of the Immaculate Conception, of Perpetual Hope, of Sorrows, among others) has the loyalty and devotion of millions of Latin Americans. The practice of venerating her was already old when the church arrived in the region half a millenium ago. Devotion to her represents a populist Roman Catholicism often independent of subtle distinctions in church doctrine or law. In every region that honors her with a shrine, statue, or pilgrimage site, the gifts and pleas left behind reflect the conditions in which her followers live. Such offerings and practices also mirror the relationship they have to their Catholicism. On the Morro da Conceição, the festa and the Virgin have been central to the community's identity throughout the twentieth century. They have also become central points of contention in a battle for control over the community's political voice, its history, and its Roman Catholicism. The fevered pitch with which this conflict was entered is not comprehensible without a glance at the larger forces that shape the festa, the Morro, the city of Recife, and the northeast.

THE SUFFERING OF A SUGAR ECONOMY

The Virgin is a repository for prayers, stories, gratitude, and longing of a people who live in a region quietly famous for its desperation. Northeast Brazil has been called "600,000 square miles of suffering" (de Castro 1969:22), "the basement of humanity" (Mesters 1985), "the largest underdeveloped area in the largest developing country in the entire Western hemisphere" (Webb 1974:1), "a concentration camp for more than three million people" (Galeano 1975:75), and a place of "sweetness and death" (Scheper-Hughes 1992:31). While richly lush, it is cruel, its beauty permanently scarred by its principle source of suffering: sugar. Because of sugar, the northeast has been a source of wealth for Brazil for centuries, but regional poverty persists. Even food is grown for export, with subsistence needs imported from southern Brazil and from abroad (Andrade 1980:30–40). Malnutrition is endemic (Reis 1981:41); an average daily intake of 1,300 calories per adult is common (Mitchell 1981; 2,700 is an adequate supply for men, 2,200 for women). The northeast has some of the highest birth and death rates in the world, and children top the death list: every year, nearly one million *nordestinos* die before the age of five (Scheper-Hughes 1989:8).[3]

The picture in Recife is not much better. According to a study released in late 1990 by Population Action International, a nonprofit research group based in Washington, DC, Recife ranks as the world's fourth most awful city.[4] It was bested in worstness by one city each in Nigeria, Zaire, and Bangladesh. According to federal and local statistics, nearly half of all Recifenses live in poverty, measured as a monthly income of 60 percent or less of one minimum salary.[5] More than 83 percent of the city's population is undernourished or malnourished (Clark 1991:182). Recife's predicament, and that of the northeast in general, is not remarkable given the staple product of the economy. Sugar fosters human misery everywhere it has taken hold. Though the Morro's Virgin is Our Lady of the Immaculate Conception (meaning hers, not her son's), the patroness of the region would more appropriately be *Nossa Senhora de Açucar* — Our Lady of Sugar — if Rome would ever declare such a saint. She would be related to *Nossa Senhora das Dores* — Our Lady of Sorrows.

The Portuguese learned to cultivate sugar from the Moors (who had learned it in India) and grew it successfully on their own in Madeira and in the Cape Verde Islands.[6] By the second decade of the sixteenth century, the ideal conditions of much of Brazil's coast made sugar the colony's first significantly profitable export, and the most successful early engenhos (sugar plantations) were in Pernambuco.[7] The soil of the northeast's littoral rainforest is particularly rich in humus and mineral salts, the warm humidity is not too intense, and predictable rains eliminate the need for irrigation. In addition, sugar proved to be one of the few crops not susceptible to the voracious *saúva*, or leaf-cutting ant, a predator that made much agriculture in colonial Brazil a nightmarish challenge (Dean 1995:79, 107–111). These conditions fostered such success with sugar that Recife was briefly the wealthiest port in the world as Europeans clamored for the increasingly popular stuff. In 1535, a pound of sugar on the world market was worth almost as much as a pound of gold (Scheper-Hughes 1992:37), and a sixfold increase in prices by the beginning of the seventeenth century kept it remarkably profitable (Frank 1969:152). By then, Pernambuco was the world's largest sugar producer (Cardoso 1983:75; Eisenberg 1979; R. Levine 1978:2).

The profits came at a price, though it was not the Portuguese colonists who paid. The first casualties of sugar were the Tabajara and Caetés, peoples indigenous to the region who were cajoled and then coerced into working the engenhos. The Roman Catholic church, which accompanied the Portuguese to the Americas, was instrumental in enslaving them; Jesuits especially were adept at founding settlements whose sole purpose was to "tame" indigenous Brazilians so that they might make better slaves. Enslaving natives was the first stable economic activity outside of sugar cultivation, and it helped alleviate the chronic labor shortage that hampered early engenho owners (Furtado 1963:43-44). The usefulness of indigenes in the cane fields, however, did not equal their initial help in harvesting brazilwood; many died of European diseases to which they had no resistance, or they rebeled, or they escaped. By 1584, most indigenous Pernambucans were gone (Cardoso 1983:67; Hemming 1978:76).

The Portuguese had been kidnapping Africans to Lisbon as slaves since 1441, and there were almost certainly African slaves on the Portuguese ships that first stumbled onto South America in 1500 (Cardoso 1983:73). As labor needs grew in their American colony, Portuguese landowners in Brazil looked to Africa. The year 1538 is estimated to be the first time people were taken directly from Africa to Brazil as slave labor (Schneider 1991:28–29); in 1559 a royal decree legalized 120 *peças de escravo* — literally, "pieces of slave" — for every working or intended engenho in Brazil.[8] By 1600, there were about 50,000 slaves working northeast engenhos. They were thought to be superior to indigenous labor because they did not die as quickly nor rebel as much, and it was believed that they were less likely to run away because, having been kidnapped from their home lands, they had nowhere to go (Dean 1995:83); nonetheless, escapes into the unexplored and mysterious interior were frequent.[9] Slave labor proved so crucial to engenho success and sugar profits that despite the high cost, their rate of import was increased; by the beginning of the eighteenth century, approximately half a million enslaved Africans were working Brazil's sugar fields (Stein and Stein 1970:42). Cattle raising in the dry interior grew with the sugar, supplying engenhos with beasts to carry burdens, to turn grinding stones, to provide fat for fuel and meat for food. Most of the sugar largess, however, did not benefit the colony at large, since 90 percent of it remained in the hands of engenho owners (Furtado 1963:17).

As long as Portugal kept her sugar technology to herself, Brazil's wealth was assured. The privilege lasted about a century. Early in 1630, fifty-six Dutch warships arrived off the Pernambucan coast; they were looking to take Recife, as a few years earlier they had taken Salvador, the nearest major port to Recife's south. The colonial governor evacuated his citizenry from Recife and from the more populous Olinda and fled inland, burning markets and engenhos behind him. He led his colonists, their slaves, and whatever livestock they could bring to the highest hill in the vicinity, called the Outeiro da Boa Vista. The Outeiro (which means foothill) was equidistant from Olinda and Recife and afforded a clear view of both towns. The surrounding forest provided ample fuel, and clean water was plentiful below the hill. The refugees built a makeshift fort, grandly named The Royal Fort of the Good Jesus, and successfully held off and harassed the Dutch for five years. Various dramas of fort life are recorded from what must have been a difficult half-decade. A young man who became a hated scoundrel after he was caught slipping letters to the Dutch was hanged for treason; a slave who had intended to use the confusion to escape became a hero after he decided to stay and fight with the Portuguese; a soldier on the eve of marriage was mourned when his wedding was postponed, first by the invasion and then by his death.[10]

The fort fell in 1635, and its inhabitants were marched to Bahia. The hill of the Royal Fort was called the Outeiro de Bagnuolo, after a Napolean count who aided his Portuguese fellows during the Fort's brief life, but over time it became known vaguely as the Morro do Arrayal — Hill of the Hamlet. When it was made the Virgin's home a few centuries later, Morro da Conceição became first its popular and then official assignation.

The Dutch were routed from Brazil in 1654, but the sugar fortunes of Portugal's largest colony were already waning. The monopoly on sugar technology had long since been broken by the Dutch, who planted the crop in their Caribbean colonies and were soon denting Portuguese profits. The northeast's economic glory faded fast; by 1675, its sugar was worth half what it had been, and it stayed cheap for much of the next century. An unpredictable series of booms and busts have marked the regional economy ever since.

The fall of Brazilian sugar supremacy prompted the first waves of what has become an old and intractable tradition in the northeast. Migration is so steady a part of life that one of the region's most famous folk art images is a clay tableau depicting a series of people walking single file, carrying sacks, pots and pans, children, and perhaps the family dog. In the last forty years, 24 million people have left the northeast in one of the greatest mass migrations in history (Sader and Silverstein 1991:39). They move from one possible home to another, pursuing work on engenhos, in gold mines, on coffee plantations, as part of the rubber boom, or in cities as maids, doormen, guards, laundresses, chauffeurs, cooks, nannies, gardeners. Some seek their own land to farm and they try the *agreste*, an inland region higher and drier than the sugar tropics and better suited to subsistence agriculture. Others venture into the *sertão*, the northeast's punishing desert. The size of France, it claims part of the interior of every northeastern state and is not an environment friendly to most crops. A few strains of cattle bred for the harsh climate seem to do well, but humans don't, and the deadliness of the sertão is legendary.

Migration was — and still is — an oft-tried solution to an untenable land sitatution in the northeast that dates from the earliest days of the Portuguese colony. To make the new American colony attractive, the Portuguese king persuaded some of his nobles to settle in Brazil. In exchange for peopling the land with colonists, warding off other Europeans, pacifying or eliminating indigenous peoples, and sending exports to the crown, these nobles were given broad powers of governance and the opportunity for hefty profits. The coast was divided into tracts approximately 200 miles long and extending inland to the Line of Tordesilhas.[11] The immense holdings were divided among family members and loyal friends, and for the most part they were controlled by a few powerful owners. A feudal plantation system with monocrop agriculture based on slave labor was the foundation of the northeast's economy from the early sixteenth century until the end of the nineteenth, with a governance style that discouraged change. "The lord of the sugar planation considered himself a miniature king," wrote northeastern historian Josué de Castro, "with an inalienable right to his lands" (1969:102).

Landowner domination in the northeast continued despite upheavals in Brazil's government. The Portuguese king escaped

Napoleon's armies by fleeing to Brazil in 1808, his entire court in tow. Ensconced in Rio de Janeiro, he opened the colony's ports to international trade, allowing manufacturing and commercial enterprises to flourish without restriction for the first time (Roett 1972:32). Rio glittered with a new sophistication under the monarch's influence, and Brazilian elites relished their novel liberties, cultural life, and intellectualism. In 1821 the king returned to his throne in Portugal, leaving behind his son Pedro as regent of Brazil. Once back in Europe, the king tried to rescind freedoms he had allowed during his Brazilian stay, but the local aristocracy resisted. After declaring the country's independence on September 7, 1822, the regent Pedro was named Emperor of Brazil, thus founding a brief American monarchy that some Brazilians wish were still in power.

In the northeast, these changes were watched with some concern, but the region's distance from the south and its relative autonomy from government influence meant that not much changed in daily life. Large landowners continued to be the rule of law in the northeast, which allowed them firm control over scarce and badly managed resources. Called *coroneis* (colonels), they were ever ready to squash rebellions, real or imagined, among growing numbers of landless peasants and restless slaves (Forman 1975:36–77; Frank 1969:154–55; R. Levine 1995:91–97; Murphy 1994:32–36). The most important trends that marked northeastern sugar production were stagnation and atrophy, as outmoded labor and land-use practices remained unchanged across centuries (Denslow 1987:121, 141). Slavery was abolished in 1888, but the conditions of engenho life were not noticeably different for former slaves; freed men and women often found themselves working on the same engenho that had enslaved them. In exchange for the right to build a small house and to till a plot of land, they pledged a given number of days' work to the engenho — and thus were transformed from slaves to indentured squatters and sharecroppers, "replacing the discipline of slavery with the discipline of hunger" (Mintz 1985:70).

Pressure from international sources squeezed Brazil's sugar industry at the end of the nineteenth century. Modernization in Caribbean sugar plantations, along with the expansion of beet sugar production in Europe, meant that demand for Brazilian sugar ebbed. To regain competitiveness, northeastern sugar growers turned to more sophisticated techniques. *Usinas*, or sugar processing plants, drew on machinery developed in Europe and North America to process cut cane (Denslow 1987:119). The increase in yield and quality was swift; engenho owners soon stopped processing their own sugar and instead grew cane to supply the usinas (Andrade 1980:97–124). The new production needs put pressure on land to the detriment of those sharecroppers farming subsistence plots. They were evicted and their plots were taken over, or they were ordered to grow sugar instead of food, or they were moved to land that was not suitable for growing food, or they were forced to work more days on behalf of engenho owners. As usinas spread, workers' conditions continued to worsen.

RELIGIOUS FERVOR FROM THE GRASSROOTS

Two particularly vivid responses to these pressures became well known in the northeast. Bandits gathered followers and roamed the backlands, brutalizing strangers and sacking rural landowners' estates. The more infamous were men like Antônio Silvino and the one-eyed Virgolino Ferreira da Silva, or "Lampião." He and his gang marauded across the region in the late nineteenth and early twentieth centuries, eventually meeting a bloody end in a dawn ambush. His head, pickled in a bottle, toured the countryside for a while and is said to rest in storage somewhere at the Federal University of Bahia. The one-eyed bandit and his taciturn lover, Maria Bonita, have become a permanent part of northeastern folktales, dances, songs, and popular art. Legend claims that he and others like him would have succeeded in toppling the strangling system of land control had they lived just a little longer.[12]

Religious and millennarian movements also attracted followers. In the 1870s, after a particularly severe drought savaged the sertão and killed half a million people just in the northeastern state of Ceará, a young priest named Cícero in the interior town of Joaseiro witnessed a miracle: a young woman's tongue ran with blood after she received the communion host. This happened several times and was interpreted as a sign of Christ. The event brought thousands for Padre Cícero's blessing and catapulted him into local power. His refusal to stop calling the event a genuine miracle eventually earned him excommunication from Rome, which ruled that there had been no miracle. He continued his priestly duties until his death in the 1930s and also held several local and state elected offices. He became, in many people's eyes, a local colonel, transforming Joaseiro into the region's most important economic center (Pang 1973–74:352). Today Joaseiro draws thousands of people from all over the country to a huge shrine of the priest, and the town's principle industry is hosting the *peregrinos*, or pilgrims (Della Cava 1970; Gross 1971; Slater 1984).[13]

Another celebrated local religious leader came into prominence in the 1890s, when an estimated 25,000 people who would today be called "disempowered" followed visionary Antônio Conselheiro to found Canudos, a settlement in the sertão of Bahia. Canudos was established after the Brazilian monarchy fell in a bloodless coup in 1889 (partly as a backlash against the abolition of slavery the year before) and the country's first republic took its place. The leaders of Brazil's fledgling republic had separated the country from any official affiliation with the church, to the mutual relief of both institutions and to the horror of those who heeded Conselheiro. This move, he predicted, was a prelude to the end of the world; only those who followed him would be spared the coming age of hell. The people of Canudos waited for the triumphant arrival of Dom Sebastião, a long-dead Portuguese king who was to ride into Brazil, restore the Brazilian monarchy, soften the hearts of stingy landowners, free the poor from their poverty, and establish a utopia.

Canudos drew adherents from all over the northeast, draining labor supplies in large numbers. Backland coroneis were increasingly disgruntled, but their attempts to curb Conselheiro's attraction were fruitless. A contingent of state military was brought in; they were repulsed. It took three separate military initiatives, the last involving nearly 9,000 state and federal troops, before Canudos was subdued by killing almost all of the original 25,000 settlers. Even today the site is unmarked and forbidden to be so, lest another charismatic leader decide to recreate something like it.[14]

Antônio Conselheiro's shortlived but passionate success at Canudos points to a significant gap in church influence in much of Brazil. Just as rural landowners opposed him, so did most clergy, who resented his successes in the face of their own largely ineffective attempts to control religious expression. For much of the northeast's history, church impact has been felt through its institutional absence, which has allowed for creative popular expressions of Catholicism that have little official encouragement. The Virgin who dominates the Morro da Conceição reflects a strong and deeply-rooted faith with all the markings of traditional Catholicism — but without much formal church guidance.

At the time Portugal colonized Brazil, the pope allowed the Iberian monarchies to appoint their own bishops and support their country's clerics. In addition, church tithes and other offerings went into national coffers, so church fortunes in Portugal and Spain — and later in the Iberian Americas — were intimately bound up with the well-being of the state. When Brazil declared independence in 1822, the Vatican gave the new nation's monarchy the same rights. A comfortable relationship between state and church throughout the colonial era meant the latter went centuries without building its own infrastructure, but rather directing its attention to those easiest to reach with limited resources. The urban middle classes and rural elites were favorite audiences, but neither the rural nor urban poor were often in contact with a priest.

Though the Roman Catholic church in Brazil was very small — so small that it would be hard to call it a significant presence in the colony (Bruneau 1974:16; Vallier 1970:44–52) — its tie to the government did not sit well with an increasingly intellectual elite after independence. The monarchy's overthrow in 1889 provided an opportunity to end the formal link between church and state.[15] The church was allowed to keep its lands, organization, and members, but little else. Vatican support for the Brazilian church came in the form of creating dioceses and appointing bishops, but the Holy See provided no financial or structural resources, and an already uninfluential body remained so. In 1889, there were only about 700 priests in the entire country (Bruneau 1974:38)

MOTHER OF GOD, PRAY FOR US

The church's small institutional size, however, did not mean that its religion was without reach. If measured by the enthusiasm given to saints' days, by statuary kept in homes, by rosaries fingered, and by prayers made, Brazilian Catholicism was thriving, even with little church encouragement. Fifteen years after the monarchy fell and the church received its independence, the festival to Nossa Senhora da

Conceição was born in Recife, one among many sites all over Brazil dedicated to Our Lady or to Roman Catholic saints.[16]

There are two stories about the festa's origins. Near the turn of the century, a ship off Recife's coast ran into trouble during a storm and started to sink. A sailor, praying fervently to Our Lady, promised that if all on board were saved he would erect a statue to her on the highest hill of the nearest land. The ship went down, but all survived, so the sailor build the statue on the nearest land — Recife — and the highest hill — the Morro. Once the statue existed, people started coming to talk to Mary on the feast of her Immaculate Conception, and thus the festa rather spontaneously came into being.

It's possible that this story has been conflated with the tale of a contemporary pilgrim who every year since the 1960s has traveled to the Virgin on December 8th by "swimming" two kilometers on his belly from a church near the bottom of the hill up the road to the monument. A newspaper described the motive behind his promessa:

> The boat was living its last moments. Water had invaded the hold and it was sinking fast. The night had no moon, the sea was stormy as never before, and tragedy was in the air. Women, children, and the wounded filled the lifeboats. The last lifeboat was setting off, dangerously full, and he found a tiny space in the prow. At daybreak, the horizon showed nothing to the nervous eyes of the survivors but sea and sky. Despair grew, worsened by hunger and thirst, after a day of sailing without destination and without news of the other lifeboats. It was then that he remembered Our Lady of the Immaculate Conception, responsible for so many miracles and the one his mother had talked about so much. He gathered all his faith and made a promessa to the saint. Two hours later, as if by magic, a ship appeared to rescue all passengers, some already near death.[17]

So faithfully does this man, thought to be a former Merchant Marine, fulfill his promessa to "swim" to the Virgin that other pilgrims look for him every year and walk beside him, helping him along the way and hoping some of his holiness will rub off on them. Surely, they reason, a man with such will has earned the Blessed Mother's esteem.

A second story of the festa's origins has more support from written records of the era. In the early 1900s, Dr. Carlos Alberto de Menezes, owner of a large textile mill on the city's outskirts, wanted to mark the fiftieth anniversary of the papal bull that proclaimed Mary's Immaculate Conception to be church dogma. Dr. Carlos, an outspokenly devout Catholic, was a board member of the local St.Vincent de Paul Society, started the first Catholic Conference of Pernambuco, and founded the Christian Workers' Federation, an organization that tried to "put into practice all the institutions and associations of economic, moral and religious order that assured to the working class their well-being, tranquility and happiness, as a result of the clear comprehension of their rights and responsibilities in a fraternal union of cooperation."[18] In the early 1900s, the Federation sold pamphlets with titles like "The Worker Question in the Light of Christian Principles" and "Professional Unionizing."[19]

When Dr. Carlos proposed a monument to Our Lady of the Immaculate Conception, Dom Luiz, Recife's archbishop, was enthusiastic, as were city leaders. Dom Luiz appointed a commission, headed by Dr. Carlos, to find land, raise money, and requisition an appropriate statue. The commission began seeking donations from local businesses, religious organizations, schools, and wealthy individuals. The local papers helped, urging people to contribute and publishing the names of generous donors.[20]

With Dom Luiz's permission, the commission decided the statue belonged on the city's highest hill, so the unpopulated Morro was chosen. There is some discrepancy about who owned the appointed land. Some sources say it was donated to the city by the church, while others say an individual family owned the land and donated it to the city, or perhaps they donated it to the church.

A "serpentine incline of a road" was cut up the hill and the land on top cleared and leveled.[21] A statue was commissioned for 20,000 francs from the firm of Vaillant Nast et Cie in Paris. The Virgin was to stand on a granite pedestal, the stones for which were cut and shipped from Rio de Janeiro. To deliver the statue to the top of the hill, a trolley track was built straight up one side of the Morro (the track was dismantled after the statue was delivered and became the hill's main staircase, the 300-step Ladeira de Apique).

The city awaited the Virgin's arrival with ornate religious festivities on the hilltop. On October 23, 1904, Dom Luiz blessed the ground and welcomed a pair of enthusiastic Capuchin monks who, with a local priest, spent two weeks on the Hill performing fifty baptisms and more than 400 weddings. Working from four in the morning until eleven at night, the three clergy also heard confessions and celebrated daily mass around a provisional altar; a small building had been erected to hold sanctified host. On November 2, All Soul's Day, they led "an enormous multitude" in procession to the local cemetery.[22]

The Virgin was delivered to the Hill from the docks on November 8. The bishop, the city's religious community, and thousands of citizens accompanied her to the top, where Dom Luiz celebrated a mass. For the rest of the month, she lay in her shipping crate, wrapped in cloth. On November 29, she was to be set on her pedestal when an interruption temporarily stopped work. Three men appeared on the Hill and told Lafayette Bandeira, the engineer in charge, that they wanted to see the Lady. He responded that no one could see her because the workers could not be delayed for any reason. This displeased one of the three men, who harangued the engineer. When Bandeira again refused, "the impudent one intensified his insolence" and pulled a knife. He would have slashed Bandeira were it not for workers who intervened. The man was wrestled to the ground and taken to the police, where he was jailed for attempted murder.[23]

On the day before the first festa, the Hill hummed with masses, rosary circles, and prayer vigils. At six in the evening Dom Luiz climbed the Hill, where he spoke to a crowd from the foot of the still shrouded though now erect monument; his departure was "led by a multitude carrying small, many colored balloons that gave the procession a brilliant and fairy-like aspect."[24]

On the feast day itself, the Great Western Railway provided extra trains between the city center and the Arrayal station.[25] The first, with thirty crammed cars, left at 5:15 in the morning, dawn barely blushing the sky. The train held city and state dignitaries, the press, members of religious orders, and several bands that played along the way, "waking inhabitants of the suburbs." The square at the foot of the Hill, already named Dom Luiz Plaza, "was decorated with streamers, foliage and arches, lending a festive air."[26] A formal procession wound its way up the Hill at six in the morning, led by the unmarried (and therefore presumably virgin) daughter of a local merchant, who was greatly honored to have such a charge given to his family. The bishop led the religious community, which included seventeen different orders and lay brotherhoods from Recife and two from Olinda, as well as numerous secular priests and seminarians. On top, to the sound of fireworks and bands playing patriotic music, the bishop parted the curtains cloaking the monument. The Virgin was serene, seemingly oblivious to the tumult around her.

After unveiling her, the bishop blessed her, then led a solemn mass, aided by priests and seminarians. After the mass, more fireworks were lit, the bands played again, and the bishop delivered a long sermon about Our Lady. It was estimated that 20,000 people came to the Morro for that first festa. In contrast to today's event, which draws mostly the poor, on that first festa the Morro "was a constant osmosis . . . of people of all classes, from the modest plebeian to the highest strata of society."[27] The numbers only slowed during the height of the day, when heat made the steep climb more difficult, but the festivities lasted well into the night. Eighty infantry soldiers and twenty cavalry maintained order, and, as has been the tradition ever since, bawdier distractions took the place of religious ones as night fell. The novelty of electric lights, powered by Great Western Railway generators, added to the air of celebration. "In the night the Hill presented a dazzling aspect," wrote one observer;

> The electric lamps placed artistically over the monument shone on high. . . , visible to the city and contemplated with admiration by all. Lamps of alcohol, distributed along the street, also produced a magnificent effect and the whole mountain, in this sprinkling of luminous lights, offered the eyes a spectacle full of shine and . . . originality.[28]

Dr. Carlos Alberto de Menezes, the man whose inspiration led to the first festa, did not see the event, for he had died of a heart attack the month before. But the tradition he helped start continues. Even the after-effects are much the same now as they were in 1904, as this newspaper ad placed the day after the first festa attests:

> Lost: Yesterday, on the occasion of the feast of Our Lady of the Immaculate Conception, at the Arrayal, a black girl called

Jardilina was lost. She wore on this occasion a cambric dress.
I ask whoever may have found her to please send her to Hos-
pício Street, number 83. Costs incurred will be paid by the
doorman.[29]

Festas in succeeding years were similarly clamorous affairs that
drew local church dignitaries, businessmen, engenho owners, their
families, and a sizable portion of the city's growing population of
poor.[30] It was organized by teams of local businessmen calling themselves colonels and captains, and the major mass of the day was always celebrated by the archbishop. Throughout the 1910s, the Great
Western Railway provided extra trains from the city center to the
Morro area on December 7 and 8. Prominent families continued to provide "the gentle young misses of the local elite" — unwed daughters, fi-
ancées, and sometimes young wives — to lead the procession.[31] The
faithful from around the city came for several days ahead, praying during the day and enjoying the makeshift bars, booths selling statuettes,
sweets, or games of chance, carousel rides, dancing, puppet shows,
and other after-dark revelries. Electric illumination, still a novelty in
much of the city, lit the Hill every year (though only for the festa). The
closing mass was marked by fireworks, military bands, choirs, the bishop's presence, and in 1920, a twenty-one-gun salute. By 1925, cars
were allowed up the Hill during the festivities. In 1926 the original road
was extended down the side of the Hill. As annual attendance swelled,
local politicians took advantage of the ready-made crowd; in 1926 the
state governor was on hand. In 1929, Dom Miguel, Dom Luiz's succes-
sor, promised an especially brilliant festa, in honor of the monument's
silver anniversary. Electricity that year was provided by Pernambuco
Tramways; the Great Western Railway had gone under.

FASHIONING A RELEVANT CHURCH

The festa fit within larger goals of Brazil's church leadership in the
early decades of the twentieth century. The split between church and
state in 1889 left some clerics wishing for more government aid and for
more effective means of making the church relevant to a larger portion
of the country. The church's most outspoken advocate was Dom
Sebastião Leme de Silveira Cintra, a former bishop of Olinda/Recife

who had worked his way up the hierarchy to become Latin America's first cardinal. Dom Leme allied himself with Getúlio Vargas, Brazil's populist dictator in power from 1930 to 1945 (and again from 1950 to 1954), to win back state support. At the same time, Dom Leme focused on parish-oriented projects, including controversial Workers' Circles, locally organized church-sponsored groups dedicated to improving the lot of laborers. There was little social infrastructure for people like urban factory workers or household domestics, so Workers' Circles attempted to answer some social needs by setting up cooperatives, pharmacies, hospitals, clinics, and schools (Burns 1980:386). They were particularly welcome in the northeast in the 1930s, when the depression's bite was made sharper by sugar policies that continued to favor growers at the expense of laborers.

Dom Leme also welcomed and encouraged the Catholic Action movement, which was finding support from the Vatican. Catholic Action targeted specific groups, most of them young, and attempted to address their needs. Besides teaching church spirituality and doctrine, Catholic Action also pointed to material problems that were impediments to good Catholicism. Groups gathered for prayer and reflection, often looking toward social reform under their motto "See, Judge, Act" (Adriance 1986:19; Cabal 1978:47; Lelotte 1947; Lernoux 1979:7). By 1933, Catholic Action groups were advertising in local Recife newspapers, with the Young Men's Catholic Action and the Young Women's Catholic Action meeting twice a week. A direct precursor to liberation theology, it found welcome adherents among people whose lives were being ravaged by the depression.

Catholic Action groups were organized regionally. In the mid-1940s, young factory workers in the south asked a priest named Hélder Câmara to be their chaplain. By 1947, Padre Hélder and his Catholic Action charges started creating a national chapter, which came into place in 1950. It was the first time a large, lay-oriented church organization made what was later called "social justice" a primary concern. It also inspired the national church to organize. The National Conference of Brazilian Bishops (*Conferência Nacional dos Bispos do Brasil*, or CNBB), the first organization of its kind in the world, was founded in 1952, in part because of Dom Hélder, who had been named bishop the year before. The CNBB allowed the Brazilian church as a whole to take "positions far more daring than many bishops would have taken on their own" (Adriance 1986:25); later it would give the Brazilian church a unified strength that would allow it openly to oppose the military government.

About the same time Catholic Action was spreading and the CNBB was being organized, an upturn on the world sugar market had dire consequences for the northeast, as rural workers and squatters were again pushed from what little land they held to make room for more sugar. The country's growing industrialization seemed to promise jobs to people whose lives were devastated by land grabs, drought, or both, and migrations to the cities increased. Often, however, migrants found themselves no better off in urban areas. Until that time, rural trade unions had been no help. Though unionization was legalized in 1944, few workers had the resources to stand up to landowners, who consistently opposed labor organizing. The Brazilian Communist Party, legal from 1945 to 1947, took some steps to organize rural workers, but the party's brief life did not give it enough time to make any headway.

Then, in 1954, came the resistance of Galiléia, a former engenho in rural Pernambuco. Before the owner moved to Recife in 1930, he divided the land into 140 plots and rented them to former engenho families who cultivated them as they wished. In 1954, the owner's son decided to use the land as a cattle ranch, and he evicted the families living there. This was not an unusual event, and custom had it that the workers simply left, but the families of Galiléia did not follow custom. They refused to be thrown off the land and formed a mutual aid society to press their cause. A Recife lawyer, Francisco Julião, an alternate state deputy for the Brazilian Socialist Party, became their champion.[32] The case attracted national attention as it made its way through the courts. In December 1959, the lands of Galiléia were expropriated by gubernatorial order and the families who had farmed them received ownership. The success of Galiléia inspired others to organize, and soon rural unions called Peasant Leagues were forming across the northeast (C. Hewitt 1980; Huizer 1972:132n; Page 1972; Palmeira 1978).

THE FESTA TRANSFORMS

Back on the Morro, the festa continued to evolve. By 1952, outsiders' perceptions of the event differed markedly from stories of earlier days.

In a December 10th article titled "The Festa of Our Lady of the Immaculate Conception and of Almost all the Sins," a journalist offered this description:

> Climbing or descending, the spectacle is invariably the same: women without shoes, rosary in hand and prayers on their lips; unhappy creatures with mutilated limbs; paralytics; all, in the end, in search of a miracle. Add to this retinue, on both sides of the street, dozens of blind people, crippled people, or simply false beggars asking for alms, and the picture is complete.
>
> The promessas, these, yes, are as varied and picturesque as possible. The lengths to which the popular imagination will go in the architecture of these promessas is incredible.
>
> For example: Amaro José Ferreira pays his promessa dearly. He climbs the hill in the following condition: on his knees, five steps forward, three steps back. He began at 4:15 in the morning, while it was still dark, and arrived at the altar at 3:10, his knees bleeding. Is there something like this in any other part of the world? Maria Angelica F., age 16, from a good family, climbed the hill on her knees to forget a young man. And she forgot . . . J. C., age 27, tubercular, made a promessa by crawling like a reptile. He made it to the top; nevertheless, how are his lungs, with all that dust? Will he live to make another promessa?
>
> There were other promessas, all picturesque — and all equally sadistic, demanding the blood of the faithful. . . . [33]
>
> One thing is incontestable: the most interesting part of the festa was the profane side. Gambling was in the open, drinking was lavish. . . .
>
> And on top of the pedestal, complacent and impassive, the image watches all of this: a sweaty, drunk, irreverent multitude lacking all devotion, climbing and descending the hill in a cloud of dust perceptible from afar and unbearable up close.
>
> It's like this every year in . . . the traditional festa of Our Lady of the Immaculate Conception and almost all the sins. [34]

Somewhere between the mid-1940s and the early 1950s, the festa lost its elite women procession leaders. By then the festa no longer drew people from all classes; the rich expressed their disdain for and fear of such an allegedly crime-ridden, dangerous place as the Morro. The event was fully transformed into a time for the city's destitute to bring their hope and sorrow to the ever-silent Blessed Mother. The Hill was a sanctuary for the poor, the festa an event organized and run by the church for its most consistently underserved constituency.

In 1954 a slightly political note was sounded, presaging days to come. The festa attracted more attention than usual that year, since it was the centennial of the Dogma of the Immaculate Conception and the fiftieth anniversary of the Morro's statue. Not for the first time, the archbishop promised in a sermon that a proper church would be built soon to augment the tiny chapel and fragile wood shelter surrounding it, making the Morro a truly grand sanctuary to Our Lady.[35] But clergy who attended to the festa and residents of the community had a more immediate concern. No public transportation served the steadily growing population of the city's highest hill. Residents pointed out that other hill communities more recently and sparsely settled had received bus service years before. Despite press attention and clergy concern, however, the Morro would wait another twenty-five years for the luxury of buses.

The festa in 1959 was one of the most infamous, and Morro residents who were there describe it vividly, as do newspaper accounts of the time. At about dawn on December 8th, in a part of the praça so crowded that it was almost impossible to move or even breathe, an elderly man suffered a heart attack and fell against a lamppost (*um poste de iluminação elétrica*). The wires of the post met, showering the crowd below with sparks. The man, struggling, cried for help and again fell, sending down another rain of sparks. Nearby pilgrims, unaware of the trouble, continued to set off firecrackers, and those near the lamppost thought the explosions were caused by the falling sparks. People panicked, pushed, and tried to run. Priests celebrating a mass from the open-air church saw the problem and took the microphones, urging people to stay calm, but their exhortations weren't heeded; "in the stampede, people were trampled, some crushed by the mass terror."[36] By the time the panic ended, four women and three children were dead and more than one hundred people hurt, some seriously.

Police on the scene commandeered all cars present to help take the victims to local hospitals. The dead were taken to the morgue, where people flocked to learn if relatives or friends were among the victims. The crowd was so big that police had to cordon off the area and let people in a few at a time. One man claimed to be a journalist so he could skip the line; when he was turned away, he pulled a gun and fired, but was promptly arrested before he hurt anyone. Two of the dead, a mother and her baby, were from a neighborhood near the Morro, and their funeral procession a day later was accompanied by hundreds. Because of the accident, festa organizers opened up the space around the square, sent the amusement park rides and variety shows to the square at the foot of the Hill, and forbade cars to climb the Hill during the days of the festa.

INTO THE CANE FIELDS

Accidental turmoil at the festa was matched by political tumult in the countryside. Francisco Julião, champion of the Peasant League unions, was thought to have communist leanings, a reputation he enhanced with well-publicized visits to Cuba immediately after the Cuban Revolution, and to China. Despite growing empathy with unjust working conditions in the cane fields, the church viewed the Leagues with some alarm. Church leaders, however, wisely decided not to meet the perceived danger of the Peasant Leagues with threats or warnings about the evils of communism. Rather, they co-opted the themes that animated the Leagues to start their own organizing efforts. These did not use the language of communism, but most of the church's goals were the same as Julião's, and soon church-sponsored unions called Peasant Syndicates rivaled the purely secular Peasant Leagues. Many Syndicate leaders had already learned organizing techniques and strategies through their work with Catholic Action.

The church's work in the rural northeast was unusual because it had never been a substantial institutional presence in the region. Priests traditionally were associated with the "big house," not the "shanties," to use the phrases of northeastern anthropologist Gilberto Freyre (1963). Catholicism flourished in rural areas, but often it wasn't mediated by a priest, a nun, or any other pastoral agent. The archbishop of Recife appointed a group of priests to work exclusively on the Syndicates, and they formed the *Serviço de Orientação Rural de Pernambuco,* or SORPE (Rural Orientation Service of Pernambuco). SORPE initially worked to form rural cooperatives, organize the Syndicates, and focus attention away from class issues toward less problematic objectives.[37] Despite initial hesitation from some rural workers, the church was surprisingly successful in its unionizing; by 1962 there were sixty church-organized rural unions just in Pernambuco (Ireland 1972:357).

The empowerment taught through Catholic Action and then through church Syndicates was applauded by church leaders, but they didn't like the idea of only unionizing without also urging people to reflect on their situations. They feared that without reflection, the unions would become just another form of paternalism (de Kadt 1970:113). It would be easier to encourage reflection, however, if people knew how to read; illiteracy in the northeast ran higher than 70 percent (124). Using Catholic Action and the Syndicates as organizing bases, Hélder Câmara launched an experimental literacy campaign, based on Paulo Freire's methods, called the Basic Education Movement (*Movimento Educação de Base,* or MEB) with the theme "Educate to Transform." MEB proved extremely successful; by the end of 1963, two years after they were started, there were 6,464 radio schools just in the northeast (de Kadt 1970:128). A MEB textbook published in 1963 demonstrates the tone of the project. While Syndicate themes did not delve into class differences and tensions, the MEB based grammar and spelling lessons on exactly such questions. The MEB text, *Viver é Lutar* (To Live Is To Struggle), is illustrated with photographs of rural workers and teaches verb conjugations with examples like "to need," "to vote," "to change." Lesson Six was typical:

O povo tem fome e doença.	The people are hungry and sick.
Por que tanta doença no povo?	Why is there so much sickness among the people?
O povo precisa de escola.	The people need schooling.
Precisa de casa e comida.	They need homes and food.
O povo precisa de trabalho.	The people need work.

E dura a vida do povo!	Life is hard for people!
O povo quer mudar de vida?[38]	Do people want to change their life?

Themes are developed as shown in Lesson Twenty:

Como são as eleiçoes no Brasil?	How do elections work in Brazil?
Muitos eleitores votam no candidato do patrão.	Many vote for the boss's candidate.
Muitos votam a troco de sapato, roupa, remédio. . . .	Many vote in exchange for shoes, clothes, medicine. . . .
Outros votam a troco de emprego ou dinheiro.	Others vote in exchange for work or money.
Esta situação pode continuar?	Can this situation continue?
Voto é consciência.	A vote is based on conscience.
Voto é liberdade.	A vote means liberty.
Consciência não se vende.	Conscience is not for sale.
Liberdade não se compra.	Liberty cannot be bought.

The church was lauded for forming the Peasant Syndicates and for creating the MEB, efforts that were no doubt aided by the practicality of goals that looked remarkably like Julião's but that were cloaked in church language. Church officials had been watching in alarm as Roman Catholic influences waned among people they couldn't reach; the church was especially leery of losing members to booming Pentecostal and fundamentalist traditions (Martin 1991:65). Its work with Syndicates and radio schools was partly an effort to keep the church relevant to Catholics by learning to go where the people were, not simply insisting people come to them.

Another effort to keep sheep in the fold involved the formation of Bible-based "communities." Around 1956 (do Passo Castro 1987:58), people in the northeast, encouraged by their priests, a nun, or a lay leader, started meeting in each other's homes, reading the Bible, and discussing its relevance to their lives. These were not founded as mere Bible-study groups, because in determining how the Bible related to their lives, group members also asked how their lives and social situations might change in response to what they were reading. By 1964 these groups had began to call themselves *comunidades eclesiais de base* (ecclesial base communities), or CEBs, in the diocese of Crateús, in Ceará (Fragoso 1982). Similar groups were forming in other parts of the region in the early 1960s (Mainwaring 1986:125; 1989:158), and in 1966 the National Brazilian Bishops' Conference (CNBB) held the first national seminar on CEBs in Rio de Janeiro.

STATE TO THE RIGHT, CHURCH FURTHER LEFT

As the church was organizing and educating northeasterners, it was also making important changes in its institutional structure. To solve the crisis of a chronic nation-wide priest shortage, nuns were given more authority within church parishes, as were members of the laity willing to serve in a limited way as priest replacements when the need arose. This fostered greater participation and narrowed the gap between the traditional role of priests and that of the laity (Mainwaring 1989:158–59). It also allowed the laity to develop a more direct relationship with the texts and rites that comprised Catholic faith and worship, which eventually allowed some Catholics to argue that mediators between the faithful and the Lord are sometimes superfluous (D. Levine 1979:63).

Changes also came from the Holy See. The institutional hierarchy gave its approval to many shifts already underway within the Brazilian church when John XXIII convened the Second Vatican Council from 1963 to 1965. Pope John made a pointed call for the church to turn outward, toward the world and toward the people it ostensibly served (Della Cava 1990; Lernoux 1979). This verified the direction in which the Brazilian church had started to move and accelerated the process. It was especially a boost for the church's already "outward" stance in Brazil, and it encouraged the Latin American church in general in its growing efforts to address widespread structural sociopolitical problems found in most of the continent; to officially commit the church to the poor; and to recognize the importance of CEBs in redefining and regenerating an institution too long associated with the ruling classes (Della Cava 1989:149), all stances taken at the 1968 meeting of the Latin American Bishops' Conference in Medellín, Colombia.

The Second Vatican Council had at least one other impact on Brazil: a young seminarian named Reginaldo was studying in Rome during the Council. In large part because of what he saw and learned through it and through the warmth of Pope John, he gradually dropped his lifelong arch-conservatism and replaced it with a liberationist Catholicism that was to set him on a collision course with conservative church powers many years later.

Brazil's church wasn't alone in its leftist leanings following World War II. The church's initiatives were, in fact, smaller efforts than those mounted by university students, urban intellectuals, trade unions, rural unions (both the Leagues and the Syndicates), and many others. But the closer these groups came to success, the greater a threat they became to existing powers, and the moderate stand of Brazil's President Goulart looked to many like weakness. On March 31, 1964, Brazil's military took over the civilian government. A few weeks later, in April 1964, Dom Hélder Câmara was appointed archbishop of Olinda and Recife. The church, Dom Hélder included, initially welcomed the coup, thinking it would calm the nation's climate of social turmoil.

Ironically, the military coup had a positive effect on the festa. Security was increased for the first time in years, and by 1967, rumors that the Hill was a safe place to be on December 8th renewed interest in the event. "The festa," noted a local paper wryly, "used to provide work for the police reporter, who was on the scene day and night, registering many muggings and homicides."[39] Because of increased police presence and more efficient organization, "scenes of violent bloodletting disappeared and the festa revived its better days . . . "[40]

The festa also provided a more varied amusement park than usual in 1967, where the most popular pastime was gambling. Though illegal, various games of chance dominated the square at the bottom of the Hill. The ferris wheel was more popular than ever, as young men tried to cajole young women clad in newly fashionable miniskirts to share the three-minute ride with them. The amusement park also included a small wax museum, a freak show, and two special exhibits — a mermaid, and a woman who turned to iron. The only significant criticism of the '67 festa was, according to one observer, the "revolting" crudity of those two displays. Temporary restaurants served meat of questionable origin — it was thought to be cat — that nonetheless tasted delicious, while beer and cachaça, the northeast's famous rum, flowed freely. And for a small fee, people could send amorous messages through the incessant loudspeakers; "many love affairs have begun through the voice of the proud D.J. between sambas and boleros."[41]

The festa's lighter moments did not presage days to come. The government grew increasingly repressive after 1968, when it used troops to squash three major strikes, effectively silencing labor for the next decade. It also went after guerilla opposition groups with decisive violence. Citing guerilla activity as a certain sign of impending anarchy, the government passed Institutional Act Number Five at the end of 1968. It allowed the dictatorship to suspend the political rights of citizens, to confiscate private property of "subversives," to rule by decree, and to try political crimes in military courts. In 1969 the National Security Law denied habeus corpus and other basic rights and allowed the government broad powers to arrest and to imprison people for "a long list of vaguely defined offenses to the nation" (Keck 1992:25). Random arrests, midnight raids, imprisonments, and tortures became commonplace. One after another, opposition groups were silenced, and the church slowly became a voice for concerns of union members, students, journalists, rural workers, and others (Barbe 1987:92–3; Beeson and Pearce 1984:90; Della Cava 1989:147; Salem 1981; Smith 1975; Stepan 1988:41n). At first the military didn't see the church as a threat, partly because the institution wasn't perceived as the source of any genuine power or broad-reaching influence, and because church/state ties had been friendly for so long that the military in effect overlooked what the church was doing. By the time the church was articulating strong criticisms of the government, it had solidified positions bolstered by those unable to speak on their own behalf, and by the church's status as a high-profile transnational institution. The military could not strike back the same way it had against most other opponents.

Because the northeast had been rife with organizing and educating efforts, it was a special target of early repressions from the military. Miguel Arraes, the governor of Pernambuco who had championed cane workers' rights by enforcing pro-union legislation, was arrested and exiled. So were Paulo Freire, the educator whose pedagogical techniques were the basis of the church's radio schools, and Peasant League organizer Francisco Julião. The radio schools were dismantled, and Syndicate and League leaders were arrested. The prison built in downtown Recife in the eighteenth century was always full, and stories of torture soon leaked from its thick white walls.

By the end of 1969, the government's control over the country was unambiguously rooted in its deft and terrifying shows of force — against individuals, organizations, and ideas. Communism and communists were continually fingered as the source of all threats; any person or cause could become a target of state violence if so labeled. Reginaldo Veloso, then a young priest recently returned from several years in Rome, felt the last vestiges of his former capitalist zeal and conservative political tendencies drained from him as he joined other Brazilian church colleagues protesting government repression and studying an alternative Catholic theology that would eventually bear the name "liberation."

THE MAKING OF A LIBERATION PRIEST

In 1968 Reginaldo found his way back to Recife, where he had started in seminary many years before. He was assigned to a parish in the northern zone of the city, near the Morro. Like the Morro, the parish was one of the *bairros da periferia* — neighborhoods on the edge. Called Macaxeira (for the yam-like crop of the same name that was once planted on that land), it was built around the area's textile factory — the same one that had attracted people to the Morro when it had opened decades earlier. It was customary for the parish priest to live in housing provided by the factory and to receive an augmented salary from the same source. Reginaldo refused both, preferring a home that equaled those of his parishioners (the one he turned down was so big that it eventually housed a school). He also insisted that he earn only the salary they did, and that he have no more amenities than they had. The factory owners protested his unorthodox demands, but Dom Hélder supported him. The Dom, however, turned down Reginaldo's request to become a worker priest — that is, to hold a job in the factory and practice his ministry through his solidarity with fellow workers.

A decade later, in 1978, he was named priest of the Morro da Conceição parish. His predecessor on the Morro had already achieved the remarkable by getting a proper church built for the parish. He did it with the help of neighborhood Encontro de Irmãos groups, the Bible-study collectives that Dom Hélder had founded in 1969, by convincing them that they themselves, with their neighbors, could build the church. All cinderblocks, wiring, wood, tiles, mortar, grating, gates, paint, and other materials were donated by community residents and local businesses. All labor was done by Morro residents. It seemed as if everyone participated, from the old women who kept pots of *cafezinho* hot and ready throughout the work day to children who fetched water and carried bricks one by one. Construction took eight months, and when it was done, the old Morro chapel was surrounded by a solid cinderblock church painted blue (in honor of the Virgin), with a wide, welcoming entrance, side doors, an altar, benches, altar cloths, a behind-the-scenes area that served as a sacristy, and a tiled roof that didn't leak. It was thus that Morro residents learned to refer to their church as their very own, meaning not just their part of an institution that claimed to serve them and to which they belonged, but a structure in which they had invested sweat and muscle and time. It was a deep commitment, reiterated in many stories over the years describing the church's creation; outside the festa, it was one of the first instances of the Morro community combining its strengths around a common cause.

Reginaldo arrived not long after the church was built, his fervor for liberationism only strengthened by his experiences in the nearby factory parish. There was much good will and excitement lingering from the successful church-building campaign, and soon Reginaldo was channeling it into equally ambitious parish projects. He formed a Center for Reading and Information; from that and the Encontro de Irmãos groups grew the Morro's residents' council, which engineered the community's first successful political effort, a campaign in 1980 to get running water to the hill. The festa itself was transformed, both organizationally and thematically. The Morro was steadily becoming a showplace parish for liberation theology, much to the delight of many parishioners — and to the dismay of others.

3

THE POLITICS OF THEOLOGY

A Special Place for Tolerance . . .

Weekends on the Morro da Conceição are noisy. Once in a while it's the noise of violence lubricated by alcohol, which exaggerates neighborly tension, unleashes normally controlled jealousy, or sends cars squealing too fast around the praça. More often it's the noise of release, of the dance hall's throbbing loudspeakers, of household radios turned high for spontaneous parties, of barroom laughter, of television blare, of muffler-less cars revving in place.

It is also the noise of people beseeching, praising, and being seized by a variety of spiritual powers. On Friday, Saturday, and Sunday nights, complex drumbeats weave through the air from all corners of the hill as people crowd the community's many *terreiros*, or places of worship, in any of several African-Brazilian religious traditions. All weekend long, fundamentalist Christians of various stripes, referred to collectively as *crentes*, or believers (the groups are also called *seitas*, or sects), exhort their neighbors to accept Jesus and to be saved.[1] Crente groups that meet in individuals' homes have portable microphone and speaker systems that they use with enthusiasm, lest their neighbors miss the chance at salvation. The neat blue-and-white Assembly of God churches, the tan Baptist ones, and the larger halls of the Universal Church of the Kingdom of God, among many others, have loudspeakers through which their members preach, sing, and pray, and though they are down the hill from the Morro praça, their calls for redemption are easy to hear.

On Sunday mornings, Catholics inside the church turn on their loudspeakers and play recordings of perky religious music around

6:00 A.M. as prelude to the worship service they're about to start. The service itself is also broadcast. At around 7:30, whether or not those inside the church are done, Catholics worshipping in the school across the street from the Saint crank up their amplifiers and microphones, filling the air with speeches, prayers, and songs. Then at 9:15 or 9:30, those inside the church begin their second service and once more blanket the community with recorded music. Often the competing loudspeakers overlap, creating a deafening cacophony. It is the preferred form of Sunday morning assault exchanged between the two groups; on one Good Friday, both kept their speakers at full volume for a good six hours with noise so loud that it shook one's ribs.

Though the Morro is nominally 95 percent Catholic, the church's presence in individual lives varies considerably. Many professed Catholics rarely enter a church and instead find spiritual expression among the chants, drums, dancing, and trances of candomblé, umbanda, or xangô, traditions with roots in African religions and the imposed Catholicism of slavery. Some regularly attend both church and a terreiro. Theologian José Comblin has claimed that if all the *maes-* and *paes-de-santo* (literally "mothers-" and "fathers-of-the-saint," or keepers of the terreiros) left Catholicism, the church would loose 80 percent of its membership in the northeast.[2]

While people step easily between Catholicism and African-Brazilian religions, there is less fluidity between Catholics and fundamentalists, but there is little overt hostility. Many households include devout Catholics, lapsed Catholics, members of a local terreiro, and committed fundamentalists living peaceably under the same roof. Once in a while the wires of Assembly of God church speakers are cut, but only after days of loud, incessant broadcasts; the wirecutter could be an irate neighbor of any, or no, religious persuasion. One nun I knew grumbled sometimes that she was sure Jesus didn't mean his message to be shouted quite so loudly, but she praised the work of many "born again" Christians in helping families cope with alcoholism, hunger, or unemployment.

The Morro's divergent religious practices were particularly clear one Saturday night on the praça. A celebration by Reginaldo's followers was going on in the school, loudspeakers at high volume. In the church, the traditional Catholics were holding a mass, and their speakers were also cranked. Near the bottom of the praça, a kindly young man thrust a piece of paper in my hand and asked if I were saved. Surprised, I realized he was with a group of Pentecostal musicians setting up guitars, drums, and — yes — loudspeakers at the praça's corner. Soon they began to sing, inviting people to Jesus and giving directions to their church down the Hill. Their music was barely audible under the din of the more powerful speakers already blaring, but they bravely continued, smiling and calm. A small crowd gathered.

Further down the street that evening I saw a group of giddy young men spill from a house and disappear around a corner. I knew them by sight and guessed that they were off to a xangô terreiro they frequented on the north foot of the Hill. They were part of the Morro's small but vibrant transvestite community, and though that night they were dressed as men, on most weekend nights they wore flawless make-up, flowing chiffon capes, and extravagant dresses they had made themselves. They went about the Hill as open couples, stepping out to the dance halls hand-in-hand and clinging to each other in the Sunday night praça socials. I never heard of them being hassled by anyone on the Morro. The first time I saw them cross-dressed and realized that they weren't comely young women but pretty young men, I was walking with an older neighbor, a very Catholic and quietly wise woman. When she saw me watching the young men and noted my surprise she said with a smile, "We have a little of everything on the Morro. That's one of the reasons this is such a special place."

. . . Except Among Catholics

Community acceptance of potentially conflicting spiritual practices and even of differing sexual orientations underscored the irony and passion of dissension between the Roman Catholics. Few on the Morro questioned the practice of allowing people to occupy different religious space, but that didn't apply when two groups wanted to occupy the same religious space in very different ways.

By the time I came to live on the Morro, the Catholics were sharply divided into two main factions: those loyal to Reginaldo, and those loyal to Reginaldo's replacement, Constante (and by extension, to the bishop, Dom José). Reginaldo's followers called themselves *A Resistência*, The Resistance. Constante's people didn't call themselves anything, except sometimes "traditional" or "true" Catholics. Within the

Resistance and the traditionalist groups, members tolerated a degree of difference among their own. Many in the traditionalist camp, for instance, participated in the church's growing charismatic movement.[3] Twice a week in a large downtown church, Padre Constante led rousing noontime charismatic masses that attracted more than a thousand people. Some Morro residents who liked that style of church were drawn to his masses on the Hill, though these were much calmer affairs, which suited those traditionalists who had no taste for foot-stomping or hand-waving and preferred a mass more staidly celebrated. But these two groups did not conflict, and saw each other making mere stylist choices.

Among the Resistance, too, there were differences. Many of the older women participated in Encontro de Irmãos groups, which by the 1990s young people sometimes teasingly called the Resistance Youth Group; most of its members were over fifty. Often in Encontro de Irmãos meetings, one person or another would sigh for the days before the division, when they felt a part of the church proper, not an enemy to it. I never heard younger Resistance members express such longing.

While each group could accept some differences within its membership, neither could accept the differences implied in the very existence of the other. This was because the differences did not hinge on separate religious institutions, but claimed opposite directions for the same institution. They argued not about how loudly they liked to pray, but about what the prayers meant, who had the right to determine that meaning, and how the meaning was made real in daily life. The confrontation was made more urgent by the community's role as a pilgrimage site: the two factions sought control of ground that was not just historically significant but also holy. The problem was further muddied by political overtones; conflicting claims were voiced more vehemently because they were linked to incompatible political positions. The Resistance proposed a rearrangement of the status quo, while the traditionalists insisted that they were not interested in replacing a grim but predictable tomorrow with an uncertain future. The drama played out themes both mundane and historic. Neighborly resentments and grudges found an outlet, theological disagreements were debated with passion, political visions of the community's role and future were hotly argued. The conflict divided families, shattered friendships of decades' duration, and carved public space into micro-territories.

Reginaldo and Dom José provide good models for the contrasting interpretations of church and faith that each side represents. The biographies and beliefs of each demonstrate how members of the same tradition can hold sharply divergent interpretations of that tradition. Each also represents, and is the result of, changes that have shaped the institution of the Roman Catholic church in the last three decades. Reginaldo and Dom José are presented here as symbols more than as individuals, for they stand as emblems of larger divisive trends, and are offered as examples of the deep division between liberation theology and its opponents. At the same time, each stands for political strategies that are anchored in the specific historical context of the northeast and of the country as a whole. Their political stands, not surprisingly, are as incompatible as their religious ones.

Two Nordestinos, Two Visions of Church

Dom José and Padre Reginaldo are men of identical passions. Christ and Roman Catholic teachings are central to their lives. They try to live as they understand Scripture teaches them to live, and the fervor of their faith is unshakable. In fact, both men will go to extremes to honor their version of that faith, and nothing will sway them from the certainty that theirs is the true understanding. Their biographies are also similar. They are both sons of the northeast; both come from large families; both entered seminary when they were thirteen years old; both entered religious orders; both were ordained in 1961; both spent time in Rome, including the years of the Second Vatican Council.

In their daily lives, however, these two men couldn't be more different. Dom José's religious passion is expressed in a zeal for obedience to and maintenance of hierarchical, institutionalized church authority, while Reginaldo believes in obedience to Biblical authority not always mediated by the institutional church, even if that puts him at odds with his superiors. Dom José honors a tradition of Catholic piety that encourages people to form a closer relationship to God and Jesus Christ through prayer, confession, spiritual discipline, and adherence to church teachings. For him, the church is a sanctuary of hope, calm, and forgiveness, an oasis of peace in a chaotic world. Reginaldo's Catholicism, however, seeks to bring people closer to God and Jesus by empowering them to restructure their lives and the lives of their communities around what he reads as Biblical teachings of liberation, not around secular (and sometimes church-inspired) habits and structures of oppression. He sees the church as a source of support, example, and inspiration for those trying to bring justice to an unjust world.

These men are not alone in their disagreements. The factions they unofficially represent are found throughout Recife, where their admirers and detractors abound and where lines of allegiance cannot necessarily be predicted by measures like income level, education, or religious upbringing.

From Sertão to Holy See and Back Again

Dom José was born in 1933 in Caruarú, a market town in the interior of Pernambuco on the edge of the sertão, the northeast's desert, where his father was a saddle maker. The senior Cardoso died in 1982 and Dom José remains close to his mother, who visits him often in Recife. He was an altar boy at a young age, and was captivated by the mystery and majesty of the mass. He entered the seminary when he was thirteen, became a Carmelite postulant, and spent part of his training years in São Paulo before he traveled to Rome. He wanted to study dogmatic theology, but when he told his superior, he remembers the man replying, "Don't be stupid. We have enough theologians. We need more canonical lawyers." He was often ridiculed in Recife for being a canon law expert, since it seemed the source of his ardor for rules and regulations. He replied rather plaintively that it wasn't his first choice, he simply did what he was told — though he admitted that he admires the discipline's orderliness. "Canon law is a church science," he told me, "and like other sciences, it doesn't contradict itself. Men have contradictions, but sciences don't."[4]

He was ordained in June 1961, then earned his doctorate in canonical law in Rome, where he lived for twenty-five years. He taught canon law at the International Carmelite Faculty and in 1971 was named head of the Carmelite order in Europe. After his first six-year term, he was re-elected to the post, but he didn't stay in Rome to finish it; the pope sent him back to Brazil in 1979 as bishop of Paracatú, a diocese in Bahia. He was there until 1985, when he was appointed to the Archdiocese of Olinda and Recife.

With fewer than a million people, the diocese of Paracatú is less than one-third the size of the diocese of Olinda and Recife, and it is mostly rural. His detractors in Recife later speculated that Dom José was assigned to Paracatú only because the pope wanted to get him back into the country as preparation for sending him to replace Dom Hélder. Dom José denies the charge. Though rumors that he was conservative preceded Dom José to Recife and some feared his coming, most Catholic clergy and lay leaders wanted to give their new bishop a fair chance. "Dom Hélder prepared us to receive the new bishop with *carinho* (affection, concern) and with intentions to journey together with him," remembered a prominent diocesan priest.[5]

Dom José soon made it clear that life in the diocese of Olinda and Recife would be different under his administration. Jorge, a former seminarian who had been close to Dom Hélder, told a story to illustrate the stark contrast between the old and new bishops. Since he had served in many masses with Dom Hélder, Jorge helped Dom José celebrate one of his first eucharists in the diocese. The time came to exchange the peace, and Jorge reached to embrace the bishop, just as he had always shared an embrace with Dom Hélder. But Dom José planted his palm in the center of the young man's chest, sternly shook his head, and then took Jorge's hand in a firm shake. "I will never forget that as long as I live," said Jorge. "It sent a chill through my whole body. I was amazed. I was stunned. I still tremble when I think of it." To Jorge, it was a clear sign that this new bishop was so different from Dom Hélder as to be incomprehensible.[6]

The situation was particularly distressing because of the sharp contrast in leadership styles between the new bishop and Dom Hélder. "Dom Hélder was very personable, while Dom José is very formal," said one priest who has worked in the diocese for many years:

> Dom José is just not as gifted in human relationships, not as sensitive to what's going on in people's lives. There's been a change of confidence among priests and people. We're more

conscious of the rule; not that the Dom [Dom Hélder] wasn't interested in keeping church law, but it was not that important. There was a feeling of freedom; you could make pastoral decisions on your own and expect to be trusted. The climate has changed.[7]

But not everyone was distressed at the changes. According to some, it was exactly Dom Hélder's relaxed leadership that had created urgent diocesan problems, and he had not heeded dangerous changes in the tone of Recife's church. Growing problems allegedly included financial mismanagement and even graft; loose sexual mores among some clergy and seminarians, including charges of homosexuality in the seminaries; and lax liturgical procedures in some parishes. The last charge particularly worried Dom José. "We have an obligation to follow the laws of the church," he explained. "Dom Hélder left those things aside. He said he wouldn't mandate, nor prohibit. You can see the results now in abuses of the liturgy."[8]

Dom José's supporters were glad to find in him a champion of moral rectitude who would right these wrongs. They saw him as a strong defender of a Catholicism that more closely resembled the way the religion was practiced in Brazil for most of the country's history, a tradition more orderly and less vulnerable to the influences of partisan politics. In his allies' memories, the "old" Catholicism included no social agitation from the pulpit, no encouragement of class struggle, no Marxist analysis of the Bible — all alleged habits of "base church" priests. Rather than rabble-rouse, said Dom José's supporters, priests must set examples with their piety and their concern for spiritual salvation. "A priest should be the presence of Jesus Christ in front of the people," explained one cleric. "In some places, there's a tendency to have the priest as an equal, as a brother. But he should serve with a certain authority, as Jesus Christ did."[9]

Dom José's primary job was to check what many saw as an out-of-control radicalism, as one priest put it, that had spread through the diocese and had been a problem since Dom Hélder's time. The conflict on the Morro was but its most vivid example. "Some things are given, are dogmas," said Dom José. "The roots of the conflict [on the Morro] are theological — in the so-called popular church, people think they should have control. Who is right? I believe I am right."[10]

THE PASSION FOR AUTHORITY: SCRIPTURE SAYS IT'S DIVINE

Through the Second Vatican Council, the church made a concerted turn toward the secular world, partly in an effort to make the institution more relevant to global problems. Dom José was in Rome during the Council. "I was considered on the progressive side," he remembered, smiling. "I didn't like the mass in Latin, and I said the eucharistic prayers in a low voice. I wanted to celebrate mass in Portuguese in a loud voice!" He was jubilant when the Pope decreed all masses were to be said in the vernacular.[11]

While Dom José applauded the Council's work, he did not take it to mean a new understanding of church laws. His Catholicism is based on his belief in a divinely dictated hierarchy that his sacred vows as priest and bishop demand he uphold. "The church is a hierarchical society by the will of Jesus Christ," he explained:

> In the Bible, some were chosen as apostles, not all. Jesus Christ chose the apostles; this is hierarchy. The Catholic hierarchy of the bishops and the pope is divine. Other degrees of the hierarchy of the church are of men and may be changed over time. Maybe some day we won't have monsignors, or cardinals. But bishops and the pope are the givens of the church.[12]

A priest cannot abrogate the rules of the church by challenging the hierarchy; this is human interference with the divine, said the bishop. A priest who opposes the hierarchy by opposing his bishop is a priest who has broken his vow of obedience and by extension broken one of his most important ties to the church.

"The people can be directed like sheep," Dom José said, "and a good pastor should understand this."[13] He does not blame the Morro confusion on the people who make up the Resistance, but on Reginaldo, who Dom José claimed abused his priestly power and who led his "sheep" astray by encouraging them to challenge their bishop and to break church and civil law. It was bad enough that they want to choose their own priest, said Dom José; they have even argued that bishops should be elected. But a congregation that chose its own priests or a body that elected its bishops would be in clear violation of

Scripture, the bishop explained, and would be mocking the power of the Holy Spirit and the sanctity of the church. "Elections wouldn't be precise," he argued. "If you had elections today, you wouldn't have the Roman Catholic church."[14] While it is true that through the sacrament of baptism, all Catholics are members of the church, and the church — understood metaphorically as the body of Christ — is made up of that membership, laity do not have the same rights as clergy. "The popular church is a heresy," asserted the bishop, "if it advocates a church without hierarchy. The church does not come from the people, it only comes from the Holy Trinity."[15]

According to Dom José, Reginaldo and his parishioners maligned the church by linking it to secular political concerns, telling people how to vote and claiming that God wants all faithful Catholics to be politically active. This was wrong, the bishop felt, for two reasons: first, because the church has no place in secular politics, and second, because one may or may not have a duty to be politically active, but that's a private interpretation of one's civic responsibility, not a Biblical mandate. The bishop was adamant that the church should work to better the world through charity and good works; it's the Catholic's duty to pray, not to agitate. The church, he believed, must not be a haven for political activists but a home for the spiritually needy.

His critics lambasted Dom José for this belief in the place and role of church structure, claiming that he was playing astute games with the church's political alliances. But the bishop consistently countered that he was only living the Gospels according to the edicts demanded of him in those texts and in his job as bishop, servant of the faith. He responded this way to most charges against him.

For instance, he was often accused of opposing the poor, a charge that made him red-faced with frustration, and he was said to have ignored the decisions of the Latin American bishops' conferences (CELAM) in Medellín, Colombia, in 1968 and Puebla, Mexico, in 1979, which supported the church's greater emphasis on issues of social injustice and economic inequity. "I agree with Puebla and Medellín about the need for the church to be in the fight for justice," he protested;

> I feel angry when people say I am against the poor. My family is poor; I know poverty, I grew up in poverty. The option for the poor is not an option, because an option implies there is a

free choice.[16] If there are nine of us here and we have one cake, we should divide the cake into nine equal parts. But if five of us are starving and four or us are drunk and overfed, then the five starving ones should get more cake. You don't have to be a Christian to defend the poor, to practice justice.[17]

The bishop also said he was not opposed to the base community movement or to liberation theology, two other accusations often leveled against him. "CEBs are very efficient, very good," he said, "with some exceptions. Remember that they're not just base communities but *ecclesial* base communities. Faith must be applied. The idea is excellent, but in some cases, you find only communities of the base, not ecclesial communities."[18] He spoke similarly about liberation theology. "There are theolog*ies* of liberation," he argued, adding:

There are positive and negative points of different liberation theologies. The main point of criticism is when a Marxist analysis is incorporated into a religious reading of reality. The Catholic Church officially doesn't accept that you can follow Marxism in the interpretation of social phenomena. If liberation theology is understood clearly, however, it is not only convenient but also necessary.[19]

CONSERVATIVE SEMINARIAN TO LIBERATION PRIEST

While Dom José has structured his life to support the church as it exists, Reginaldo has dedicated himself to challenging it. He was born in 1938 in the northeast, the eldest of five sons. Reginaldo's early childhood was marked by his mother's death from tuberculosis when he was eight; he vividly remembers the doctor placing a small candle between her clasped hands moments after she died, and has felt her absence all his life. His religious formation was shaped by his paternal grandmother, who encouraged him to lead prayers of the rosary in May, the Month of Mary, when he was nine years old. He also served as an altar boy at the local church.

His father, a bakery owner, was not wealthy, but he was hardly poor. Reginaldo was close to his father, who was involved in local politics through the *União Democrática Nacional* (National Democratic

Union).[20] The party represented, in Reginaldo's words, "the rural aristocracy and *latifundiários*," or landowners, and "was more connected with the vision of the rich." The elder Veloso often took Reginaldo to political rallies, where the boy was impressed by the impassioned speakers and the charged atmosphere. He remembered his father as a good boss to his workers, and when he died, hundreds came to the funeral to praise him. "They said," recalled the priest, "that surely he had stairs straight to heaven because of all the good he did for the poor."[21]

He was thirteen when he began his religious studies in Recife. After several years there, he enrolled at the Gregorian University in Rome, where he lived for seven years. He recalled that in Rome, his future adversary José Cardoso (not yet a bishop) was "nobody special," someone he did not know well. Reginaldo was ordained in December 1961.

In contrast to Dom José's early obedience to his teachers' commands, Reginaldo opposed authority even as a youngster. While he was a seminary student in Brazil, he had a philosophy teacher who treated some pupils unfairly while favoring others. Reginaldo challenged the teacher and the two had an argument in front of the class. "I don't remember the specifics," Reginaldo said, "but we had a conflict and I made him look ridiculous."[22] Reginaldo was forced to kneel in front of everyone as punishment, but he continued to mock the teacher while his back was turned, making the man even angrier.

Reginaldo claimed that the event presaged his current relations with Dom José, but his attitude toward oppressive authority was limited to classroom spats until much later. When he first went to Rome, Reginaldo said he was staunchly conservative, even reactionary. He opposed socialism and communism, thinking them evil, antireligious doctrines; the church itself "taught a radical anticommunism," recalled the priest.[23] He defended the 1964 military takeover in Brazil to doubtful friends in Rome. He pointed to the United States as a shining example of the promise of free-market capitalism and a model to which Brazil should aspire.

These ideas began to change during the Second Vatican Council. He met clerics and laity from all over the world who, as he said, "discussed different human realities" with him.[24] He greatly admired Pope John XXIII, who nearly caused a scandal by inviting Nikita Khrushchev, seen as an icon of godless communism, for a Vatican visit. The Council,

Reginaldo said, had a vision that was more anticapitalist and more open to some socialist ideas. It was through hours of conversation, reading, and observation of Council proceedings that gradually he began to soften his opposition to communism and to socialism. The process continued when he returned to Brazil in 1966, when military repression was growing harsher and popular protest was beginning to meet serious reprisals.

Not long after he returned from Rome he took a three-month course at the Superior Institute of Pastoral Liturgy, a seminary in Rio de Janeiro. "As incredible as it seems," he wrote in an autobiographical statement more than twenty years later, "that helped me open my eyes and see Brazilian reality more clearly, and see with real clarity the serious demands placed on the Church." In Rio he studied "a new theology" and learned "a new pedagogy made of participation, democratization of the word, collective construction of knowledge."[25]

In 1968, back in Recife, he was appointed to the parish of Macaxeira, near the Morro da Conceição. That was the year the dictatorship moved into its most brutal phase. The church reacted strongly, condemning the government in statements distributed around the world. As Reginaldo watched these developments with increasing concern, his reassessment of life and politics in Brazil, which had started at the Vatican Council and continued in Rio de Janeiro, took a significant turn. In Macaxeira, he worked with a priest named Alberto, who was active with a Catholic Action group. In his native Italy, Alberto had been a worker priest — that is, a priest who worked alongside his parishioners in the factory. The inspiration he found in Alberto's example completed the process of Reginaldo's "conversion." In 1969, he participated in a demonstration protesting the expulsion of two American priests from Brazil. He was apprehended by the police and would have been arrested, had Dom Hélder not intervened. Already a maverick, Reginaldo's political activity attracted the attention of local authorities. It was bold for a priest to participate in a public protest demonstration, and his rescue by Dom Hélder made him even more visible. Dom Hélder himself was under increasing fire from Brazil's government; newspaper editorials in Recife demanded his expulsion from the country.

When Padre Antônio Henrique, a close associate of Dom Hélder's, was assassinated in 1969, Reginaldo was one of thousands who took part in protest demonstrations at the young priest's burial. During the event, police pulled Reginaldo aside to inform him that he was under surveillance. Occasionally, military police showed up at Reginaldo's mass to confiscate a weekly protest journal the priest edited and handed out in his celebrations. In 1973, he was kidnapped by the military; Dom Hélder once again intervened, and Reginaldo was released after several days. While in jail he was shown all the literature that had been taken from him in the preceding four years as proof that he was, indeed, being closely watched. In 1978, Reginaldo was named to the parish of the Morro da Conceição, where he built on the work of his predecessor and continued to organize the annual festa. "It took a new turn," he said proudly, "enriching the community with a reflection on the larger problems of the population."[26]

THE PASSION FOR AUTHORITY: SCRIPTURE SAYS IT'S INDIVIDUAL

Reginaldo and Dom José do not disagree that the Bible is the most important source of Christian spirituality and that one finds in the Bible the mandates meant to guide Christians' lives. That both men root their Catholicism in the Bible, however, does not mean they read the book the same way — indeed, it seems as if they read two entirely different Bibles. The priest and the bishop disagree about the text's teachings on many issues, but especially where it addresses obedience, hierarchy, the legitimization of authority, the appropriate role of a priest, and the responsibilities of lay Catholics.

For Reginaldo, the Bible does not institutionalize authority but instead is intended to liberate the people for whom the Bible was written — to his thinking, the poor and the oppressed. It is a document, he said, that grew "from the experience of an oppressed people who had great thirst for justice."[27] The Bible does not dictate clerical authority that must be followed blindly, but demands that one understand Biblical teachings through conscientious reflection on one's life, one's material realities, and one's duties as a Christian. Reginaldo agrees that Catholics must obey the pope and his local representatives, the bishops, but one must first follow the Gospels and one's conscience. This can have radical consequences. As Reginaldo explained, "To follow the Gospels, one must be willing to fight all types of oppression, especially religious oppression and even when it comes from within the church."[28] The priest believes that one of Jesus's principal ministries involved challenging local religious leaders whose power had been corrupted and whose spiritual honesty was suspect. "There is a parallel between Caiaphas and Pilate and some bishops today," said the priest.[29]

Reginaldo's stance has echoes in history, since these were among the precepts of the Reformation set in motion by Martin Luther in 1517. But Reginaldo, a son of the church, will not consider leaving it:

> It's important to stay within the Catholic church. History put me here. Wherever history puts you, you must take up the fight there. Through the Gospels, I must work for change from within, or we'll be buried by oppressive economic and political structures. Others who have a commitment to the church of the people have not left the Catholic church; neither could I.[30]

Reginaldo's Catholicism is found in such Bible passages as: "He has sent me to bring good news to the poor. He has sent me to proclaim liberty to the captives and recovery of sight to the blind, to set free the oppressed and announce that the time has come when the Lord will save his people" (Luke 4:18–19). According to Reginaldo, a responsible Christian must challenge the structures that cause most people to live in poverty, illiteracy, poor health, and inadequate housing while a minority lives in wealth. He believes that the church belongs squarely on the side of the poor, advocating for them and working on their behalf. Both individual Catholics and the church as an institution, he feels, have a sacred responsibility to challenge political systems, economic relationships between nations, government policies at all levels, and local patterns of patronage, among other things, to begin creating a more just society, in keeping with God's intentions. His is an understanding of Christian theology that closely follows the thinking of liberation theologians like Peruvian Gustavo Gutiérrez (1973) and Mexican José Porfiro Miranda (1981), among others.

As practiced in Recife and on the Morro, these criticisms find expressions in leftist political trends and especially in the Partido dos Trabalhadores (Workers' Party), or PT, a national coalition of disparate leftist groups and alliances formed in 1979. The PT rose from regional obscurity to national prominence in only a decade, in part because of its success in building on the grassroots networks of CEBs and other local-level church organizations.[31] Reginaldo was accused of using his pulpit to preach PT doctrine. He admits that the ideas of the PT come closest to his aspirations of a Christian model of society. He was asked several times to be a candidate for office in PT campaigns, but he always refused and is not officially affiliated with the party.

Some critics charged Reginaldo with alienating wealthier patrons by preaching against them. "We used to have rich and middle-class people helping with the festa," complained one woman, "but no more. Reginaldo drove them away by telling them there was something wrong with them because they were better off than we are. But we need help from people like that. It's just another way Reginaldo hurt the community."[32]

"I have tried to teach things that to me are evident in the Gospels," responded the priest. "The rich in our economic system represent injustice and oppression." Reginaldo says he invited the rich to become conscious of the oppressive role they play, and to seek salvation by making a commitment to the poor. "I think it is simple and clear," he claims, "but poor people who make an 'option for the rich' think I don't want connections with the rich, that I want to reject their help."[33]

The priest was also accused of practicing Marxism, but his reading of Marx, like that of many followers of liberation theology, did not embrace the thinker's entire *oeuvre* so much as borrow from his analytic methodology. Much of the intention behind Marx's teachings, Reginaldo asserted, "coincides strongly with Biblical teaching." He cited the prophet Isaiah as an explicit Biblical denunciation of exploitation that one also finds in Marx's writings. The passage says, in part,

> My people will build houses and live in them, plant vineyards and eat their fruit; they will not build for others to live in or plant for others to eat. They will be as long-lived as a tree, and my chosen ones will enjoy the fruit of their labour. They will not toil to no purpose, or raise children for misfortune, because they and their issue after them are a race blessed by the Lord. (Isaiah 65:21–23)[34]

Reginaldo noted similar teachings elsewhere in the Bible. Acts, for instance, says, "All believers agreed to hold everything in common: they began to sell their property and possessions and distribute to every-one according to his need" (Acts 2:44–45). Marx, said Reginaldo, wrote about how to create a just and fraternal society, and his work offers valuable insights about class relations, labor processes, and possibili-ties for structural, society-wide change. "We benefit from this, espe-cially in Latin America" he explained, "through a sociological analysis that takes advantage of . . . many intuitions from Marx. . . , whose thought is like you find in the Prophets, like you find in the Apostles, in the Gospels."[35]

This view angered his critics, who saw in Reginaldo a clergyman who abused his priestly vows, betrayed the church, and (at best) mis-led or (at worst) lied to his congregation. He, after all, was an educated man, they said; he "turned the heads" of those seduced by his charisma. His fans, however, saw in Reginaldo's analyses a clear expla-nation of the poverty, political injustice, and unequal power relations that have adversely effected the Morro since the community was first settled. They saw in the priest a man whose vows put him in the trenches with the unfortunate and forgotten, whose battle with the bishop was martyr-like, and whose encouragement of Morro residents to fight for their community enabled them to better their lives materi-ally and spiritually.

THE REBEL PRIEST: FAITH REDEEMED OR TRUST BETRAYED?

Few of the Morro's active Catholics expressed neutrality toward Regi-naldo. They were either dedicated advocates or passionate opponents of the priest. Many in the Resistance pointed out that before Reginaldo came to the Morro, they were alienated from the Roman Catholic church and felt it irrelevant to their lives and problems. Dona Luiza, who directs the local elementary school, said that even though she was raised in the church, as an adult she didn't participate in church activi-ties. Then Reginaldo asked her to take part in a mass for young people. She did so reluctantly. "I didn't like Reginaldo much when he first came," she recalled. "I thought he was a show-off. I went to the masses, but I didn't get involved." Then he asked her to attend a meeting to help organize the Center for Reading and Information a year or so after he arrived. "I didn't want to go because I still didn't like him much," she said. "But I went anyway, liked the idea, and left the meeting as the

Center's director."[36] It was the first of many community projects on which she worked, and was the beginning of a steady friendship with Reginaldo. She also started attending church worship services regularly for the first time in years.

Others were similarly attracted. Reginaldo's sermons about social concerns and his descriptions of a Jesus who wanted to help them solve concrete problems drew many formerly disaffected Catholics into active participation in church affairs. A youth group formed by Reginaldo's predecessor was expanded; as their activities in the community grew, so did their numbers, and eventually there were close to seventy active participants. "There is a different energy on the Morro," explained a former seminarian who had recently moved to the community. "People can be more involved. Things have changed here."[37]

Dona Hilda, who has lived on the Morro for close to fifty years, told of houses destroyed by winter rains one year that Reginaldo helped rebuild. This was around the same time that the community was wrestling with the city to get running water.

> When part of my house fell, Reginaldo held a raffle to raise money to rebuild my house and four others. He paid the workers to work each day. The boys who smoked *maconha* [marijuana] carried everything, built my house. The water arrived at the same time. I turned on the faucet in the street, the boys took a bath, I made a big soup — I'm proud to say that my house was built by *marginais* [marginals, thieves]. I thank first God, then Reginaldo. The house is well made.[38]

Dona Hilda was especially happy that local youth were involved in the construction project. As the self-appointed grandmother to many young men on her block, she had spent years trying to keep them away from the darker temptations of Recife and trying to woo back those who already were lost to smoking maconha, sniffing glue, and committing petty crimes. It was a miracle to her that Reginaldo inspired some of these boys to rebuild houses, and she was grateful that for a time, at least, they were off the streets, working hard, and earning an honest wage. Because of this she saw Reginaldo as a man dedicated to all the members of his parish, even those who seemed to have no use for him and who were rejected by the larger community.

While many on the Morro told stories of their renewed interest in the church because of Reginaldo's influence, praised him for his efforts to reach even the most unreachable among them, and declared loyalty until death to the priest they saw as a man of God in the best sense, not everyone was so enthused. Hiring young thugs to rebuild houses at church expense, said detractors like Seu Azul, was the wrong way to broaden the church's reach and a waste of resources besides. Seu Azul was born and raised on the Morro and remembered what he called its better days as the time before Reginaldo's tenure. He and many of his colleagues also felt it was preposterous that Reginaldo encouraged people toward greater political involvement. In their eyes, he transformed the church from a sanctuary to a political center, using the space for worship services that sounded like get-out-the-vote drives, and also allowing representatives of the Workers' Party to hold rallies and meetings in the church. It started, explained Seu Azul's mother, when Reginaldo urged the community Bible-study groups to lobby local government for water for the Hill. When the mayor came to the Hill to give a speech around the time of the water campaign, residents heckled him; Reginaldo was among them. Though the lobbying effort was successful and today the entire Hill enjoys running water at least a few days a week, many people were appalled at the group's tactics. "The image of our community became ugly in the rest of the city," said Rui, a twenty-eight-year-old traditionalist who grew up on the Morro. "They [Reginaldo's parishioners] only knew how to criticize and complain, messing with politics, with city hall."[39]

Shortly after the water campaign, Reginaldo brought more shame to the Morro, according to those who didn't like him. In 1980 he wrote a song protesting the deportation of an Italian priest, which landed him in jail for several days and in national newspapers for several weeks, a fact his supporters pointed to with pride and his detractors with derision.[40] For supporters, the event indicated a man willing to put himself at risk to speak the truth. For detractors, it was proof that since the early years of his work on the Morro, Reginaldo showed signs of unhealthy rebelliousness and a need for the spotlight.

This latter group was angered further when Reginaldo gave the annual festa a decidedly political cast, preaching, praying, and singing about women's rights, Brazil's foreign debt, the destruction of the Amazon; they resented that he invited people from outside the Morro and even outside Recife to come to the festa and talk about human rights abuses, unionizing, and land struggles. His work even attracted activists from other parts of the city who decided to settle on the Hill because of what he was doing with the church. "People from the Morro were more and more alienated," asserted one young man. "Reginaldo never did anything for this community. He only destroyed. The Morro used to be a united community. On Sundays, everyone went to church; people helped each other. Then Reginaldo came, and the divisions started."[41]

Perhaps worst of all, alleged his foes, he changed the very nature of the mass. It was no longer a time of quiet prayer, reverence, and brief escape from the trauma and drudgery of daily life. They claimed that it became a reminder of the neighborhood's poverty, crime, hunger, chronic unemployment, illiteracy. By making the mass a time to concentrate on community woes, they said, he sullied the one place where people could find refuge from exactly those concerns. Many finally fled Reginaldo's church in disgust, finding that one of their few sources of retreat and spiritual sustenance had been cheapened by material concerns. Some attended weekly mass in other parishes; others left the Catholic church and sought comfort among fundamentalist traditions; still others simply stopped going to church at all. There was even a feeling that Reginaldo was the source of a growing anarchy and loss of control over community life. Marí, a married woman in her late thirties who had grown up on the Morro and was now raising her own two children on the Hill, put it this way:

> I got involved in the church [with Reginaldo] because a friend asked me to, but I didn't stay long. I heard things, I became very alarmed. I saw that it wasn't religion, it was politics. Reginaldo changed a lot of things in the community. We always had kids in the streets, but not like today. Reginaldo gave them too much liberty. . . . We never had people who smelled glue, kids on the loose. Today there are mothers without any commitment to their children. This didn't exist before.[42]

Reginaldo finally lost what legitimacy he still had with his disillusioned parishioners when he stood up to Dom José, and many said with a sigh that the ensuing conflict between the bishop and the Resistance was an unfortunate but unsurprising result of Reginaldo's *jeito*, his style or way of being. The bishop showed ample patience, said the priest's detractors, before the situation forced him to make some difficult and unpopular decisions, like calling the police. Marí's explanation echoed that of others who support the bishop:

> Many people don't know what happened on the Morro. It's like when there's a husband and wife. Who orders the house? The husband. If the husband says he doesn't want his wife to go out dancing, and she goes anyway, then he can put her out of the house. Just like with the bishop and Reginaldo. The bishop told him not to do politics; he did politics anyway, so he was put out of the house. He was told he could return if he'd ask public pardon, but he won't. For this, just this, it's confused the entire community. It only depends on him asking pardon, but he won't. Where's Christ in that? Even Christ on the cross, on earth — He asked pardon for everyone, but Reginaldo can't even just for himself. It's very sad.[43]

The most damning accusation was expressed quietly, but insistently, by those who most dislike the priest. "Reginaldo got money from outside Brazil," went one popular sentiment, "and many people profited from that. People who had nothing now have good jobs, phones, two houses, even a car. Why do you think so many people wanted to work with him?" When asked why many people still follow Reginaldo, many of his opponents pursed their lips in scorn and made the perhaps universal thumb-rubbing-finger hand sign for "money." People even said that the modest house Reginaldo was slowly building as a place to retire in the countryside was paid for by money he stole from the church.

Such accusations brought sighs from Reginaldo. "That's the way people normally analyze,"[44] he said wearily. "No one is in the [Resistance] struggle for financial gain." The Resistance has, however, attracted monies and other support from sympathizers in southern Brazil and abroad. These resources do not go into individual pockets, but they help the Resistance maintain the fight.

TRANSCENDENT SON OF MAN, IMMANENT SON OF GOD

The theological arguments that Dom José or Reginaldo might use to support their positions were not cited by Morro residents in explaining their allegiance to one side or the other, but at the heart of the community strife lay a fundamental disagreement about the teachings of Jesus and the nature of God as described in the Bible. The contradiction was expressed in polarities that rarely, if ever, allowed for middle ground. A series of questions best elaborates the dilemma. Did Jesus teach first that one must be submissive to the will of God by choosing prayer and contemplation over proclamation and action? Or did Jesus teach that one must be submissive to the will of God by choosing prayerful action over mere contemplation? Is the will of God best elucidated through the teachings of the Roman Catholic church, or does the church impede a Christian's ability to understand Christ's teachings by insisting that only church authority may fully explain the Bible's meanings? Was Jesus a revolutionary who taught his followers how to overturn unjust political systems, or a prophet who taught how to withstand the insults of life's injustice by offering a path to other-worldly salvation? Did Jesus stress material change as a means of spiritual illumination, or spirituality as a means of freedom from material concerns? Did Jesus become incarnate as a carpenter and fisherman to show special concern for the poor, or to show the need for humility in earthly endeavors?

These questions point to the tension between an image of Jesus Transcendent, teaching a spirituality that points away from this world toward a heavenly refuge, and a Jesus Immanent, teaching a spirituality that points to the inherent dignity of this world and the necessity of struggling to better it through what liberation theologians call "orthopraxy." This means a course of action chosen through reflection, prayer, and a study of the Bible. The first position asks: What must Christians do to make themselves right in God's eyes? The second asks: What must Christians do to make the world right in God's eyes?

Theologians who advocate one position or another do not make their arguments this simple. Traditional theologians believe strongly that the church and faithful Roman Catholics must help others in need and must act to alleviate suffering. Liberation theologians believe in the vitality and efficacy of prayer and of a disciplined spiritual practice. But helping the poor, for traditionalists, doesn't necessarily mean working to topple social structures that create poverty. Mere prayer, contemplation, or charity, for the liberationists, doesn't satisfy all that God demands of faithful Catholics.

In the conflict on the Morro da Conceição, those who subscribe to Reginaldo's style of religiosity have learned from him and from others who believe that a liberationist way of "being church" empowers them to question and to act in a realm that includes the political but that also transcends it. If one is doing hands-on organizing work sanctioned by a priest, work that he has helped reveal as God's work, it takes on a new gravity. For many on the Morro engaged in community- or city-level activism, the realization that they have the ability, strength, and intelligence for sustained, organized work has been a personal and collective liberation.

Everyone I spoke with who was caught by Reginaldo's vision and leadership style had gone through an experience that I call a "conversion" to a liberationist model of church and engagement, not unlike the change Reginaldo went through during and after the Second Vatican Council. Many on the Morro were moved by Reginaldo's dedication to the community and his quiet passion about the need to fight for people's spiritual *and* material needs. They were also moved by his inclusion of even the least among them. Dona Luisa told a story of Reginaldo's return from jail after he had been incarcerated for writing a song in defense of the deported Italian priest. The event erased the doubts she still had about Reginaldo, and sealed her loyalty to him.

> Vicente was a man in the community who was not quite right in the head. He picked through the garbage for food, lived on the praça — kids were always taunting him, throwing stones at him. He never bathed. He would come to the door of the school and we knew he was there without looking because we could smell him. We always gave him clothes from the festa. Sometimes someone would grab him and give him a bath and a haircut.
>
> When Reginaldo was released from prison, people lined up to greet him and hug him. Vicente was in the line, too, though

no one would stand too close to him. I stood a little way off to see what Reginaldo would do with Vicente. When he came up to hug Reginaldo, he was crying and saying, "Is it you, sir, is it really you?" Reginaldo said, "It's me, Vicente, it's me" and opened his arms wide and hugged Vicente longer than anyone, stink and filth and all, and Vicente cried and cried. Other priests not only wouldn't go near Vicente, they kicked him out of the church. From then on I really trusted Reginaldo.

When Vicente got sick, we took up a collection and then took him to the hospital. He died there. We laid out his body in the parish house and hired someone to clean and dress it. Then we brought the body to the church — it was a tumult! Everyone on the Morro wanted to pay homage to Vicente. Everyone brought at least a plant; the kids cried when they heard he had died, and they stole flowers to put on his coffin. It was a funeral more beautiful than any I'd ever seen. There were so many people![45]

Dona Luisa finally believed Reginaldo's sincerity by the way he treated a community outcast. His warm embrace of a man so smelly that no one else would even stand close to him redeemed her faith in the message of Christianity that Reginaldo preached. Through him, she moved toward an understanding of faith that grounded the Bible and Jesus's examples in concrete, daily realities.

For those whose Catholicism was less materially involved, however, this very grounding served to evacuate Jesus from the church. Women and men whose lives provided little relief from the countless daily indignities of relentless poverty found that Reginaldo had removed their one sure solace and replaced it with reminders of the very problems from which they needed relief. Reginaldo did not bolster their faith; he betrayed it. People he encouraged toward greater political involvement often proposed ideas about the community's relationship with city and state government that seemed sure to anger those in power and thereby to jeopardize the community's potential future gains. While Reginaldo often attracted people who had long ago broken their relationship with the church, he created a new group of disaffected, those whose Jesus offered salvation by transcending worldly concerns, not by wallowing in them.

POLITICAL IMPLICATIONS

The influence of both Dom José and Reginaldo extended well beyond the church. The bishop was an ally of people long used to exercising power through formal and behind-the-scenes venues. He represented, and acted on behalf of, a vertical authority structure that has marked Brazil's history since the colonial era and that, throughout the worst days of the dictatorship, effectively silenced organized protests and individual activists, making opposition to the government a dangerous position. Reginaldo stood with people historically lacking weight in political struggles. His work challenged the tradition of power hierarchy and advocated a horizontal, inclusive style of religious expression, community involvement, and decision making.

The bishop protested Reginaldo's work in part because, he claimed, the priest was too overtly political in his pastoral responsibilities. His sermons, his prayers, the songs he wrote for worship services, and his position outside the church in political contexts — electoral campaigns, lobbying initiatives, protest rallies — were not appropriate for clergy, said the bishop. According to church rules, priests (or monks or nuns) may not hold public office, take public political stands, or be formally affiliated with a political party. The church, Dom José argued, is above politics. Liberation-minded Recifenses always scoffed at this claim, saying the church is and always has been intensely political, if politics is measured in the institution's influence in secular affairs. The argument, they point out, would have more weight if the church had actually kept clear of secular involvement during its nearly 500 years in Brazil, but its political machinations started early.

During all sixty-six years of the imperial era, priests regularly held parliamentary office. After the monarchy was overthrown, priests and bishops worked for political parties or government offices in the Old Republic (between 1889 and 1930). Under Getúlio Vargas' rule, from 1930 to 1945, the cardinal of Latin American himself — Dom Sebastião Leme, formerly archbishop of Olinda and Recife — worked side-by-side with the dictator to reclaim privileges lost to the church after 1889. During that era priests held office; the most famous was Padre Cícero of Joaseiro, a state senator from Ceará and one of the most powerful men in the region. From 1945 to 1964, priests and bishops often advocated social reforms and programs that were addressed in electoral arenas, and after 1964 the church spoke in tones that were often overtly political when it opposed the military regime.[46]

Dom José's claim about the church as an apolitical presence was not seriously entertained by many in his diocese; even those who supported him admitted that the church had at least some political role in Brazilian society simply because it is an important national institution. But the bishop held to his stand and was particularly incensed when he believed those under his watch did not heed his request to stay out of the political limelight. A Workers' Party candidate ran a television commercial in the Recife area that included jubilant Franciscan monks apparently giving him their endorsement in a celebratory rally. The bishop countered with harsh reprimands to the order, and went on television himself to denounce the commercial and offer an indirect endorsement of the opposing candidate, a conservative who won the election.

Reginaldo tried the bishop's patience in similar ways; the priest's stark criticisms of Dom José in the local press across several years also did not endear him to the bishop. Though Dom José didn't say so, Reginaldo's billboard may have been the last straw. In the back of the Morro church, on top of the stage that divides the church from the soccer field and that serves as the staging area for the large masses during the festa every December, a large billboard usually sports a church-related theme. During the presidential elections of 1989, Reginaldo used the billboard to suggest the following: "Think before you vote. Are you a boss or a worker? Of the candidates for president, which is a boss and which is a worker? Will you vote for the boss?" An Electoral Court judge ruled that the billboard had to come down because it represented free advertising for the Workers' Party, but it stayed up throughout the festa that occurred immediately before the 1989 presidential run-off election. It reached a large audience — exactly Reginaldo's intention.

DEMISE OF A PRIEST, RISE OF RESISTANCE

Dom José had a powerful recourse against Reginaldo, and the billboard destroyed any lingering hesitation he may have felt in using it. Immediately after the festa of 1989, while Reginaldo was taking a few days' holiday with family in another state, Dom José delivered a letter to

Reginaldo's home informing him that he had been suspended on grounds that the priest had violated canon code 1373. The code forbids a priest to disobey his superior and forbids him to incite his congregation against church authority. Dom José alleged that, despite several warnings, Reginaldo had not changed unacceptable behavior; the bishop said the suspension was his only recourse. It meant that in the diocese of Olinda and Recife, Reginaldo could not perform any of the functions for which he had been ordained: he could not celebrate mass, hear confession, nor perform baptisms, confirmations, weddings, or burials. He could not, in short, be a priest. In addition to suspending Reginaldo, Dom José ordered him to leave the Morro da Conceição and to turn over the parish keys.

Word leaked before Reginaldo found out; the news electrified the priest's supporters, who contacted the press. "When I came home from work that day," remembers Zé João, "the saint was draped in black, the bells were tolling, people were running around like a war was on or like someone big had died. We had a meeting that night and decided not to accept Reginaldo's suspension."[47]

The priest was expected home the next day, and a contingent of about a hundred supporters went to meet him at the city bus station. One television station decided to get a jump on its competition and persuaded the state police to intercept his bus. About an hour south of Recife, the bus was pulled over and a camera crew climbed aboard, their bright lights surprising the passengers — and their news stunning the priest. When he arrived, his supporters carried him on their shoulders, gave him the keys to the Morro church, and posed for the cameras. Reginaldo blasted the bishop, calling him "pathologic" and saying he acted so arbitrarily because he suffered from an inferiority complex. He said the bishop was paranoid and in need of psychiatric help. "Since he's paranoid," said the priest, "it may be that he'll commit even worse abuses, but I pray to God that doesn't happen. I hope he manages to sleep well every night, like I always do." When the crowd delivered Reginaldo to the Morro, parishioners opened the church and rang the bells. "They want to finish the church of the people," Reginaldo told them, "but they are fooling themselves, because you are proof that this will not happen."[48]

Reginaldo's supporters took to calling themselves The Resistance. They decided they would agree to his suspension if they had a say in choosing his replacement. The bishop agreed to negotiate with them, despite protests from his advisers, who said he was setting a dangerous precedent. Across ten months, the group and the bishop met. The Resistance offered a list of twelve acceptable candidates. The bishop offered a priest named Constante. The Resistance suggested that Constante be named assistant to one of their candidates.

During this time, the Resistance continued to use the church in twice-weekly celebrations. Reginaldo coordinated them, but a sympathetic priest from another parish actually ran them. When Dom José learned that priests were holding mass for the Resistance, he forbade all ordained persons in his diocese from participating. Graffiti around the Morro and throughout the city called him a devil and demanded his ouster. A banner strung over the doors of the Morro church prayed for deliverance from the bishop. A rumor started that the pope was on the verge of replacing Dom José for his ineptitude. "Rome will tire of Dom José because he's missing something in the head," maintained one priest. "Rome will waken to this eventually. They'll remove him." He echoed a cherished belief that many shared.

Without priests to consecrate the host (that is, to bless the unleavened bread fundamental to the Catholic mass and that church teaching says becomes Christ's flesh once blessed), Morro Resistance worship services were called Celebrations of the Word. Communion was included, but consecration was not. A small group took unconsecrated host to a priest in another parish twice a month. That priest included the Morro's host in his parish's eucharist, thus consecrating it, and then the Morro contingent brought it home to use in Resistance celebrations. The identity of the priest willing to consecrate Morro host remained a carefully guarded secret; it was always assumed to be a cleric who liked and supported Reginaldo.[49]

Through the months of negotiations with the bishop, the "rebel" masses and the priestless celebrations, media coverage played an important role. Recife's three daily papers provided frequent updates on the situation. Mention occasionally was made in Brazil's papers of record in Rio de Janeiro and São Paulo and circulated to other cities through the country's wire services. Local television also followed the story, especially TV Viva, an alternative public station in nearby Olinda. Later, national and international secular and church publications carried stories about the Morro.[50]

The Resistance was given positive coverage by all sources, with the exception of Recife's oldest daily paper, the *Diário de Pernambuco*. TV Viva especially depicted Dom José as a tyrant and Reginaldo as a hero. Dom José became exceptionally media shy, refusing to give interviews or explain himself to the press because he felt his words were distorted. "I know that most of the news reports aren't very exact," he once sighed. "I have a permanent complaint against the media. Some in the group that doesn't agree with me [the Resistance] have a very good ability to manipulate the media."[51] The bishop's refusal to talk to reporters created a classic catch-22: the press didn't like being refused, so coverage of Dom José grew more unflattering, which confirmed his decision to refuse interviews.

The Resistance group quickly realized that they couldn't let just anyone talk to reporters, so they named two spokespersons, Dona Luisa and Zé João. Dona Luisa, the extremely articulate director of the Morro elementary school, could make strong statements in a quiet way that made them sound reasonable. Zé João, a government bureaucrat and union organizer and also very articulate, was an amiable young man who could make complete strangers feel like friends. Both also turned out to be telegenic, a pragmatic plus for a group seeking all the media attention it could get. The church hierarchy and many laity in and outside the Morro disagreed with Resistance positions, but letters from Recife, southern Brazil, Europe and Canada made it seem like the rest of the world wholeheartedly supported the group.

On September 5, 1990, Dom José sent his assistant and Padre Constante, his choice of replacement priest, to the Morro, perhaps thinking that if they simply appeared, the assistant could install the priest and the problem would be resolved. Just to be safe, a pair of policemen accompanied them. When the quartet found the church and parish house locked, they went to Dona Luisa and asked for the keys. She said she didn't have them, nor did she know where they were. This was technically true, though she probably could have guessed: Whenever the church was used in the months following Reginaldo's suspension, one person was assigned to lock the building and take the key. He or she then quietly gave the key to another loyalist. The second key holder gave it to a third a few days later, and again the transfer was secret. Only the current key holder and the immediately preceding one knew who had the key at any given moment.

Keys had become a potent symbol in the Resistance and among liberation-minded Catholics throughout the city. The Resistance claimed that Peter, the first pope, had received the keys to the church from Jesus in the form of instruction, and that Peter had then passed them to the people, not to an institution. No bishop, they said, Dom José included, held the true keys to the church, and the Resistance intended to drive home their point by refusing to turn over the keys to the church on the Morro. "Dom José tried to break up the church," asserted one older Morro woman, "but the people don't have to ask for the key, they already have the key." A local musician who wrote a song about the key explained simply, "We didn't give the key to Dom José because it's Peter's key."[52]

News spread fast that Constante and the bishop's assistant were on the Hill with two cops, and a small, angry crowd gathered at the church entrance. The clerics tried to talk with them, but were told they were unwelcome and that the church on the Morro would never belong to the bishop so they might as well leave. Constante and the assistant soon saw that their effort was fruitless, and they drove away under a hail of catcalls.

In response to Constante's unexpected visit, the Resistance organized a twenty-four-hour vigil at the church. Negotiations between Dom José and Reginaldo's supporters were scheduled to continue, but it was ominous that Constante had made an appearance on the Hill with the bishop's right-hand man and the police, especially since the bishop himself had just left for a month in Rome. It seemed the bishop meant to install his priest but not to be around to assume the consequences. Many people, including Dona Luisa and Zé João, still believed the bishop would work to resolve the problem in harmony with the community, but others felt their trust dwindling. At least with an organized vigil in front of the church, the Resistance group reasoned, the bishop could never again take the community by surprise.

A Declaration of War

The next meeting scheduled between Dom José and Resistance organizers, for October 19, 1990, never took place. That morning at about 10:00 A.M., Constante came to the Morro with the bishop's assistant once again. This time, however, the clerics brought more than just a pair of cops; they arrived with five trucks of fully armed, helmeted riot police.

After initial moments of astonishment and disbelief, the group on watch in front of the church scattered to tell the rest of the Morro that the community was under siege. The troops quickly formed one ring around the church and another around the parish house. They cut open the lock on the church gates and accompanied Constante inside, where the bishop's assistant officially installed him as the new priest of the parish. Forming a tight circle around the priest, the soldiers escorted him across the praça to the parish house, broke open that lock, and stood guard outside while the priest surveyed the building.

The Resistance vigil keepers phoned the press and dispatched messengers to other parts of the city. Soon, an outraged crowd of several hundred was chanting and screaming and taunting the police. Old women fell to their knees in prayer in the middle of the melee. Young men wept and cursed. "I was on the bus coming to the Morro when someone told me, 'The Morro is on fire,'" remembered Zé João. "When the bus arrived, I couldn't believe it. People nearly did set things on fire. Like the saying goes, in the hour of rage, you use what you have in your hand."[53]

The chaos was soon heightened by television crews and print journalists. Two television reporters interviewed a dazed Constante. They asked him if he was glad to be there, and he said he didn't know. They asked how the problem would be resolved, and he said he didn't know. They asked several other questions, and the disheveled priest kept saying "I don't know." Then one reporter paused briefly and asked, "What is your name?" to which the priest, with a slight smile, replied, "I forget."

When Reginaldo appeared on camera, he was tight-lipped with anger, and though the crowd jostled and bounced against him, he did not move. He soundly condemned the bishop for having sent soldiers against the people. He said he didn't know how Constante could still call himself a man of God after allowing himself to be delivered to the Hill so violently. The community would never accept Constante as their priest, he promised, adding that the man was doomed to an isolated time in a hostile place if he really intended to attempt leadership of the Morro parish.

A throaty rendition of the song about the key rang out across the praça. Some young people started pelting the soldiers with stones, but Reginaldo stopped them. The line of troops around the church held, but the helmeted soldiers, nightsticks drawn and gun holsters un-snapped, looked distinctly nervous. One said that though he felt the church's actions were wrong, he would obey his commanding officer and do what he was told. Some in the crowd tried to talk the soldiers into stepping down from the church steps and joining their rebellion. Two men pushed some soldiers too far and despite Reginaldo's pro-tests were thrown to the ground, handcuffed, and rushed to jail.

Constante and the bishop's assistant finally climbed back into their car, which was parked near the church doors, and tried to leave. Police had to help them walk even the few feet to their car to insure they would get there unmolested. The car circled the praça toward the road leading away from the Morro, and the crowd ran to meet it as it sped away. They threw rocks, bottles, and jeers of "Judas!" and "Trai-tor!" Most of the police left with the clergy, but one van and five cops stayed behind.

The residents' council had long been planning to hold a mass cele-brating their tenth anniversary the following Sunday. There was some discussion about if they should proceed, given the events of that Fri-day, but the group decided that, now more than ever, they must cele-brate a mass. Hundreds of people from across the city who had seen the Morro violence on the television news and on the front pages of the papers came to the Hill for the event.

The mass couldn't be celebrated inside the church, since the po-lice had replaced the lock, so the Resistance decided to hold it directly in front of the church. A foreign-born priest and leading figure in the lo-cal grassroots church communities, in full vestments and unmindful of ever-present TV cameras, led the celebration.

Though the church was locked, many knew that the two side doors wouldn't hold against even slight pressure, and the police had neglected to secure those entrances. Near the end of the mass a loose line-dance formed and moved slowly around the church building. With the police occupied in watching the crowd, some of the dancers led the circle to the side doors. The doors opened after a few gentle pushes, just as the dancers anticipated, and they danced into the church amid shouts of joy. A good part of the line was inside, through the church, and out the opposite door before the soldiers realized what was happening. Later there were accusations that the dancers had stolen things from the church — the chalice, some robes, some Bibles — but the dancers said they touched nothing. They simply relished the ease with which they hoodwinked the police and could stand once more, even briefly, in their church as its proprietors, singing and dancing and laughing at the guards. The police were placed on twenty-four-hour watch in front of the church.

THE CITY REACTS

Dom José's decision to use police force to "take back" the Morro church allowed him to put his priest into the community, a goal he had been unable to reach through discussions with the Resistance. The action was seen by some as a sure sign that the bishop's time in Recife was limited, since the pope could not possibly approve of such a drastic step. Others said they had heard that the bishop had acted on the pope's orders. Dom José had been in Rome only the month before and had consulted with the pope about the situation on the Morro. When asked, Dom José said, "I knew what to do. I spoke to the pope and to the second in command."[54] In Dom José's mind, the church on the Morro clearly belonged to the diocese, and the group holding it was breaking a civil law by denying access of a lawful property owner — in this case, the institutional church — to its own property. In translating the problem into a civil affair, the bishop then saw the logic of calling in a secular authority — the police.

It wasn't the first time Dom José had used the police to solve what he saw as a problem of trespass; when he responded to the Morro by calling the police, many in Recife felt their worst fears about him confirmed. He seemed to be a man who would quickly resort to force when threatened. It didn't help that at the very moment the police were cutting the Morro church lock, the bishop was making his first public appearance after his trip to Rome by celebrating a mass for the region's military forces. Dom José had first called police to silence protesters, more than a year earlier.[55] Some saw this action as proof that he had no legitimacy among the people and therefore relied on force as the only means he had to get his way. After the initial public shock, however, and a few articles in the paper, the event became merely one more scandal in Dom José's rocky early years in Recife — until the police raid on the Morro.

The Morro was much more visible and its residents more articulate than those Recife Catholics who had met police summoned by Dom José, so the bishop's decision to call in the troops had wider reverberations. As a celebrated religious pilgrimage site, the Morro was famous far beyond the city. It was also known locally as one of Recife's two most politically organized communities and had allies among activists and clergy throughout the city, northeast Brazil, and beyond.[56] Because it was so well organized, Morro residents met obstacles with tenacity and often with success, and they knew how to exert pressure. And as Reginaldo and the Resistance participants had learned, there was a wide network of hostility toward Dom José. The bishop's decision to call police to the Morro da Conceição would not go unanswered.

One of the first responses came from a group of priests, unofficially nicknamed *Os Padres Rebeldes* (The Rebel Priests) or *57 Rebeldes* (57 Rebels). They gathered immediately after the police arrived on the Morro and drafted a public letter of protest. They were *envergonhados* (ashamed), they wrote, that their bishop once again had resorted to police force to impose his will. A group of more than five hundred laity also published their disapproval in the press, in a letter called "Laity in Solidarity with the Morro da Conceição."

Shortly after the police escorted Constante to the Morro church, posters appeared all over town announcing a rally and march against the bishop on October 30th. The event was to protest Dom José's action on the Morro, to call for his ouster, and to demand "the right to be church" (*Pelo Direito de Ser Igreja*). About 3,000 people participated, making it one of the city's biggest demonstrations that year. At the head of the march was a tall wooden cross, draped with a plain white stole and a large white paper key. Many of the marchers wore similar keys around their necks. In the middle of the march was the sound car, a station wagon with speakers bristling from its roof that is the most important part of any Brazilian political demonstration. It wound its way through downtown Recife (without detours provided for irate drivers) and ended with speeches and street theater outside the Palace of the Manguinhos, Dom José's residence. Dom José had anticipated the demonstration by going to Caruarú, his hometown in the state's interior. He left instructions for his staff to videotape the event in front of the palace, which they did discretely. He later explained that he used the video to learn the faces of his enemies, as he considered the marchers. Any nuns or priests in the crowd that day were wise to remain out of a camera's eye.

WHAT ABOUT THE FESTA?

In early November — two weeks and three days after the police "invasion," as the Resistance called it — the community hosted a meeting of priests and lay representatives from nearby parishes. Reginaldo's suspension and the ensuing conflict had split the parishes into those who supported him and those who supported the bishop (one parish tried to reconcile with both, an idea that met with derision from all sides). The parishes that turned their backs on Reginaldo were headed by priests recently appointed by the bishop; they did not attend this meeting.

The meeting concerned the upcoming festa, the festival to the Virgin Mary, due to start in just over three weeks. Every year it took months of planning and work from hundreds of volunteers to ready the community for the nine days of religious events and festivities that led up to the Feast of the Immaculate Conception, on December 8th. This year, however, the community's attention had been devoted to the confusion that followed Reginaldo's suspension, and the festa remained unorganized, a potentially disastrous situation. There was no indication from the bishop what plans were in place for the 1990 festa, and Morro residents were growing anxious, because they knew that regardless of the community's readiness or the official church's preparations, thousands of pilgrims would start arriving at the end of the month.

The people now calling themselves the Resistance had run the festa since before Reginaldo had come to the parish, and they felt they were logically the best ones to run it on such short notice this year. At the meeting, with thirty-five people from four parishes, there were two predominant attitudes. Some felt they should ignore the whole affair, not offer any help, and let the official church — that is, the bishop — flounder. "They have taken away our resources, therefore we won't take responsibility," said one man. They proposed alerting the newspapers to warn the public that this year's festa would surely be a travesty because of Dom José. The bishop, noted this faction, hated negative publicity, and would be especially humiliated when the reasons for such a dismal festa were made known.

Others argued that they should "open their hands" and try once more to negotiate with the bishop. They were concerned about the security of the event, which would be threatened without a strong organizational infrastructure. The festa, they reasoned, should be a time of cease-fire.

The meeting became a shouting match before a decision could be reached. Representatives of the Morro decided to inform Dom José that the people of the Morro — that is, the Resistance, though they would not call themselves that to the bishop — would run this year's festa, thereby insuring a successful event, if the bishop would give them complete organizational freedom. If he were not amenable to this idea, they offered a second proposal: get a neutral religious order to run the affair.

They met with the bishop on November 9th to present their idea. He rejected it as too unilateral. The group also tried to re-open negotiations about Constante. They proposed that the local head of the Carmelites, the religious order to which Dom José belonged, take charge of the Morro, with Constante acting as auxiliary priest. Then Reginaldo would retire immediately. This proposal was also refused; negotiations about Reginaldo, the bishop said, were closed. The group left the meeting certain that the festa was doomed. Unbeknownst to them, the bishop had another scheme, and it was brilliant.

On November 15th, Dom José announced that Frei Damião, a Capuchin monk, would be present for all nine days leading up to the feast day itself and would celebrate the rousing last mass on the final day. Already ninety years old, the monk was famous in the northeast for his "missions," journeys throughout the region to preach the word of God and to exhort all people of faith to practice their Catholicism, renounce sin, and to live God-fearing lives. Despite the venom of some of his messages, which condemned kissing, miniskirts, Protestantism, women wearing trousers, and adultery with equal ardor (Fonseca et al. 1977), he was beloved, even venerated, and considered a saint (or, as one source put it, "a living anachronism"). It guaranteed the festa's success. Dom José knew that regardless of trouble on the Morro, plans made by the Resistance, or his own damaged reputation, people would come from miles for the chance to receive a blessing from Frei Damião.

The Resistance immediately cried foul, claiming that the Frei was being used to manipulate people to come to the festa even if their better instincts told them not to. Saying they represented the sentiments of the majority of Recife's Catholic community, the Resistance asked all Catholics of good conscience to stay away from the festa as a protest to Dom José — but clearly, Frei Damião would be hard to resist. They said he was once more just a pawn, since he was already a tool of conservative politicians; for during the 1989 presidential campaign, Fernando Collor de Mello had traveled the northeast with the monk at his side, despite condemnation from many Catholic leaders in the area.[57] The monk was quoted as praising Collor for having given him a new green Ford, complete with air conditioning, in exchange for his help on the campaign trail. Some later said it was Frei Damião's presence that carried the northeast for Collor and that gave him the edge by which he won the election. The bishop's choice to trot out Damião for the festa was yet one more example of how people with power manipulate popular religion against the poor, claimed some. "He was used," one older Morro woman said later about the little monk. "He's too old to know what was going on."[58]

The Resistance published a protest in the form of a xeroxed blue leaflet that was handed out around the city. Dom José, said the tract, "resolved to impose his will of iron and fire, putting a priest on the Morro we don't want because he doesn't deserve our trust." It accused the bishop of "blowing smoke in the eyes of the people" and blasted those on the hill who had decided to work in the festa. "Half a dozen traitors to our cause are trying to tempt those of less conscience . . . to 'close the hole' at the last minute on a festa they have no right to improvise." It concluded ominously, "God grant that nothing evil befall the beloved and suffering people of the Virgin, and that they not use Frei Damião, as he was used by the politicians, to deceive our people of good faith. The ancient saint [Frei Damião] deserves respect."[59]

Despite ominous predictions to the contrary from Resistance members, the festa proceeded without any significant problems. The "half dozen traitors" referred to by the Resistance turned out to be several hundred volunteers from the Morro and surrounding neighborhoods who worked in the festa. "I decided to work the festa," explained a fifty-seven-year-old woman who had been a devoted ally of Reginaldo, "because I don't work for Reginaldo or for Constante, but because I have faith in Our Lady. Now people [in the Resistance] won't speak to me."[60] Many Morro residents couldn't afford to miss the opportunity to make some money by selling confections or statuettes at booths outside their homes, or by renting that space to vendors who paid a handsome fee.

The only clear sign of suffering was found among some who had decided to boycott the festa in support of Reginaldo and of the Resistance, but for whom the decision was heavy. Many women from neighboring communities who usually climbed the hill before dawn on the last day of the festa to attend the first mass had promised the Virgin that they would make that journey every year in thanks for her protection and help. The women didn't want to anger their friends on the Morro, but they also didn't want to disappoint the Virgin. It was a difficult choice, and in small meetings to decide whether or not they would attend the festa, many wept openly in frustration and confusion. Should one risk neighbors' scorn or risk angering the Mother of God? A nun who worked with the women suggested they go to the Morro and explain to any detractors that they went not to support Constante or the bishop, but to pay homage to Mary like they did every year. The women, however, were certain that Morro friends would refuse to speak to them ever again if they went, regardless of their motives. Most decided to honor the Resistance request that they stay home, but it was an uneasy choice.

For most Recifenses, the festa was as big a draw as ever. A sizable police presence insured order, and the city provided help in clean-up and maintenance. The Resistance said if Frei Damião hadn't been there, no one would have come, but most came because they'd always come, because it was the time of year when they came to "talk to Mary," as one man explained. The conflict of the community was irrelevant to the majority of pilgrims. Neither the Resistance nor the official church held their hearts. An informal straw poll near the end of the festa revealed that many had only a vague idea that there was trouble on the Hill, and even those who knew some details were not concerned by them.

Each day of the nine-day event, Frei Damião was propped in a chair at the back of the church to hear confessions, to bless people, and to give advice. The line to see him was always long. He sat in the chair for hours, but probably he didn't dispense many blessings because he mostly slept, his hunched back bending his head deep onto his chest, his cross dangling loosely from his hands. His slumber didn't stop the people on line, who whispered their confessions anyway, then kissed his cross or hand or robe. When he entered or left the church, guided by a younger Capuchin monk, a police escort had to shield him from the crowd that clamored to touch him.

On the last day of the festa, the Frei was to celebrate the biggest mass with Dom José, who would preach. The mass was held on the large stage built behind the church over the soccer field. Frei Damião sat on stage in a regal-looking chair that dwarfed his diminutive frame. When the bishop formally introduced him to roaring cheers from the crowd of several thousand, the ancient monk had to be helped to his feet and steadied. He didn't have the strength to wave, so the bishop took the Frei's wrist, held it aloft, and waved it back and forth, making the old man's hand waggle and jerk. Some in the Resistance later said it symbolized the bishop's manipulation of the monk, and of the festa.

4

THE DANGER OF STORIES

TIME AND POWER

A telling profile of Recife is found in a survey of its neighborhood names. A vibrant, crowded community not far from the Morro da Conceição is called Nova Descoberta — New Discovery. Its optimism matches names like Alto do Ceu (Hill of Heaven), Alto da Bondade (Hill of Goodwill), and Vila dos Milagres (Villa of Miracles). Other neighborhoods have specifically religious names, like Ilha de Deus (Island of God) and Piedade (Piety); of course, there are many communities named for saints. There are neighborhoods with allegedly indigenous names, like Apipucos, Beberibe, and Genipapú. At least one neighborhood not far from the Morro, called Monteiro, is named for the engenho that was once there. Some neighborhood names are neutral, derived from a prominent landmark or building, like Torre (Tower), Casa Amarela (Yellow House), Casa Forte (Strong House), Mustardinha (Little Mustard), Passarinho (Little Bird), and Várzea (Marsh). Then there are names that reflect history, pride, even irony — like Linha do Tiro (Line of Fire), Remédios (Medicine), Brasília Teimosa (Stubborn Brasilia), Cidade Operária (Workers' City), Iraque, and Vietnam.

Standing on a corner in downtown Recife and watching the destination names of city buses is like catching brief, enigmatic glimpses of the city's history. There are stories behind all the neighborhood names, though not all the stories are still remembered. Many names came into being informally, eventually finding official recognition as they were noted on city maps. Particularly through those places named casually by their inhabitants, the neighborhoods of Recife indicate the ability of just plain folks to have a voice in their own history by designating a piece of geography that knows their presence.

One of the biggest sources of contention on the Morro da Conceição concerned the community's immediate history. Many facts about Reginaldo's tenure on the Hill, his removal by the bishop, and the arrival of the police were not debated. The meanings of those facts, however, were fiercely contested. There was also intense controversy about who had the right to determine what those meanings were.

It's easy to see the conflict on the Morro da Conceição as a battle already done, with the winners and losers long ago determined. The bishop wanted the community's church back in diocesan hands, wanted his appointed priest on the Hill, and wanted Reginaldo gone. The first two goals he achieved on October 19, 1990. Since that day, there have been twice as many weekly masses in the church as there were during Reginaldo's tenure, construction of a new church building has been completed, and attendance at Sunday church services is up. Several festas have come and gone without significant disruptions or decline in attendance. Reginaldo's continuing presence, while an annoyance, does not significantly interfere with the Morro church proper. Reginaldo's alternative worship celebrations continue to fill Sunday mornings and Wednesday nights with amplified music, prayer, and exhortations to stay true to the fight, but a steadily shrinking number of people heed the call.

Tensions on the Hill, however, have not subsided. Controversy about who has rights to the church building and who draws a bigger Sunday crowd are important, but — in part because these are no longer actively debatable questions — dissension thrives in other arenas. The continuation of hostilities points to a larger struggle that is unresolved and that will stay unresolved as long as competing points of view can find an audience.

Still up for grabs is the future history of this conflict and of the community itself, and whoever can construct and perpetuate the version of events that is recounted years hence will be the ultimate victors in the Morro contest. It is a profound and simple problem. It fuels ongoing debates, maintains their intensity, and, for a while at least, raised this conflict from a community squabble to a confrontation watched by different audiences around the world.

The way in which this fight is remembered and retold to succeeding audiences and even succeeding generations will redeem questionable choices. Hard-held positions will no longer look stubborn but noble; sacrifices will not be imprudent but brave; decisions that entailed considerable risk will not seem poorly conceived but daringly foresighted. The faction that wins the passionate, slow-motion contest of owning the "true" account of what has happened on the Morro da Conceição will be fully justified in pointing to their opponents as fools and heretics while claiming their own prescience and even divine guidance (though both sides already claim the latter). This part of the friction is subtler but more consequential than debates over whether the bishop has the moral right to celebrate mass in the Morro church, or whether Reginaldo risked excommunication by his refusal to obey his superior.[1]

Many who engaged with Recife's progressive Catholic church learned to value their own points of view and their abilities in ways they hadn't before. Those who learned to organize, to demand, to critique, to build, to lobby, to boycott, to demonstrate, to publicize, and to persist were not about to retreat from these skills or from the needs these skills were meant to answer. Those who were alienated by the liberationist church were not blind to their neighbors' efforts, and though traditionalists did not agree with the goals, they saw the effectiveness of the techniques and started using them.

Dom José has powerful allies. The institution of the church, from Rome to Recife, supports him. History supports him. The police, military, judges, and local elites support him. But lined up against him is a much more inchoate force that has several factors in its favor. It is patient. It is unpredictable. And its impact will be known over a long stretch of time, not in the immediate moment. This is the force of narrative history, self-conscious and otherwise, as created by those with a stake in the Morro conflict. Dom Hélder's legacy was to teach Recife's poor, both progressives and conservatives, that they can be players in their future history. Both are members of the community; both have an investment in what is told and understood about their stories years hence.

A partner to the narratives comes in the form of rituals. Narrative and ritual comprise the two primary tools used in this struggle for the future history of events. Narratives, either fragments or whole stories, trace the changes Reginaldo brought to the community; recount events leading up to the day the police came, including that day itself;

interpret specific events by laying blame and accusation on the opposing faction; tell stories of events since the police arrived and Constante
was put in charge of the parish; maintain daily, ongoing tensions; and
prove the errors of *o lado de lá* (the other side) with emphatic accent
on competing meanings and causal links between events. Rituals, particularly those integral to Roman Catholicism, bolster each side's
claims while underscoring their belief that they alone are honoring
God's, Mary's, and Jesus's true intentions for their religious expression. This chapter explores the war of narratives that animated the
Morro, especially in the year or so after the police raid; the next chapter looks at the use of ritual as it strengthens the faith and determination of one side over the other.

TIMELESS AND TIMELY HISTORIES AT ODDS

The community's contested narratives, played out in daily Morro life,
take place simultaneously on at least four different levels. First, they
point to a cosmic understanding, a timeless place where Truth is
thought to be changeless and enduring. This is the place of sacred
texts, of God and of Mary, of heaven. It is in part an eschatological
level, because it stands beyond time and beyond history.

Second, there is local understanding, or the interpretation of local
history. This usually moves between analysis of Recife's popular movements during and since the dictatorship, and analysis of Morro history
before and after Reginaldo arrived. This is smaller than cosmic understanding, but no less philosophical. It ties Morro residents to larger
alliances and frames the current conflict in a context of other, perhaps
more urgent struggles, like the dangerous one that the dictatorship
created for many opposed to the military in the late 1960s through the
mid-1980s.

Local understanding is bigger and less specific than the third
level, which is event understanding. This is the level at which specific
events that already occurred are still being contested. That the events
happened is not open to question, but they are continually interpreted
and reinterpreted. Event understanding marries the recent past — the
events that took place — with constant reworkings of those events.

Fourth, there is daily understanding, in which ongoing tales are
created and debated. This is the most explosive level because it is

where the conflict is most actively played out. It is where the other levels of understanding coalesce. Also at the daily level, issues of identity are felt most keenly as residents vie for the power to shape the community's identity by asserting their own in opposition to that of their opponents.

These four levels of understanding are not mutually exclusive. Sometimes a story will stress one or more of these levels; other times reference will be made to one level in explaining another. This is particularly true when people point to their cosmic understanding in explaining a local or event understanding.

Timeless, or cosmic, understanding underscores some of the most profound contrasts between Morro residents, especially as they revealed these contrasts across many long talks with me. No one, except the leaders, accuses anyone else of misunderstanding God, but the understandings are starkly dissimilar and reveal incompatible beliefs about God.

GOD IN TIME

The Morro's Resistance faction conceives of God as an active agent in secular history, reflecting liberationist conceptions of God's role in human affairs. Liberation theology insists that spiritual and secular history coincide and actually depend on each other, giving sacred affairs a more human immediacy and in turn linking human concerns more intimately with an immanent God. Liberationist exegeses of the Bible reveal a God active in human endeavors, giving shape to human history with a dynamic presence in particular moments of that history. Liberation theologians especially like the book of Exodus as evidence of this (Levenson 1991). In the books of the New Testament, they claim Jesus's historical circumstances and his continual references to the poor and downtrodden as proof of God's proximity in contemporary struggles.

Though the Bible's canon is closed, liberationists argue that its message is no less concretely or historically valid today than it was when Jesus lived. Because of this, they assert that some church teachings need modification. They especially stress a new understanding of Catholic eschatology, or teachings about the end of time. For example, the "Kingdom of God" is betrayed, they say, through practices of oppression; the Bible's historical contemporaneity demands concerted work against such practices. By couching the Lord's Prayer, which calls for making the Kingdom real, in a history coincident with exploitative conditions of modernity, liberationists believe they and all committed Christians are called to eradicate social and economic injustices, which are seen as concrete realities hostile to God's intentions.

History is thus malleable. This reading of Christianity's past, its present, and its basic tenets gives individuals more agency and greater responsibility, since the course of history is waiting to be determined by the actions of those in the present. Individual Christians are urged toward a new meaning of redemption, say liberationists, since God's salvific grace is felt through struggles in history. The union organizer, the striking domestic worker, the agrarian activist, the pastoral agent are living in closer harmony with God through their choices to work and to sacrifice for change. This also redeems humanity, which experiences the fruits of God's love through and with those who work the way God intends. And the church, in its commitment to this work and to this understanding of God's presence in time and in human history, is also redeemed and even is forgiven for centuries of a sin-filled history.

This liberationist interpretation of history sheds harsh light on the Roman Catholic church's nearly two millennia of existence. Liberationists point to the Catholicism of, say, Dom José and accuse it of historical inauthenticity. They say it is bound up with political choices made across hundreds of years that have allied the church with oppressive forces, especially in Latin America. They claim the bishop's faith is grounded in an institution that is as much an accident of history as a source of God's revealed truth. Following the Second Vatican Council, liberationists stress that the church is first and foremost the People of God, an emphasis that they say must realign the church's power in favor of oppressed peoples and against structures that cause and/or perpetuate oppression.

GOD OUTSIDE TIME

Traditionalists appreciate and believe in the strength of God's immanence in the world today, but not at the expense of his transcendence. God does move within human history but ultimately stands outside and beyond it; God cannot be reduced to historical concerns, though he encompasses them. The call for a Kingdom of God means all must live according to God's teachings in this life so that all gain entry into his Kingdom in the next, into the place to which Jesus referred at his trial when he told Pontius Pilate, "My kingdom is not of this world" (John 18:36). Because of Jesus's death on the cross, the world has already been redeemed, so there is no need for continual redemption. Rather, individuals must heed Jesus's call to obey the Father through him. It is not necessary to change the world to know God's grace, but to follow the Ten Commandments and to love one's neighbor.

While liberation theology proposes a christology that understands Jesus's life in social conditions very like those found today in much of Latin America, traditionalists point to the danger of historicizing Jesus out of the universality that underscores the truth of his teachings. Such a tendency would run the risk of making Jesus a mere figure in history and thereby would deny him the status of a divine being who transcends history and is therefore relevant in all times and all places.

Traditionalists view the Catholicism of, say, Reginaldo as a blasphemous break with Scripture, with the institutional church, and with historical precedent. The church, described in pre–Vatican II language as both the Bride and Body of Christ, exists as Jesus's earthly representation, guided through time and in history by the Holy Spirit.

It is true that, like any human institution, the church has erred, say traditionalists, but its history in Latin America cannot be understood as a travesty or as a failure; the place is, after all, largely Roman Catholic. And though traditionalists acknowledge that different choices would be made if the church arrived to evangelize today, a new evangelization project slated to peak in the year 2000 is designed to rejuvenate the faith, to restore the lapsed, and to help assuage global suffering.[2] They argue that it is indeed the church's goal to eradicate poverty and misery, but not through direct political engagement; this would debase the institution's sanctity and cheapen its voice, making it just one among many political agendas, no less and no more heard than any other of comparable international reach.

ON THE MORRO: HERE, NOW, AND THE TRUTH

The Morro's struggle for its future history blends these cosmic understandings with local, event, and daily understandings on a community level, moving from theology — the epistemological bedrock of the con-flict — to concerns about who has the true knowledge of what has been happening on the Hill, who has the power to determine the truth of that knowledge, and who has the right to that power — three very different issues.

The language each side uses is often the same, as are the variables such language describes. In local understanding, everyone agrees on the basic facts of what has taken place on the Hill since Reginaldo was named priest of the parish. But the meanings, implications, and impact of those events are hotly debated in local and event understandings. It is in the continuing daily play of stories — daily understanding — that power is claimed, opposed, or maintained, as narratives become prisms through which community identity is refracted.

The stories reflect on and continually recreate the neighborhood's recent past. In arguing different pasts, competing factions simultane-ously push toward different futures, since the way forward is deter-mined by the way already traveled. Dramatic incidents like the police arrival and the festas are combed and analyzed and interpreted end-lessly, reinforcing the strength of the speaking group while denigrating the opposition. Simpler events are no less scrutinized: who sits with whom at the local bar, or even which bar someone is seen frequenting, becomes the stuff of gossip, the elaboration of an ongoing tale, or an entirely new story.

Local, event, and daily understandings are made clearer in the tales themselves. What follows are three separate stories that illustrate central issues in the conflict, each told from two perspectives; this makes six stories, since neither teller would ever admit the validity of the other's "version." The stories are based on identical factual circum-stances. I heard them many, many times during my fieldwork, and from many different sources. The first two are set in January 1991, a little more than a year after Reginaldo was suspended, and illustrate cosmic, local, and event understandings. The second two take place in May 1991, at the end of the Month of Mary, revealing event and daily under-standings. The last are in October 1991, when Constante was readying the ground to construct the new church building on the Morro, and are examples of cosmic and daily understandings. The stories are not mine, but are composites compiled from interviews, casual conversa-tions, observations, speeches, sermons, and overheard exchanges.[3]

The stories address and attempt to answer the three questions that were central to the Morro's identity and understanding of itself as a community, especially in the year after the police raid: Who has the true knowledge of what is happening on the Hill? Who has the power to determine the truth of that knowledge? Who has the right to that power? I will explore these concerns after the stories.

Story One, January 1991: Tradition and Balance Restored

We are a poor place; like Jesus says, "The poor you shall always have with you," but Reginaldo didn't think like that. He is stubborn and hard-headed, and from the beginning he involved the community in different problems. He got the Bible-study groups to form a residents' council, and then they made spectacles of themselves in demonstrations at city hall, demanding water. We've had a bad name up here ever since, thanks to them. It's a joke that they're called a residents' council; they don't represent any residents! It's full of outsiders and homosexuals and thieves. That's typical of Reginaldo's riffraff.

It got worse when Reginaldo reorganized the festa. The festa is sacred, a time for prayers and devotion, but Reginaldo turned it into politics by getting all those people from outside to come talk against the government and against the rich. We're poor and we're going to stay poor if we anger wealthy people who might help us. In the festa before last [1989], Reginaldo even used a billboard outside the church to tell people how to vote.

It was too much for Dom José. He suspended Reginaldo after that. He had to. For a long time he had warned Reginaldo to stop bringing politics into the church, but Reginaldo never listened. A priest is like a soldier in the army: he has to obey his superior. When he disobeyed Dom José, Reginaldo broke his vows as a priest, and in doing that he broke with Scripture. Dom José was very agreeable about it; after the suspension, he negotiated with Reginaldo's supporters, but that was a mistake because they are too radical and violent.

Finally, the bishop called in the police. He had no choice

— those people wouldn't let his new priest into the church. They wouldn't even give Dom José the keys to the church building. They said they didn't know where the keys were, but that was a lie because they had been using the church for meetings and masses, breaking the law by trespassing. That meant the police had to come. The whole thing just shows how badly people are brainwashed by Reginaldo. In a way it's not their fault — he's got their heads so turned around they can't even think right any more.

It's been a big headache, but at least the festa this past December [1990] was back to normal. Thanks to Padre Constante, it was one of the best ever. Reginaldo only has a handful of followers now, and all the people who left way back when he first came have returned to church. Clearly, this is a sign that the Virgin Mary is on our side.

The tellers of this tale, active Morro traditionalists, reveal an image of themselves and the Morro that asserts the truth of their understanding of events through sympathy with the bishop, and by assigning most of the blame for the community chaos to Reginaldo. His followers, though radical, have had their heads "turned" (*ele virou as cabeças deles*; he turned their heads) by the charismatic leader. In part because the bishop is allied with the traditionalists, they are a powerful faction, which lends to the strength of their interpretation of events, and to their legitimacy.

They also reveal a distinct set of relationships with the state that adds weight to their claims. They believe that one who is impoverished is best helped out of that poverty, or at least helped to bear it, by appealing to traditional patron/client relationships that have been part of Brazil's political landscape for centuries. Reginaldo threatened that relationship by fostering a more activist, participatory approach to problem solving, and many traditionalists were upset by his brazen break with tradition. They were appalled when he used a similar approach to reorient the festa away from prayerfulness toward what they saw as politicization, further jeopardizing potentially useful ties with Recife's wealthier classes.

The bishop rescued the community from its shameful and disturbing circumstances. A bishop who doesn't hesitate to call in the troops displays no ambiguities about the strength of his determination to get his way, and those who support him find ample space in the shadow of that determination, simultaneously shoring up the bishop's position and creating the opportunity to seek future favors in exchange for that support. The state has helped restore a balance of power that the traditionalists felt they had lost to Reginaldo and his followers, and though everyone will admit the police action was dramatic, the tellers of this tale see its logic and necessity. This story points to the traditionalists' reassertion of their claim to hold the orthodoxy of Roman Catholic faith and practice and to know the proper community relationship to church and state authority. This allows them to become determiners of the community's future, and gives muscle to their tellings and interpretations of various stories.

The traditionalists see proof of their success in the festa, once again restored to its traditional place in community dynamics as nine days of piety and popular devotion, void of the noxious political tones of Reginaldo's years. They also see evidence of their success in their count of how many people attend which worship service: the ones in the church or the ones with Reginaldo. They count their numbers rising and his dwindling. Finally, appealing to the most immediate heavenly representative and placing their fight in a larger cosmic scheme, they are certain that Mary is their ally.

Story Two, January 1991: The Illegitimization of Power

This community has always been poor, but that's not God's will. Reginaldo, a simple man of tremendous faith, helped us see that. He helped us understand that our poverty is the result of exploitation of countries like Brazil by rich countries like the United States. Reginaldo showed that Jesus is on the side of the oppressed, not the rich. That means the real church works in the world for the poor and is not locked under the control of elite men who know nothing about the realities of the popular classes.

There would be no residents' council on the Morro if it weren't for Reginaldo, which means there would be no water, no paved streets, no buses, no garbage pick-up. With his encouragement, the residents' council started a day-care center, literacy classes, mothers' clubs, an herbal medicine post, and a school for mentally handicapped children. People who hadn't been to church in years started coming back because of Reginaldo. He even organized the festa and made it mean more than just lighting candles and praying.

But not everyone liked Reginaldo's work. One of his biggest enemies was Dom José. For years that devil was looking for any excuse to suspend Reginaldo, and he finally got him on charges of disobedience. That's absurd; Reginaldo obeys Scripture, which is a higher authority than any bishop. Everyone on the Morro supported Reginaldo, but agreed to go along with the suspension if the bishop would let us have a say in choosing the new priest. Then, on a day we were to meet with him to negotiate, Dom José used troops of armed military police to bring his new priest to the Morro. It was awful — people were screaming and weeping and throwing things. If it weren't for Reginaldo telling people not to get violent, there would have been a riot. Any bishop who would call police against his own people has no right to be bishop, and any priest who would go along with him can't be a real priest.

No one accepts the bishop's man; no one goes to his masses. The community keeps telling Dom José that if he'd get rid of the new guy and replace him with anybody else, there will be no more tension. But he doesn't listen. The last festa was a travesty, with people from outside the Morro running things and even getting paid for it, when it had always been done by volunteers. But the new priest has to bring in outsiders, because no one here pays any attention to him. Everyone attends Reginaldo's celebrations of Resistance in the square, which is a clear sign that the Virgin Mary is on our side.

This story, told by Resistance group members and their supporters, illustrates the "immanentized eschaton" — that is, a definition of the sacred broadened to include what was formerly "merely" secular. Community poverty is seen as a wrong to be righted and is no longer addressed through appeals to old-fashioned paternalistic ties, but through analysis and strategic action. Reginaldo is a model of piety and humility, giving weight to his words. He is not a cause of problems but a teacher of liberation who awoke Morro residents to their inherent dignity and untapped political potential. By grounding the festa in everyday concerns, he opened church language and support to people who had been disaffected by what they saw as its hollowness and irrelevance.

The Resistance group sees the state as an entity to be manipulated, sometimes feared, and most often opposed, especially in achieving local services and rights to self-governance through the residents' council. By aligning himself with the state, Dom José destroyed his legitimacy with the Resistance group. It was a truly dastardly act, in their eyes, in part because it so broke with the pattern established by Dom Hélder. By calling the police, Dom José re-established the church's alliance with a punitive power all too familiar to the city's poor. His action was seen as a tacit blessing of a pernicious and sometimes terrifying force.

A digression here about police/community relations helps explain this. The police in Brazil have at best an ambivalent relationship with neighborhoods like the Morro, whose residents don't make much money and who sometimes find work in the informal sector — even the illegal informal sector. When police arrive, residents view them with healthy suspicion. On the Morro, for instance, police occasionally show up just before dawn, out of uniform, in groups of three or four. For the residents of the Hill, this means death. Between January and June of 1991, there were several death-squad killings in the area that comprises the Morro parish. One happened on a walkway just off the praça, near Dona Hilda's home (she of water lobbying, who applauded the church hiring pot-smoking young men to help rebuild her house). On March 19, 1991, at about 5:00 A.M., four men burst into the home of eighteen-year-old Aureliano Gusmão, dragged him out into the street by his hair, and, in front of his screaming mother, younger siblings, and neighbors, killed him with a shot to the head. He was allegedly involved in a car theft ring; his obituary used his name only as a caption to a picture of him, referring to him throughout merely as a "marginal."

This murder, and others like it, chilled all who heard of it, but there were no formal protests. The victims' names were merely added to the list of area deaths announced in three daily fifteen-minute broadcasts on a local radio station. Walking the Morro or any of the city's poorer neighborhoods in the early morning, or at noon, or in the late afternoon, one hears the loud, insistent radio voice blaring from nearly every home as the macabre chronicle is read with the professional urgency of a horse race or an auction. The murders on the Morro are understood as more of the casual violence of Recife's urban ghettos, where death — from death squads, drunken brawls, vengeance feuds, traffic accidents, malnutrition, marital disputes — comes cheap and easy for the poor, and where it is clear that accountability for violent crime depends entirely on who is the perpetrator and who is the victim.

When Dom José called riot police to the Morro to enforce his will, the Resistance group disavowed any possibility of trusting him in the future, since he proclaimed his willingness to use a strength whose deadly force had already been felt too often on the Morro and in neighborhoods like it.

Resistance Morro residents cited numerical success in their worship services as proof that Padre Constante, Reginaldo's replacement, has no popular support. Like their traditionalist counterparts, they claimed Mary, the nearest and dearest heavenly representative, as a sure ally, obviously bolstering their certainty in the rightness of their cause.

The discrepancies in attendance counts was not unusual. Each side used its own counts to shore up its argument, and the numbers they quoted never agreed with my own counts of how many people were attending which worship service. For example, on the Sunday after the 1990 festa, the Resistance group held a worship celebration in the school just off the southern end of the praça. I counted roughly three hundred participants, some (but not all) from other parts of the city. It was a goodly number that seemed larger and more vibrant than usual in the cramped school space because of television lights, cameras, and news crews. The church worship service that started a little later drew nearly seventy people, a respectable showing for the day after the festa and considering that Padre Constante, Reginaldo's replacement, had only been celebrating mass on the Hill for a little over a month.

Later, however, Resistance members told local media that more than five hundred people came to their celebration, while only "two or three" were in the church. They pointed to the evening's newscast as proof. During the Resistance celebration, the camera crew filmed the inside of the church. They filmed at least half an hour before the church service was scheduled to start, so obviously there were not many people in the nave. But the newscast didn't note the difference in schedule; it only showed the image of the near-empty church in contrast with the exuberant event in the school.

The traditionalists said that only a handful of people in the school service were from the Morro and that most in attendance were from outside the community, while the more than one hundred people they claimed were inside the church during the church service were all Morro residents. They said that the newscast was a typical distortion by a media outlet that blatantly supported Reginaldo, and that everyone knew it could not be trusted.

Story Three, May 1991: Mary and the Co-opted Children

We started that evening at the dance hall, down by Dona Luca's place. There were hundreds of us, all the people from the CEBs, from the Morro and the adjacent neighborhoods. We were so joyful; it was the end of May, and we had been meeting all month in neighbors' homes to pray the rosary and share our strength and solidarity. This was the last celebration, with a procession through the community to the Virgin to crown Her with flowers and show Her our love and faith. We had a sound car, and the children led us, dressed in white. A little girl carried the Bible, people from Encontro de Irmãos [Meeting of Brothers] walked behind her with candles and banners, and four women carried the Virgin (a small replica of the statue) together on Her platform. Different people took turns animating us, leading us in songs and in the Ave Maria, which we said at every stop. It was beautiful! We went slowly, full of reverence.

We knew Constante had scheduled his Month of Mary closing celebration at the same time but had canceled it, a victory for us. He knew we would draw more people, of course, since we hold the heart of the community and he never will.

When we got to the feet of the saint we crowned the Virgin. Then *Resisteatro* (Resistheater) did a play about the history of women in Brazil. They couldn't use the microphone, so they asked us to be quiet so they could be heard. But the children who had been playing in the praça were making such noise that it was almost impossible to hear. So Cecilia went over to ask them to quiet down. That's when she learned what happened. She was so angry! After Resisteatro finished, Cecilia went straight to the microphone and told us what had happened. She said, "I want you to know how low they will stoop to undermine us. I want to tell you the newest sign that they are never to be trusted. The children are making so much noise because they have been paid to make noise! They have been paid with cola and popcorn." Cecilia didn't say who could have done this, but we knew. Only Dona Bene and Nilton are capable of such deceit.

People from here told members of the Encontro de Irmãos sector meeting the next day, and Zé João put it on the Voice of the Morro radio program he does every Saturday night. It's just more proof of the other side's evil. Thank God, Jesus Christ was with us and helped us overcome their attempts to *atrapalhar* [disturb, confuse, interrupt].

This story blends cosmic understanding with daily understanding so that a sense of martyrdom, a Resistance group *leitmotif*, is strengthened. In part because the evening had drawn people from all over the Morro parish, the alleged attempt to disrupt their activity was seen as an assault on the corporate identity of the entire Resistance effort and so reverberated wider than it might have otherwise. It also coincided with two opportunities to share information with wider audiences. Once a month the Encontro de Irmãos sector meeting draws a few dozen people, mostly older women, to different parts of Casa Amarela, the city zone in which the Morro is located, to discuss the state of the Encontro groups, future events, and any problems. News of the alleged bribe quickly traveled into neighborhoods across Casa Amarela. It also happened that Zé João's radio program, broadcast on the Morro once a week, was scheduled for the next day, so anyone who hadn't already heard the tale could listen to the young man's voice of calm outrage spilling from the praça speakers. Two days later it was Sunday, and again the story was repeated through loudspeakers across the praça during the Resistance celebration.

That the alleged bribe happened during an occasion of prayer and reverence dedicated to Mary first provoked pride but then group enmity toward a common foe. They saw their celebration marred by the Virgin's enemies, defined as anyone who opposes the Resistance *luta*, or struggle.

Making the accusation specific to Dona Bene and Nilton speaks to a daily understanding on the Morro. Dona Bene, a dynamic woman in her late forties, was close to Reginaldo, as was Nilton, a flamboyant man in his mid-thirties, but both had a falling out with the priest and now support Constante. Dona Bene's final break with Reginaldo came the same time the police arrived; she is believed to be a spy and a traitor. Resistance people rarely speak of her by name, but only say The Traitor; everyone knows to whom the title refers. Resistance people believe she was leaking information about them and their plans to the bishop during the ten months they tried to negotiate with Dom José. Since she "switched sides" from Reginaldo to Constante on the day the police arrived, no Resistance member doubts her betrayal.

Nilton had been disillusioned with Reginaldo for some time before the trouble escalated. He and Dona Bene are close friends. Nilton was appointed head of the Morro's state-funded health post after a conservative government was elected in 1989. He used his position in part to attract resources for children's events. For instance, he organized dance competitions for the São João festival, and had large groups of children practicing several nights a week for months before. Even Resistance parents sent their kids; it was too much fun to only sit and watch, despite Nilton's habit of continually making wisecracks and deprecatory remarks about the Resistance, Reginaldo, Dona Luisa, and Zé João. It's easy to understand why Dona Bene and Nilton would immediately be suspects in the bribe scandal.

The alleged bribe also points to the difficulties inherent in sharing the praça area on which the Virgin stands, a communal space that each side claims is theirs to use (though it was eventually made off-limits to the Resistance). Resistance people hated to see Constante and his allies in what they felt was their church, celebrating the eucharist at their altar. But traditionalists equally hated to see Reginaldo and his troop singing songs and praying miked petitions to Jesus, Mary, and God at the very feet of the saint herself. The praça area in general is carved into microterritories. Traditionalists hold the health post, one of the state schools, a corner bar, and the church building. The Resistance holds the larger state school, two bars, and they did "hold" the statue in that they had free access to her, until several months after this incident.

The bribe may, in fact, have existed nowhere but in the clever imagination of the twelve-year-old who reported it to Cecilia, but no matter: as soon as she heard it, Cecilia decided it was unquestionably true, one more confirmation of the despicable character of the opposition. The story served the level of daily understanding, in that it fueled outrage toward opponents and hardened the Resistance group even more firmly against any possibility of reconciliation. It strengthened their anger toward their enemies, their sense of loyalty to each other, and let them put their fists in the air, figuratively speaking, in righteous indignation. The affair soon moved into the realm of event understanding as Reginaldo's supporters added it to their ever-growing oral annals of resistance.

I tried to learn if the children had actually been bribed to make noise to throw off the Resistance celebration; gentle questioning of several Morro traditionalists brought vehement indignation and heated denials, and generally took the form of the following response-story.

Story Four, June 1991: The Noise of Fools

O lado de lá [the side over there; the other side] says we incited the children against them, that we bribed children with soda and popcorn to make noise. Ha! Those people are crazy. They're paranoid. They're just looking for an excuse to continue to harass us with their microphones on Sunday morning and to disrupt us by having those children make so much noise. They're the ones whose kids make noise, those thieving *Meninos da Santa* [Children of the Saint]. It's a false charge. It's absurd! It's slander, is what it is. As if we would ever bribe children! That's exactly the kind of thing *they* would do to annoy *us,* but we would never stoop so low. Though it's not a bad idea, if we'd have been badly educated enough to think of such a thing, as badly educated as they are, maybe we could have done it! Then to spread it all over as if it's truth . . . and accusing Nilton and Dona Bene — Nilton gives his life to those kids!

That group makes fools of themselves all by themselves. They don't need any help from us to look like idiots! All that huge noise in front of the Virgin — it hurts my heart every time I see it. It must pain the Virgin so, to see such lies. It's a travesty. It's a heresy! And they use these lies they make up as an excuse to interfere with our mass inside the church. Have you ever heard of such a thing? Incredible.

Charged with a devious act, traditionalists could not simply ignore their accusers. This was especially true when two of their strongest leaders — Dona Bene and Nilton — were the accused. It was important to the traditionalists that their reputation not be defiled with such an ugly accusation as bribing children. They had the church back, and more people attended every week, but they had not been returned to power very long, and they were only as strong as their bishop. Furthermore, Reginaldo's side had allies throughout the region and outside the country.

Once again, spatial considerations came into play, because the area in front of Mary's statue is the most sacred place on the Hill, and for the traditionalists, the Resistance presence felt like an occupying force that had invaded the home of a loved one. Traditionalists also could note that the praça is full of children at any hour of the day, and that their play is usually loud, even raucous. To disapprove of a normal community rhythm was bad enough; to then accuse two leaders of encouraging more formal distraction was to stoop very low indeed.

The problem of the praça was partly solved about ten months later, and leads to the last pair of tales.

Story Five, March 1992: The Virgin Rescued

They started building the fence around the church and the Virgin right after the [1991] festa. It was in the plans for the general outlay of the square for decades, but there was never money. Finally, thanks to Constante, money came through, and not a moment too soon. The fence had to be built. People on Reginaldo's side kept holding those mockeries of the mass at the feet of the Virgin, and tourists who came to see Our

Lady were completely confused. When Reginaldo's people weren't making all that noise, the children were hassling the tourists — one woman was mugged as she prayed. If the fence hadn't been built when it was, those kids probably would have committed a more serious crime. People can see the saint every day from eight in the morning until midnight; Alexandre has the key and makes sure the area stays safe. He's such an honest and reliable man, the perfect person to attend the gate; he and his family have lived right on the praça for nearly fifty years.

This is a significant milestone for the traditionalists, and they tell this tale with broad smiles, sometimes rocking back and forth and nodding with satisfaction. At last they are able to bolster their power with a physical symbol of it, a ten-foot-tall, cast-iron, spike-tipped fence embedded in concrete. It both provides and dramatically proves a deepened security in their command over church and community affairs because it gives them complete control over the most important space of the Hill, the area immediately in front of the Virgin. It also encloses the 1906 chapel and the new church, planned by Reginaldo but completed by Constante. The old church, built around the chapel tower with volunteered community labor and materials, was torn down. There was not much protest about this because it was already in plans laid out by Reginaldo in the late 1980s but stopped when his trouble with the bishop intensified. The traditionalists acted on those plans in October 1991, and the old blue cinderblock church was replaced by a blonde brick circular structure topped with a sloping cement roof in time for the 1991 festa. But they made the project their own by fencing it all in, and the surety of their decision was reinforced by their funding: the city kicked in money and labor, and posted a brightly colored billboard at the foot of the Hill near the main road proclaiming that the city's *Mais Trabalha; Mais Você!* (More Work; More You!) improvement campaign had come to the Morro church. Because of the fence, the Resistance can no longer hold celebrations at the feet of the saint and is relegated to the state school that Dona Luisa heads, or on nights when there are classes, to a space above her house that CEB monies and volunteer work renovated into a tiny chapel.

By building a fence, the traditionalists also control the children who play around the saint. *Os Meninos da Santa*, or The Children of the Saint, had been organized by Dona Luisa, a key figure in the Resistance group, to provide children with a more orderly means of earning tips for putting people's gifts high up the statue, closer to the Virgin (this was before a stair allowed people to climb to the Virgin's feet on their own). The children wore blue T-shirts decorated with a picture of the Virgin's face, sold Virgin trinkets and *fitas* — brightly colored ribbons to be worn on the wrist that say *Lembrança de Nossa Senhora da Conceição* (Remembrance of Our Lady of the Immaculate Conception) — and were considered a supreme nuisance by traditionalists. Before Dona Luisa organized the children, they fought with each other for the right to carry promessas up the statue or to guard a tourist's car, and often the promessa payer or the tourist was caught in the scuffle. But her supervision of them slacked off when the crisis started, and soon there were accusations that the children disrupted reverential moments in front of the statue and even robbed people at prayer. The most irksome fact about the children was that they had been organized by Dona Luisa, who had lived on the Hill all her life, a fact that robbed traditionalists of the taunt that the Resistance was made up exclusively of people from outside the community.

Traditionalists weren't prone to gloat, and even though the fence makes them happy, they point to the community's older history and claim that the fence was always meant to be built, since it was in the church's original plans for the praça. I was never able to find anyone who had a set of the plans nor learn where they might be kept, but was repeatedly assured by many people that they had seen the lay-out and, yes, there was supposed to be a fence. Older residents said that when they first moved to the Morro as children in the 1920s or 1930s, a straggly barbed-wire fence already enclosed the chapel and the saint. That fence was too flimsy to withstand the pushes and twists of several festas and a steadily growing population. The new fence, however, is built to last.

Alexandre, nicknamed the Gatekeeper, is an unemployed man in his late forties who has lived within a stone's throw of the statue since he was a small child. He is colorful, full of fiercely held opinions about a wide range of subjects. He takes no guff from anyone, which makes him a good gatekeeper, and his status as a nearly lifelong Morro resident adds to his appeal.

Story Six, March 1992: A New Berlin Wall

They started building the fence right after the last festa, and for only one reason: to keep out the community. They know they don't have the support of Morro residents, and they didn't want to let people have access to the saint the way it's always been. They've locked up the Virgin out of fear. They're afraid people will hear the truth in Reginaldo's celebrations, which we held right under the saint's gaze. They're afraid of the Meninos da Santa. And they're afraid of people of Afro-Brazilian traditions like candomblé, who come to the saint to pay homage to Iemanjá as Mary. Alexandre, that deadbeat, even charged the candomblé people a fee to get inside; no wonder they broke down the fence and nearly trampled him. It's ironic that in Europe, the Berlin Wall came down, but in Recife, the Morro wall went up.

The Resistance reacted strongly to the fence. Doninha, an avowed Marxist and Resistance supporter in her mid-thirties who lives near the praça and was raised on the Morro, sat outside her house all night after construction workers built an elaborate barbed-wire fence around the immediate construction area to protect supplies and equipment left behind. She looked at the fence — or, as it was immediately called, the Wall — and wept. In the morning I found her clinging to it, eyes red. Not noticing her sadness, I asked if I could photograph her at the Wall. She dissolved into tears and turned away, shaking her head. I quickly put down the camera and apologized. She said it was the saddest day of her life. She said that closing the Morro church behind a wall, fencing off the praça's heart — it was too much. The depth of her feeling was surprising because, while she supported Reginaldo and the Resistance cause, her relationship with the church even during Reginaldo's tenure was ambivalent, and her moments of Roman Catholic piety were always tempered by her fast-held Marxist sentiments.

The Resistance charged the traditionalists with acting in bad faith, and once again proclaimed their own righteousness — the Wall was meant to prevent people from hearing their truth, what they believed was *the* truth. It was one more indication of the traditionalists' fear and insecurity. It was also one more indication of their illegitimacy. Alexandre is a particular foe of the Resistance, and to charge him with graft and even thievery in his role as gatekeeper indicates the depth of their distrust of him, and the place at which economic impropriety is usually claimed. On both sides, it is reserved for the most despised members of the opposition. Were he employed (he works as gatekeeper for free), Alexandre would not be as vulnerable to the indictment that he charged people money to get to the Virgin, an egregious and even unthinkable act. His status as a man without a job leaves him more vulnerable to charges by people who imagine ways he might try to get cash.

Resistance members also see traditionalists as less tolerant of Afro-Brazilian religions like candomblé, making their complaint against Alexandre more credible. They see themselves as models of tolerance and goodwill; Reginaldo invited candomblé practitioners to share some of the formal presentations in the festa's novena over the years, yet another choice that angered traditionalists.

The story also reinforces Resistance distrust of the state. Many Resistance members complained bitterly that Constante and his supporters are in bed with corrupt politicians, for how else would they have wrangled building materials and labor out of a stingy local government for a new church and a fence, while hillsides without retaining walls were ready to collapse in the next winter rains, the buses still didn't run often enough, the roads were falling apart, water still ran only sporadically, there was inadequate electricity on side streets, and garbage collection was haphazard at best. The new church and fence were more proof that the government was not to be trusted.

The story about Alexandre and the candomblé adherents may or may not have been true. It was reported in the local paper, but the only source quoted throughout was Doninha, one of Alexandre's most passionate enemies. Like the story of the bribed children, the truth of the accusation was quickly irrelevant, since everyone responded as if it were true. The Resistance perpetuated it as sure proof of the traditionalists' evil. Alexandre was angered and hurt by the accusation and reacted by refusing to speak to reporters (or to the visiting anthropologist) about anything ever again.

CONTESTED WEALTH

Several issues are revealed in these stories. Traditional Morro Catholics believe, on the one hand, the sacred is dirtied when linked to politics. They see a clear line dividing sacred and secular, and to blur or to erase that line is to tempt heresy and simultaneously to deprive many Catholics of one of their few sanctuaries. This is the bishop's view; he said he reacted the only way he could when Reginaldo went too far. For Resistance Morro Catholics, on the other hand, almost anything secular may also be sacred, since they understand the Bible to say that the entire world and all that happens in it is God's province. Traditionalists think the Resistance people deserve excommunication; Resistance people think the traditionalists have sold out to the status quo.

The stories also engage residents in daily confrontations about wealth — not only material wealth, but the immaterial wealth of reputation, custom, and definitions of tradition. It is true that the most volatile accusations that fly between the groups at odds always mention ill-gotten gains. Traditionalists say Reginaldo's supporters have access to resources no one else has because Reginaldo's pockets are padded by aid from European and Canadian sympathizers. Resistance people say traditionalists have jobs and resources no one else has because they butter up local politicians and so are granted illicit favors. They even deny traditionalists their claim to tradition. "We are the real traditionalists," one woman explained, "because our way of being church is like the very early church, based on conciliation and sharing resources. The people who here call themselves traditionalists believe in a version of church that is not authentic."[4]

Though each side can point to examples that support these accusations, the general homogeneity of everyone's poverty belies the claims. And they are not the charges lobbed most frequently. Rather, each faction levels charges that the other has no truth in its stories, that its religious practices are corrupt, and that it blasphemes tradition and local heritage. In other words, the factions are fighting in part for control of tradition and custom, their shared noncorporeal property.

Discourse can be an instrument and effect of power, or a point of resistance to undermine power (Foucault 1980). These sets of stories are both, since the power at several levels is still contested. Legiti-mated hegemony within the community of the Morro da Conceição does not currently exist, since neither faction recognizes the other's right to any power or to determine the Morro's shape and future. The traditionalists, however, did enjoy the favor of city and state officials when conservatives won the 1989 elections, and legitimacy was con-ferred on them by powers outside the Morro through program funds and support in building the new church.

Chapter 5 illustrates how ritual practices have developed to sup-plement and to bolster contentious narratives, and how rituals help channel tensions that might otherwise cause the conflict to escalate beyond the relatively comfortable place its participants have created for it.

RITUALIZING DISSENSION

WORDS OF MY MOUTH, MEDITATIONS OF MY HEART

There is perhaps no more basic nor more complicated expression of faith than prayer. It invokes, calls down blessings, supplicates, and beseeches; adores, glorifies, worships; celebrates and laments; rages and curses. Through prayer one can "cut a deal" (cf. Burkert 1987) with Mary by setting up a promessa, or lay one's heart bare in an intimacy no mere human could ever provide, or seek signs of the holy. Prayer can be an immediate mediation between the sacred and the everyday, an instant link between one's mundane existence and a redemptive, salvific power. It can help maintain or restore balance in times of stress or threat; it can provide an outlet for private torments that will brook no other audience, not even the sympathetic ear of a friend.

Prayer plays all these roles in the life of a Morro Catholic. It is both intensely personal and often public. It can take the form of a conversation with God, Mary, Jesus, or any of a host of saints. There are always people kneeling or standing in front of the Virgin, praying to Mary. They are unself-conscious and devout. During the festa, they number in the hundreds. People who never attend church can have an active prayer life.[1] One festa-goer cheerfully explained that the only connection he had with any formal church worship all year was at the festa, which he attended so that he could "talk to Mary" on her feast day.

Prayer is both a private and shared event during the mass. People pray by themselves before the mass begins, and once it starts they pray together in recitations of the Nicene or Apostles Creed, the Lord's Prayer, and the Confession. These prayers describe central tenets of Roman Catholic faith; most people have them memorized since childhood. During the mass and during confession, prayer can be a time to look to the priest for guidance, as he prays on behalf of members of the community or for an individual seeking forgiveness for sins. Padre Constante explained early in his Morro tenure that praying alone is good and is something one ought to do every day, but a priest's prayers are more directly linked to God, so praying in church with a priest during the mass is a better way to get a prayer heard.

Many people believe prayers said in church are more efficacious even if they are not said as part of the mass but are simply said inside a church nave. This is because the body of Christ is in the church, locked behind the altar in a vault called the tabernacle. When the elements are transubstantiated, or transformed from bread and wine into flesh and blood (more on this shortly), any remaining bread — now body — is preserved in the tabernacle until the next mass. To be inside the church, then, is to be inside a space that also holds Jesus Christ.[2] Older women of the Morro's Encontro de Irmãos often regretted that they could not go inside the Morro church to "sit with Jesus" and pray, as one woman put it (cf. Campbell-Jones 1980, who tells a similar story). They did not go inside the church because they were afraid neighbors would see and think they were "traitors" to the Resistance.

The repetitious nature of some prayers can be incantatory, echoing at least one definition of prayer that equates it with charms (Fallaize 1919). Certainly the Hail Marys of the rosary form a meditative repetition, and people praying the cycle seem transported as they gaze into space or close their eyes, their fingers steadily tracking the prayers on their rosary beads. The same quality sometimes comes over a mass when people are responding to formal prayers of intercession.

Moreover, within Catholicism, prayer is inclusive. Anyone and everyone may pray. This is not true of all religious traditions (see, for instance, Metcalf 1989), and Resistance worship services allow more room for people to say a prayer when they are moved to do so than is normal in a conventional mass. The priest in a conventional mass has the right to say some of the prayers alone, especially when he is consecrating the elements. But sometimes habit can override a priest's insistence on following the rules. At a mass I attended in Paraiba, the state north of Pernambuco, a priest stopped in the middle and sternly informed the congregation that the pope had issued a directive forbidding people to pray with the priest at the consecration. He in effect told everyone to shut up until the Lord's Prayer. As he launched into that part of the mass, however, more than half the assembled worshipers prayed right along with him, just as they had always done, ignoring the priest's glare.

On the Morro, the content of someone's prayers gives signs of her or his depth of involvement in the community strife. Among the Resistance, prayers can become "political," a word I must put in quotes because its definition on the Hill is so troublesome. When Reginaldo was suspended, a black banner was draped across the locked church doors that read, "O Lord, deliver us from this devil bishop." Another draped the Virgin, saying "Our Mother, your people do not fail you; they fight." A prayer requesting Dom José's ouster was sung and chanted throughout the protest march in downtown Recife shortly after the police took the Morro church building. Resistance people pray for God to guide the Pope to replace Dom José, for Padre Constante to leave the Morro, for strength in their struggle, for community peace (praying for harmony while at the same time asking for strength to maintain the struggle sounds contradictory; by harmony, several Resistance members explained, they mean prayers that the Morro traditionalists will desert Constante and join the Resistance). They also pray that street children will no longer be brutalized, that hunger in the northeast and in the world will end, that war in the former Yugoslavia will end.

Traditionalists on the Morro scoff at some of these prayers; they think it's absurd and disrespectful, to say the least, to pray against the bishop. Their prayers are less ambitious; they pray for restored community harmony, for patience with their neighbors, for a reunited church. Their prayers are also harder to know; communal prayers are not spoken aloud during the mass because Constante follows the list of intercessions provided by the diocese. I learned that asking a person about her or his prayers is, for some, a question so intimate that it is unanswerable. I was prying into a relationship of profound, lifelong importance that had deeply private elements; it would have been less rude to inquire about the person's sex life.

One of the most important functions of prayer is to mediate between narratives and rituals. Prayers are part of the central rites in Catholicism and in many other religious traditions, Christian and otherwise, and can be ritualized and formal. For instance, they can take the form of theological stories, as when they repeat the fundamentals

of the faith in the Nicene Creed. They can tell the tale of a special figure, like in the Ave Maria. But they can also allow room for individuals
to add their own voices to an ongoing event, in this case the ritual of
the mass itself, and so personalize and make intimate something that
could become rote. In this, prayers reveal details about individual
lives, especially in Resistance celebrations, when a prayer is a thanksgiving or a petition for help. At one Resistance New Year's Eve worship
service, for instance, members of the community were asked to say
prayers of thanksgiving for things that had happened in the year that
was ending. People gave thanks for new babies, marriages, cured illnesses, for the continuing strength of their cause. Next they were
asked to say prayers for changes they wanted in their lives in the coming year. People asked for an end to the community's divisions, for better health, for a job.

Then one very old man, eyes closed and head bent, said loudly
and slowly, "I want a wife!" The group burst into laughter; the man, who
had spoken with great sincerity, raised his head in surprise, then
smiled. An occasional participant in Resistance events, he was stiff
with age, nearly deaf, and his clothes were always stained and badly
patched. He had been a widower for a few years and was clearly worse
off for being alone. He didn't get a wife that next year, but everyone remembered his prayer with affectionate chuckles.

Hell, Fire, and Brimstone

Preaching is a kind of formalized prayer. One preaches to and on behalf
of a group — a sermon is not a sermon without an audience. Sermons
are as varied as prayers. In the Roman Catholic and many other Christian traditions, sermons are supposed to be wrapped around the day's
Bible readings, culling useful moral teachings from sometimes obscure
passages with the assistance of vignettes, exhortations, theological reflections, or discussions of church law. In Roman Catholicism, the traditional preacher is the priest, a man trained in theology and
homiletics, or the art of sermon-giving. The sermon moves the worship
act between three planes of spiritual reality. The congregants sit in
rows at the lowest level, heads tilted up toward the priest, who is
sometimes elevated at the altar area or in a pulpit (though there are no
elevated pulpits on the Morro). The priest, who has helped direct

people's prayers to God at still a higher level, now moves the flow back toward the people by giving them divinely inspired guidance. He is higher than the people and so closer to God, but not so removed from the people as to be out of their reach. In the sermon he is their intercessor, standing between them and God, helping move their prayers up to God and conversely moving holy messages from God down to them. This describes the spatial arrangements of Padre Constante's mass on the Morro. It does not describe the Resistance celebrations, however, where participants sit in a circle and anyone can preach.

Catholics the world over, Roman and otherwise, follow a similar lectionary, or list of prescribed readings, that draws on three Biblical sources: the Old Testament, the Psalms, and the New Testament. Every Sunday, preachers may build their sermons on one Old Testament reading, one psalm, and two readings from the New Testament, one of which will be from a Gospel (the books of Matthew, Mark, Luke, or John). Sometimes a parish will choose to leave out either the Old Testament lesson or the non-Gospel New Testament selection. This is up to the discretion of individual parishes or dioceses. The lectionary is broken into three-year cycles; in one cycle is a complete reading of the Bible.

On the Morro, as one might predict, the conflicting factions have very different preaching styles. Sunday morning Resistance celebrations have mini-homilies after each Bible reading (not including the psalms). The Resistance liturgical organizers call the homilies a *reflexão* (reflection) or *comentário* (commentary). It is in large part because there are three "sermonettes," each of which can run the length of a traditional sermon, that the Sunday Resistance celebrations usually last at least two hours, guaranteeing that they bump up against the starting hour of the church mass.

Bible readings and sermons are done by different members of the Resistance community. If the organizers for a given Sunday are young people, then chances are three young people will read and reflect. If the Encontro de Irmãos is organizing, their members will read and reflect. The reflections are always prepared in advance. Sometimes Reginaldo will do one or all three, especially if he wants to impart a special message or alert people to a special cause for concern. Usually, however, he lets the participants decide who will reflect.

The Gospels, the holiest sources of the Christian tradition, are handled with care, and are conventionally the purview of deacons or priests (males) only. Resistance celebrations offer a significant break with Roman Catholic liturgical tradition when laity and especially women read Gospel lessons. The Bible is held high as the reader both offers himself or herself as a worthy purveyor of the sacred message, and gives thanks for the wisdom that Jesus imparts through the apostles' writings. In some churches the Gospel is chanted, a further indication that it isn't a normal text even within the Bible.

Resistance sermon themes almost always include the righteousness of the conflict, citing Bible passages that prove God is on their side and that sometimes prove the vile nature of *o lado de lá* (the other side). Various Bible lessons are understood to support the continuous Resistance assertion that "*Nos somos a igreja* (We are the church)." Because of this, the sermons are powerful sources of continuing tension. Dona Bene successfully obliterated Resistance sermons, piped over the praça P.A. system, when she took control of the church speaker system for several months. As soon as the Resistance celebration was well under way, she cranked the volume on a small collection of recorded church music and immediately no one could hear anything but amplified muffle from the Resistance speakers. A select contingent of Resistance members complained to Padre Constante, who said that since he wasn't on the Hill at the time (he celebrates mass at another community immediately before his 10:00 A.M. Morro mass), there was nothing he could do, but after a while he spoke to Dona Bene and the church speakers weren't turned on quite so early. But she, Alexandre the Gatekeeper, and Rogério, a young man who lives in the parish house, always listen closely to the Resistance homilies, and if they hear any talk against Dom José or Padre Constante, the church speakers start blasting. "We can't let them speak against the church or our priest," explained Dona Bene simply. "It is an insult to the Virgin."

The traditional church never offers three sermons during a mass. There is one sermon, and Padre Constante preaches it. Sometimes he will involve the congregation by asking people direct questions, but usually he will develop a simple theme drawn from the day's readings. He has never spoken against the Resistance group by name, but more than once has warned his listeners against them. One Sunday, for example, he noted that tourists arriving on the Hill for the first time had asked him what all the noise was about, what the group was doing in the school. It looked like a mass, but why in the school? Constante explained to his church audience that he told the tourists the group in the school was only bent on sowing confusion. They call themselves Roman Catholic, but they are not, said Constante, because they stand against their bishop, and it is not possible to do this and still be a Catholic. He reminded his parishioners that one must extend brotherly love, charity, and especially forgiveness to all Christians, and he supposed the group in the school — he called them *os outros* (the others) — was Christian, even if they weren't Catholic. But then, he said, it's hard to tell, since good Christians are obedient to Scripture, and those "others" were not.

Such not-so-subtle invective gives Morro traditionalists permission to continue scorning their Resistance neighbors, just as Resistance criticism of Constante and Dom José allows them to continue castigating the traditionalists. One must extend Christian forgiveness and brotherly love to fellow Christians, but if the people in question are not Christian, then one is not Biblically mandated to forgive them. By defining the Resistance as *os outros* and exempting them from a category of people to whom forgiveness must be extended, Padre Constante encourages the conflict to continue. Reginaldo does the same by denying any validity to all traditionalists' worship services and by naming the traditionalists as traitors.

Do This in Remembrance of Me

Roman Catholics the world over share a set of symbols and rites that comprise the mass, their principal worship event. The core element of the mass — the consecration of wine and bread, and their subsequent transformation into blood and flesh — has proven particularly enduring; in Christian lore, it was instituted by Jesus on the night before his execution and has been perpetuated across nearly twenty centuries (Shepherd 1965). The mass, more technically called the eucharist, is a re-enactment of Jesus's last evening meal, which he shared with his disciples (described in the Bible in Matthew 26:26–29; Mark 14:22–25; Luke 22:15–20; I Corinthians 11:23–26).

Over the years, some aspects of the eucharist have changed. It was thought originally to have been communally celebrated with no leader claiming special responsibilities or authority, but by the late fourth century it was dispensed by a cadre of elite priests, and its simplicity was replaced by growing pomp. It moved from house to church, from table to altar, from evening to morning, from communion to adoration (Rouillard 1982:146–56).

More recent changes happened through the reforms of the Second Vatican Council. Formerly said in Latin, the mass was translated into the vernacular in the early 1960s. This was significant, because it allowed people direct access to the words of the ritual and the Bible readings in it; these were formerly mediated exclusively through the priest. One Morro woman in her late forties who was raised in the church remembered when it was different. "We didn't have the Gospels for the people," she recalled, "only the priest had them." She remembered that many people didn't know how to read, and that after the liturgical switch to local languages, literacy classes were started to encourage Bible reading.

Other changes were structural. The altar, where the consecration act takes place, was pulled away from the back of the sanctuary and moved closer to the congregation. The priest no longer stood with his back to his audience when he said the prayers and transformed bread and wine into flesh and blood; instead, he faced the people so they saw exactly what he was doing, and a mystery formerly beyond the ken of laity was slightly clarified.

But many of the trappings of Catholicism have remained relatively unchanged since Constantine converted to Christianity and it was proclaimed the Roman Empire's official religion in the fourth century.[3] The vestments priests wear are modeled on clothing of the imperial Roman court, and genuflection was originally a way of showing respect to the emperor. The classic shape of a cathedral is an imitation of Roman assembly halls called basilica. Constantine made a gift of a palace to the Bishop of Rome that remained the headquarters of Roman Catholicism until 1308. Constantine declared December 25th Christ's birthday, usurping the day of worship formerly dedicated to Mithrais, a sun god, and he set aside the first day of every week, formerly the Day of the Sun, to worship the Christian deity. The church's governance system, dioceses headed by bishops, was based on an imperial organizational scheme (Herr 1985).[4]

The basic pattern of the eucharist, too, has remained remarkably unchanged. Indeed,

the fourth century . . . is the formative age of historic christian worship, which brought changes the effects of which
were never undone in the East or the catholic West at all
. . . [T]he essential outline of the christian eucharist . . . had
been fixed for all time before the middle of the second century, and probably by the end of the first. (Dix 1954:303)

The central symbols are bread and wine. The rite is traditionally led by
a male priest, who alone occupies the most sacred ritual space behind
the altar during the consecration. The actual eucharist, the blessing of
the bread and wine, happens in the second part of the service after the
synaxis, or the Bible readings and sermon. The most important part of
the eucharist blessing draws down God's power to transform mere
bread into flesh and mere wine into blood, and the priest then shares
the changed substances with the faithful.

The tenacity of this ritual opens it to many interpretations. It is a
shared meal, a communal exchange, a rite of incorporation, a ritual of
defense, a re-enactment of Jesus's death and resurrection, a pardon of
sins. It can even be seen as the vestige and perhaps the re-enactment
of an ancient cannibalistic sacrifice ritual in which the flesh and blood
of a victim are consumed by the group for the good of the group. The
basic language of the eucharist is unambiguous, though many Catholics
and other Christians who partake of it are uncomfortable with the la-
bels "cannibalistic" and "sacrifice ritual." There is a sense that contemporary Christians want distance from what was likely a messy, sensual
foretradition to today's eucharist, with blood flowing across the altar
from the slit throat of an animal. One theologian has declared, "The
Christian altar has nothing to do with the sacrificial altars of other
cults" (Richter 1990:145), though Christianity grows out of Judaism, an
agrarian-based tradition that shared sacrifice elements with other
agrarian cultures of the day. Gregory Dix, a pre-eminent eucharistic
scholar, distinguished a sacrifice from the remembrance of a sacrifice;
he maintained that the eucharist is the latter (1954:241–47). But a different voice declares:

The notion of "covenant blood" definitely introduces sacrificial overtones into the Last Supper event. The liturgy of
Christ's life and death is presented as a covenant sacrifice

which elevates the earlier Mosaic event . . . and endows it with its authentic meaning. (Ratzinger 1966:71–72)[5]

Even Leach claims that "sacrifice in Christianity appears only in vicarious symbolic form as a reference to mythology" (1976:92). Campbell-Jones protests (1980), saying that if the Nuer of Africa, as described by Evans-Pritchard, can substitute a cucumber for an ox and still be thought to engage in sacrifice, then why can't bread and wine substituted for flesh and blood also be a sacrifice? Douglas points out that Roman Catholic doctrine on the subject, spelled out in Pope Paul VI's encyclical *Mysterium Fidei*, is "as uncompromising as any West African fetishist's that the deity is located in a specific object, place and time and under the control of a specific formula" (1970:46–47).

Like rites in other religions that have survived centuries of tumult, the eucharist's strength comes precisely from the powerful and ancient simplicity of its central elements and from the timelessness of its ritual rhythms. These elements are open to vastly different understandings and interpretations on the Morro, as each side looks to verify its position by the integrity of its spiritual practices.

TIMELESS AND TIMELY

The various levels of understanding that Morro residents bring to narrative telling and interpretation they also bring to the eucharist, which is infused with several time elements. The first is immortal time, or timeless time; the next is enduring time; then there is cyclical time; last comes immediate or repetitious time. Illuminating these several levels of time clarifies aspects of each side's position.

Through immortal or timeless time, ritual participants are taught that the God they beseech through the body and blood of Jesus Christ is timeless, ageless, forever. Because Jesus is also God, partaking of him is to partake of this agelessness, or immortality. For believers, time is not an unstoppable force, but a trivial, human measure that God transcends and that they, too, transcend by eating God. This is not unique to the Christian experience; as Maurice Bloch notes in another context, "Ritual makes the passage of time, the change in personnel, the change in situation, inexpressible and therefore irrelevant. . . . Ritual can create a world of hazy timelessness in antithesis to another world, which is caricatured the better to deny it" (1986:184). On the Morro, this sense of timelessness permeates the conflict. There is no hurry for settlement, despite protests to the contrary, because God will be the final judge. Since those committed to one faction or the other already believe God will validate their choices, they don't need him to rush.

Next comes enduring time, which ties participants to both deep secular history and to a sacred event. Leach notes that the purpose of ritual activity is to bring about a transition from normal time to abnormal time at the beginning of the ceremony, and to move back from abnormal to normal time at the end (1976:83). The "abnormal" time of the eucharist is what I call enduring time. At each re-enactment of the death and revivication of Jesus, participants are sharing in a centuries-old rite. Some of the richest images of the ritual are direct ties to this past. The representation of flesh and blood as bread and wine; the sacred text of the Bible; the priests' ritual clothes; even the shape of many ritual spaces are centuries old (Shepherd 1965). The eucharistic prayer itself is a recitation of the "institution narrative" (Dix 1954:239), that is, the story of how the eucharist came to be and what it means; this is called the anamnesis, "considered in the Latin West as the sacramental 'formula' through which the priest, acting *in persona Christi*, performs the sacrament" (Meyendorff 1966:52–53).

Then there is cyclical time. The church year revolves around a cycle of seasons that are marked by different events in Christ's life, and there are small but sure alterations in the eucharist as the church seasons pass. There are two main cycles of feasts and holy days, the high points of which are Easter and Christmas. Often parishes hold their biggest Easter celebration on Easter eve, observing the transition from the gloom of *Sexta-feira Santa*, or Good Friday — when Jesus was tried and executed — to his resurrection two days later. Lent is meant to bring a time of contemplation and quietude (in Brazil and in many other countries, it is also a time to recover from carnival). The month of May is always dedicated to Mary, when active Brazilian Catholics take part in a more frequent cycle of rosary prayers. September is Bible month. Advent, the four Sundays preceding Christmas, marks the beginning of the church year and preparation for the birth of Christ.

Finally, there is immediate or repetitious time, which also involves the pattern of the liturgy. Participants depend on the sure repetition of the liturgical process every time they partake of the ritual. The speed, intonation, and enthusiasm of the priest can vary, as can the size of the congregation, the hour of the event, the day being marked — a Sunday, a weekday, a feast day, a wedding, among other occasions. But the eucharistic prayers will be said with the same words and gestures, every time. Immediate time also concerns participation in the ritual. Many believers attend the ritual every Sunday; a few attend every day (they leave the Morro for daily mass). This implies that the ritual works best if it punctuates people's lives at steady, predictable intervals.

IN REMEMBRANCE OF WHOM?

On the Morro, different meanings are culled from eucharistic ritual, and they point to yet another set of divergences between *o lado de lá e o lado de cá* (that side and this side). For Resistance members, the sharing of bread-made-flesh is a vital commensality that binds them in their unity and reminds them of their strength together. The sacrifice represented by the ritual is both that of Jesus on their behalf and that of the group for itself, through and with Jesus. His presence in the shared host is literal and symbolic; his divinity is acknowledged, but his humanity is more frequently cited.[6] The reflections, or sermons, after the Bible readings, especially after the Gospel, note the material conditions of Jesus's life, his poverty, the simplicity of his disciples, the oppressive government structure of Jesus's time.

Resistance celebrations on Sunday mornings and Wednesday nights can play a little loose with eucharistic interpretations because they are not, strictly speaking, eucharistic. There is no wine present, and the host is not consecrated in the ritual. This is because Reginaldo cannot perform the consecration or any other sacramental function in the Olinda/Recife diocese, having been suspended from his priestly vows, and all other clerics have been forbidden from participating in Resistance celebrations.[7] At the moment during the ritual that the host would normally be consecrated, it is brought in solemn procession from the home of a nearby member. It is dedicated to a theme — group solidarity, peace in Northern Ireland, an end to war — and distributed by two or three people, often women. Participants approach to take the host just as if they were in church, forming two or three lines and walking with bowed heads.

Some of the older women have said they miss the proper mass. Dona Ana, a widow in her fifties who has lived on the Morro for more than thirty years, said she cried often in the first few months the group was no longer inside the church, but said she grew accustomed to services in the school. She preferred them at the feet of the saint, however, because at least she was closer to Our Lady.

Though the host is not consecrated, Resistance worship services don't lack spirit; they are true celebrations. They take place in the common area of the school Dona Luisa heads, a space that has a roof and two walls. Young children, sometimes dogs, and an occasional chicken run in and out at will. The celebrations are accompanied by drums, guitars, and enthusiastic singing. Everyone sits in an oblong circle on chairs dragged from the classrooms; a makeshift altar of saw-horses and wood covered with white linen is at one end. Sometimes the Gospel reading is offered with a dance. One especially moving celebration was organized by the Encontro de Irmãos groups, and as they prepared to read the day's Scripture, all the older people gathered in the middle of the space and did a simple dance, one woman holding the Bible high over her head. The exchange of the peace is always boisterous, as everyone tries to hug everyone else at least once. Intercessory prayers, when people ask God's help for specific problems or give thanks for specific events, can go on a long time and often become personal testimonies about individual lives. Occasionally personal gifts of poetry written for the day or a letter of support from a distant place are shared during the intercession.

There are elements in the celebration that are true to a normal mass. Names are given to the coordinator, and he or she reads them in a long list as the celebration starts. They are for people who have just died, or died a week, three months, a year, or seven years before. The pattern of the celebration follows the same pattern as a normal mass. There is an opening song, the greeting to God called the gloria, a gathering of the group through a collect, another song, then the Bible readings. This is followed by recitation of the Nicene Creed, the intercessory prayers, a confession, and the exchange of the peace. Then the ritual moves into preparation for communion, which includes a prayer of thanksgiving, the sanctus, the Lord's Prayer, communion itself, a post-meal prayer, and a dismissal blessing. This pattern is punctuated by differences not necessarily particular to the Resistance celebrations but that mark "popular" masses. There are calls for people from outside the community to stand up and to tell where they are from and accept a welcome. There are often many more songs than usual, and people are likely to clap and to sway with the rousing music. There is more noise and motion.

Mass among the Morro traditionalists is more staid, and the orthodoxy of the liturgy is honored. People sit on rows of benches that face the altar. The service is conducted by the priest, who follows the prayers and songs in a small leaflet with the day's readings that each congregant also uses. An assistant is nearby to start the speakers when it's time to sing a song. The songs are sometimes unfamiliar to the congregants, and without the recordings no one would know the melody. The exchange of the peace consists of handshakes with people sitting nearby. The priest alone gives the sermon. Intercessory prayers come from the list on the leaflet and the congregants participate only in their responses. During communion, the priest and a congregant distribute the host. Here, like in the Resistance celebrations, the congregant helping with the host is likely to be a woman.

For the traditionalists, the eucharist is a source of release, even momentary escape, rather than a commensal bonding experience. Communicants concentrate more on their individual relationship with Jesus, strengthened by his presence in the sacramental elements. Jesus's divinity, not his humanity, is the more important factor during their time in church. It is important to participants that the traditional masses are calmer than Resistance celebrations. There is a sense that the confusion of the outside world is left on the threshold when one enters the church. No one offers personal testimonies about the injustices they have suffered during the week, no one urges the assembled to pray for the goals of what sometimes seem like local political squabbles, no one talks against city government for not building retaining walls before the winter rains or prays for the success of a bus driver's strike. Those are real concerns, but they are left where they should be left — outside the hour of the mass. The entire focus of the traditional worship service is the eucharist, and congregants can concentrate on that without distractions. It is not that traditionalists don't worry about real problems, or that they are escapists. But for many of them, the mass is a time to gain sustenance from Jesus through the host, to be restored and blessed and reminded that there is another, brighter future waiting for them. They still struggle with the traumas of this life, and some are active in local politics or community organizing efforts (though not through the Morro residents' council, a Resistance stronghold). Those activities, however, are for their weekdays, not their Sunday worship attention.

The differences between traditional and Resistance worship services do not merely indicate differences in preference or ritual style:

> One of the frames or contextual questions that continues to be important for the student of religions is that which seeks to identify the *religious* element underlying rituals and other phenomena. I use the word "contextuality" to mean that which places the phenomenon in terms of the believer's perceptions of a total context — that is, the Sacred or ultimate. (Clothey 1988:152)

The two groups hold separate definitions of the sacred, and this guides their ritual, personal, and political behaviors. If the sacred is most keenly known inside the church and particularly during the eucharist, it behooves believers to keep that space undefiled by certain categories of worldly concerns. Certainly people bring their suffering, fears, and hopes into church, and these are often grounded in problems going on in their lives outside of church, but for the most part they are personal concerns. It is right to bring them to church, and to request help from Jesus or Mary when outside church; prayer is not limited to church, and most people on the Morro have pictures and statuary of Jesus, Mary, and various saints in their homes. But there are other categories of the mundane that do not belong in church precisely because they do not and should not have a relationship with the sacred. These include concerns that are more properly consigned to the realm of material discontent or prideful efforts to get personal attention. Traditionalists believe that bringing such themes into the space and time that is set aside to sit humbly and needfully before one's Creator is to besmirch, even to foul that space and time, to denigrate the deity, and to confuse classifications of events and needs that are properly set apart.[8]

Resistance definitions of the sacred are broader. Reginaldo illustrated this in a sermon discussing the eucharist:

We need the nourishment of Jesus to always be better husbands and wives, better fathers and mothers, better children, better brothers and sisters. We need the nourishment of Jesus to be better catechists, better participants in the Encontro de Irmãos, better members of the residents' council, better participants in the political struggle, in the struggle for a better neighborhood, in union struggles. We need the nourishment of Jesus so that, in the name of love, putting our lives at the service of others, we can construct a different world.[9]

According to many who adhere to liberation theology, the sacred includes not just the daily and the mundane but also the actively political. If Jesus teaches about a new world and a reign of peace and justice, then his followers are beholden to work for that new world in a very literal sense. Changing the world involves the tools of politics, according to this model, so the struggle for a union, for the residents' council, can have a sacred tone. If those arenas themselves don't quite qualify as sacred, then at least one's work within them can qualify as blessed, assuming one enters the work with a proper spirit and dedication to Jesus and to the eventual realization of his kingdom.

But this broadened understanding of the sacred does not satisfy everyone in the Resistance, and it indicates the potential plurality of voices within an effort that presents itself as completely united. One woman who has lived on the Morro for nearly thirty years and who is an active participant with the Resistance expressed the sentiments of more than a few when she quietly said that, though she believed in the struggle, she wished they would stop to evaluate what they're doing. "The struggle seems to be going on for its own sake," she said, "not for any higher goals, and it could go on forever, but what for?" She continued,

Reginaldo is not the church, nor the host, nor our faith. . . . He should say, "Let's stop, let's reflect." He should say he's leaving and let people figure out what to do. But he will never do this. He sees people from all over the world supporting us, sending us letters, but really we're isolated. The pope won't say anything. People say the pope will remove Padre Constante, but this will never happen. Dom José and the pope won't say, "Ah, you're suffering so much!" Never. The community already put Dom José down too low. And I don't have the courage to open my mouth, or people [in the Resistance] will be completely on top of me. Reginaldo is very stubborn. He wants to destroy himself and everyone else.[10]

CLEANSED AND INITIATED, OR, BAPTISM AND CONFIRMATION

Baptism, the sacrament that makes a human a Christian, may take place among Roman Catholics when a baby is a few weeks old. A priest blesses the infant with consecrated oil and then pours holy water on its head three times — in the name of the Father, the Son, and the Holy Spirit. The child is then Christian; if the rite has been done in a Roman Catholic context, she or he is also now Roman Catholic and will go to Jesus at death. In Brazil, baptism is sometimes put off for several years until a suitable set of godparents can be found, a white dress or suit bought, and a photographer hired — expensive propositions for ghetto dwellers. Baptism is important, however, because without it, a child will not go to heaven if she or he dies. In regions with high infant mortality, it is sometimes the practice to baptize a child after it has died, a possible aberration of the theology but a tremendous reassurance to the parents (Scheper-Hughes 1989).[11]

Like the eucharist, baptism is explained in the Bible. The water purifies by removing the taint of original sin and initiates the person into a life in Christ, freed from fears of death. In this, like the eucharist, it is a rite of passage. Confirmation, or first communion, is also a rite of passage, but one made consciously as an adolescent, not made on behalf of a baby. Confirmation requires lengthy training. One is allowed to take communion — eat the bread and drink the wine — only after detailed instruction into the beliefs and teachings of the Roman church. The training takes up to two years and is done by catechists, or people who teach children Catholicism by teaching them the catechism, the codified instructions of the church. The instructions are often presented in question-and-answer form.

The student, called the catechumen, will be a full member of the church after she or he has completed the training, and first communion is a special occasion. Again, white clothes are the custom (though not a requirement). Another set of godparents are chosen, photographs taken, family gathered from far away. Usually a group of catechumens who have been studying together for the previous two years go through the first communion rite together, rather like an age-set initiation rite. Parents want pictures of their child receiving the host for the first time, and a picture of her or him with the priest who performed the rite. With all the families, godparents, and photographers filling the church, the service has an air of festive near-chaos.

As one would expect, traditionalists and the Resistance have dissimilar approaches to baptism and to first communion. A family may baptize their child at the Morro church by visiting the parish office during the week, registering, and paying a fee. The following Sunday after the mass, Constante will perform the baptism. People like to baptize their children on the Morro because of Mary's proximity.

The Resistance cannot baptize, but their *Equipe de Batismo*, or Baptism Committee, prepares parents of baptismal candidates with a month-long series of weekly meetings. This custom started when Reginaldo was priest. The idea, he explained, was to educate parents about being witnesses to the profundity of the commitment implied in baptism, and to encourage a more active participation in the church as the child grew. It should be a solemn decision to dedicate one's child to Christ, he said, not one made only because it is a cultural habit. After the parents are duly instructed, they are sent to a parish down the Hill where a priest sympathetic to the Resistance will baptize the baby or child.

Reginaldo's baptism style drew many people when he was priest precisely because he was a priest, but the time commitment was a burden many parents resented. Now that he is no longer the parish vicar, people who do not want to go to Constante are more likely to go to another parish than to work with the Resistance Baptism Committee, which imposes what many parents believe are unnecessary complications on a simple process.

The Resistance group had a cohort of children in the middle of their catechetical training when the schism opened. Their catechists continued to teach the children, and when they were ready for their first communion, Resistance members chipped in, rented a bus, and held the celebration in the church of a nearby parish. There were dozens of children, because the four parishes in that sector of the diocese that were still speaking to each other had decided to give first communion to all their candidates at the same time. Hundreds of people filled the church, several priests officiated, and the camera-toting anthropologist was put in charge of photographing Morro children. Dona Luisa had the last word of the day; she took the microphone after the service and after a brief talk about the immense success of the day, put her fist in the air and led chants of *Viva nossa luta!* (Long live our struggle!). This got back to Dom José, who saw it as further evidence of the depraved and heretical tone of the Resistance.[12]

Tools Of Conflict

Like narratives, rituals mark and maintain the continuing tension on the Morro. Both are tools of conflict that appeal to residents' reason, emotion, and faith. Like narratives, rituals are used competitively, each side claiming the true version, the more honest orthodoxy, the more powerful allies and historical precedents. Resistance members cherish an idea of early Christian practice and worship that was conciliatory, not hierarchical. Traditionalists equally cherish an idea of Jesus's teachings that establishes hierarchy and mandates obedience to his divine will.

The rituals are crucial tools in perpetuating the struggle by keeping tensions manageable (cf. Turner 1957:301–302). Through the rituals, participants "deal with their frazzled emotions and their hostilities in ways that do not endanger the social order" (Kertzer 1988:133); in this case, the social "order" is steady disorder.

WHAT IT BECOMES

In Recife, like in many tropical cities, dust, sweat, and humidity mingle in a soundless force that sometimes feels like another element of nature. Dust carried by ocean wind and river breezes is kept in motion by an army of buses disgorging brown plumes of exhaust. Dust and bus smog settle across everything in a fine grey gauze, which sweat congeals into a thin gel on the neck and forehead and in the creases where limbs bend. Humidity adds a sense of suffocation, not just of one's breath but of the skin itself. Rain is no relief, only making sweat bead and trickle faster, and giving the dust a mudlike quality that stains buildings as it streaks windows and eyeglasses.

A continually moving throng of people adds to the intensity. Young office workers in ironed T-shirts and sturdy shoes carry papers in bright plastic folders. Businessmen with open collars and no ties lean toward each other as they speak. Teenage students in uniforms gambol from or meander to school. Men and women of all ages stand inside small wooden stalls, patiently selling everything from sugarcane juice to aluminum cookware. At the river's edge, young men in shorts sink up to their knees in low-tide mud as they harvest crabs to sell. Young women with babies, isolated old women, deformed men beg on the city's many bridges, plaintive in their rags and punished by the sun. Variously uniformed police in dull-colored fatigues and black boots stroll with alert langour; their presence means that the small bands of shoeless, shirtless children scatter in well-learned fear. The street is home to these children, who swoop in and out of vision like birds. If police are not around and they stop, they may beg; if they keep moving, they may grab what they're after.

A continual aroma serves as an olfactory accent to the crowds and to the grit. Even on clear days it rises from the gutters, a steady smell of rotting oranges, something like sour milk, and a slight but sharp top note of urine, all blended on wafts of wood smoke, sea air, and fetid river mud. Combined with the sweet fragrance of sugarcane-based car exhaust, the effect is unique to Brazil's urban northeast. Each city has its own smell, and though Recife's resembles Salvador's to the south and Natal's to the north, it has an aromatic signature all its own, at once acrid and pleasingly sweet.

The smell of Recife varies somewhat from neighborhood to neighborhood, but to me as an outsider, it never became invisible the way the smell of one's home disappears. Native Recifenses, on or off the Morro, occasionally commented on some addition to the usual scents, like a smouldering pile of trash or a flatbed truck piled high with rotting cow bones, but for the most part they did not notice anything special about the city's aromas. When I asked them to describe the smell of Recife, many were puzzled by the request, and I realized that I'd have as hard a time describing the general smell of New York City or of the towns where I grew up.

Sometimes our different perceptions of the religious disagreements on the Morro felt to me like our different sensitivities to Recife's smells; as an outsider, I was continually amazed at the depth of discord among residents of the Hill. They, too, noted the passion of the acrimony, but they understood parts of it as inevitable expressions of feuds that in some cases had been brewing a long time. There was a taken-for-granted quality to the fight that did not detract from its more sensational moments but that allowed its perpetuation for quite a while. I want to highlight the mundanity, as I call it, of the conflict because it points to similarities that the two factions shared. These were as important as their differences, because without similarities between the two sides and in their tactics, the conflict would have evolved into two unrelated causes. The samenesses allowed the conflict to continue, and kept participants engaged in its tormented conversation.

Indeed, the metaphor of conversation is useful here, because the conflict represented many overlapping conversations at once. The religious disagreements were the first contexts, but political incompatibilities were also crucial, and the conflict that the Morro represents cannot be understood without looking at them, which I do here. Those conversations also resonated within and were mediated by larger trends within Brazil's political life, within the church, and within liberation theology, in Brazil and elsewhere, and as such deserve a glance. Finally, I want to end this story by talking about the situation today, a temporary conclusion to a drama that in many ways started centuries ago and that will continue into the distant future.

BLESSED BE THE TIES THAT BIND

It is true that in worship style, understanding of Roman Catholic faith, and interpretation of the Hill's recent history, the two factions that define the Morro conflict have little in common. The same is true in their political practice and ideology. But many of the strategies used to perpetuate the conflict reveal Resistance members and traditionalists to be as much alike as they are different.

One effective tactic was their shared use of print and broadcast media. For example, there were two radio efforts: *A Voz do Morro* (The Voice of the Morro), run by a combination of Resistance and residents' council members, and *A Verdade do Morro* (The Truth of the Morro), run by traditionalists. A Voz started through the residents' council and used the community's public address system, which consists of bull-horn-style loudspeakers hung from lampposts around the hill. The original loudspeakers were put up by the city many years ago as part of the festa infrastructure, and the residents' council added more. A Voz broadcasts on Friday evenings, then all day and evening Saturday.

It was subject to government regulations about broadcasting rights, which meant the residents' council was supposed to pay a fee for their broadcast license. When they first started A Voz, they ignored the licensing requirement and said they would never need to worry about it because no one in authority would ever find out about their broadcasts. After all, they reasoned, we're puny; the government couldn't possibly care. But someone — probably traditionalist leader Nilton, if the broad hints he dropped were true — reported A Voz, and the council was told to pay the licensing fee or get off the loudspeakers. Resistance supporters thought the radio effort was surely doomed, but Zé João came up with the necessary funds from money that the CEB organization received through Reginaldo from supporters in Europe.

The traditionalists were not to be left without their own radio. If the Resistance could spew their opinions all over the Hill through loudspeakers, traditionalists eagerly countered with the same technique. Starting Sunday morning at 6:30 with the broadcast of the early mass (and with a brief pause for the Resistance celebration, though not always), A Verdade do Morro, the traditionalists' broadcast, used the church speakers to fill the praça with sound. After the masses were over, A Verdade played their own music and kept listeners informed of community news and upcoming church events.

Neither faction limited itself to Morro media, a strategy that would have denied access to and response from larger outside audiences. Both Morro factions had sympathetic outlets, and each outlet spoke to a different constituency. *O Diário de Pernambuco*, which claims to be the oldest continuously published newspaper in Latin America, sided with the traditionalists, while *O Jornal do Comércio* liked the Resistance. *O Diário* regularly published letters from Recifenses who condemned Reginaldo for his disobedience and stubbornness. Editorials blamed him and his followers for ruining the festa, driving away wealthier patrons, and embarrassing the city. A vivid sign of *O Diário*'s views was its almost weekly mention of Frei Damião, the tiny ninety-something Capuchin monk who was brought to the 1990 Morro festa to insure its success. In contrast, *O Jornal* seemed enamored with the Morro Resistance and printed scathing articles and editorials against Dom José. Just as *O Diário* had its Roman Catholic saint-like hero, so did *O Jornal*, reporting almost weekly on the doings of Dom Hélder Câmara.

Every time the Morro was mentioned in a story in either paper, clippings of the article made their way around the community. The weekly national news magazine *Veja* (Look) published a detailed story about the Morro soon after the police raid. It ran several pages and was illustrated with vivid photographs of the key players. Several residents bought that issue of the magazine, or made xeroxes of friends' copies. At the end of December 1990, *Time* magazine's international edition carried a story complete with photos of the church, Reginaldo, and Dom José. The printed stories were prized possessions, and swelled the already detailed archives that both the residents' council and the CEB council had maintained for several years. While harder to come by than television and radio reports, the printed coverage had a permanence that residents on both sides valued.

Cost and general lack of reading skills, however, meant that most Morro residents relied on broadcast media for their news. And though it was harder to influence, they also sought coverage on those media for their side of the conflict. A good friend of Nilton's, twenty-eight-year-old Rui, was interviewed on a city radio station about the Morro. Rui was active among the traditionalists and, like Alexandre the Gate-keeper, was an outspoken man with strong opinions. He made good use of the radio exposure both to explain the traditionalists' perspective and to slam the Resistance. He called Zé João a liar and Dona Luisa a cheat, and said Reginaldo had stolen money from church funds after he had been suspended. Rui played the hero for Morro traditionalists, but not without consequences. Several months later, when the newspaper *O Jornal* reported Doninha's accusation that Alexandre charged people a fee to see the Virgin, rumors circulated that she was getting revenge for Rui's radio slanders.

Padre Constante went on a morning television news talk-show to explain a development project he and the city government were working out for the Morro. The two newspapers also reported the plans, which proposed developing the Morro as a major local tourist site along the lines of Olinda, the sixteenth-century settlement five kilometers north. Tourists, drawn by the Virgin, already visited the Morro with some frequency; especially on Sunday mornings, a few busloads of them often filled the praça. The idea of transforming the Morro into a tourist center, then, was not completely farfetched, but the comparison to Olinda was a stretch. The old part of Olinda has been relatively well kept for years and has an air of colorful, faded elegance. There are even the requisite pricey shops selling regional handicrafts and a couple of swanky restaurants, and it is considered home to one of the oldest, most "genuine" expressions of *carnaval* in the country.

In a given year, the festa probably drew nearly as large a number of people to the Hill as visited Olinda, but pilgrims don't spend money like tourists. The Morro, with its very different history and focus, could not appeal to Olinda's visitors. Highlighting the Morro's status as a tourist attraction, rather than as a pilgrimage site, would necessitate changes like covering the praça with grass and forbidding the almost twenty-four-hour soccer games — an unthinkable prohibition — as well as upgrading the run-down children's play area at the west end of the praça, painting the chapel and the statue (the new church was not built yet), and knocking down some homes around the praça so the view to the ocean would be unobstructed. The traditionalists, who supported the plan, called these community improvements. Resistance members and the residents' council called them government impositions.

The plan was a threat to the balance of geographies that the conflict had established. An unprecedented meeting was held between the two groups and city representatives. Residents' council members, unofficially led by Cecilia, told the city that the community didn't need to be turned into a tourist site, which they said would only benefit middle-class people from other places, but did need real infrastructural help, like more retaining walls and more regularly running water. The city official said he didn't know that these were lacking and promised that they would be provided as part of the plan. Cecilia still objected, saying there was no way that the residents' council would allow people's homes to be torn down. She asked where displaced residents would go and was told that housing would be provided for them. She pointed out that there wasn't room on the Morro to build more homes; where would the displaced people live? Probably to the west in Nova Descoberta, the government officials said. No, replied Cecilia and the rest of the residents' council members, that's not good enough. Traditionalists at the meeting, meanwhile, were mostly silent. At one point Nilton got up and said he was present as a representative of the Morro church, and said that even though some people believed there were two priests in the community, there was really only one, Padre Constante. The meeting ended with no resolution, but the residents' council members were pleased with their reception.

The traditionalists apparently were not so pleased, because a few days later a small contingent of them went to city hall. They explained to the city official who had been to the Morro that the community was in a tremendous state of dissension, so the city's representatives should be cautious about what they said and how they interpreted what they had heard on the Hill. This seemed to impress the city official; the next word the residents' council heard was that there would be no further discussion because the community was too full of conflict.

There was some speculation that Constante had encouraged the development plan. He had often complained that the Morro looked grungy and worn-down, and showed a contempt for the place that marked him as an outsider even to some who wanted to like him. Dona Bene started to grumble that he was discontent with the Morro's looks because he was from a well-off family in the south and didn't like poor places. "*Ele não é da gente,*" she said often as time passed and she grew disillusioned with him, "He's not one of us."

The newspapers covered the story of the would-be tourist site, but as the city's plans seemed to stall and the residents' council remained opposed to them, media and neighborhood interest faded. Traditionalists shook their heads and said that once again, the council had proven itself an obstacle to helping the community. "*Eles tem cabeças duras,*" clucked the traditionalists, "They have hard heads." They even charged that council opposition to the plan and the resulting publicity had cost them what little they had left of a good reputation.

Nilton, however, said the problem was older than the tourist park controversy. Months before, he had gone to the city with a plan to develop the Morro São João festivities. For several years, Nilton had dedicated himself to the community's children from April through June, rehearsing them in the dances that comprised the height of São João on the Morro.[1] This year, he wanted city support to elaborate his work and to provide more activities for the kids. He wrote a detailed scheme that he said had impressed the official who reviewed it. According to Nilton, the man was on the verge of approving the plans when he asked, almost as an afterthought, "What community did you say you're from?" "The Morro da Conceição," replied Nilton. Nilton reported that when the official heard the name Morro, he jumped up and yelled, "No! I won't have anything to do with the Morro! It's too much trouble!"

THE PRESSURE OF THREATS

Besides sharing a sophisticated ability to win media allies and use various news sources creatively, the two factions had other tactics in common. They both used ostracism and the threat of it to keep their own members in line, and they gave harsh punishment to those who were too friendly with people on the "other side." An alleged transgressor's loyalty was questioned, and she or he was warned to stay away from the opposition. If she persisted, she was shunned and even, in some cases, publicly ridiculed. Members of each side feared this, especially because some had been victims. Dona Leonarda, an older woman who had moved to the Morro with her family from another neighborhood twenty years earlier, was an integral part of the Resistance and a leader in the Morro's Encontro de Irmãos groups. Unfortunately, she was seen talking too often to people with traditionalist affinities. Many of them had been involved with the Encontro groups, too, and over the years the women had formed a bond. Dona Leonarda realized that she had to choose between them and the Resistance members. She said she spent nearly a year on the fringes of Reginaldo's group until her humble persistence convinced people she was still loyal. It was exactly this fear that kept Dona Ana and other Encontro de Irmão members out of the church even when they very much wanted to sit in the same space as the tabernacle, which held sanctified bread — or, as they believed, Jesus himself. Dona Luca, a retired laundress and mother of three whose entire family was part of the Resistance, responded strongly to the women who wanted to sit with Jesus. She explained,

> For me it's different. When I see people like them entering the church — people who were seminary trained — when I see that face of Constante filled with *maldade* [wickedness, malice], with those hands doing evil, it's a sacrilege against the Most Holy Sacrament. Because of this I can't enter the church.

One woman from an adjacent Morro parish, Dona Glorinha, did try to enter a Morro chapel for a mass in December of 1990. The celebration was started by CEB coordinators, but Constante showed up unannounced, kicked them out, and said mass himself. Dona Glorinha decided to stay because, she explained later, she felt a strong need for a mass. When she left the chapel, she was greeted by dozens of Reginaldo's supporters, who jeered at her and chanted, "*Traidora!* [Traitor!]" She claimed that even Reginaldo himself was calling her names. The event traumatized her. She never returned to a CEB event, nor did she frequent Constante's masses, but attended services off the Hill when she could find someone to give her a lift.

Seu Mateus, a man who had been loyal to Reginaldo for more than a decade and to the Resistance since its inception, confessed that he still very much liked Dona Bene, who had been his friend for years, but he was afraid to talk to her because of what he'd seen happen to Dona

Leonarda. Seu Mateus was at particular risk, because he lived in another community where the priest had warned that anyone who attended the Resistance celebrations would no longer be considered part of his parish. If he alienated the Resistance, he would lose his only church home and one of his most important social networks.

Many people told me in the intimacy of interviews that they were concerned and even alarmed by some Resistance decisions but were afraid to say anything for fear they would be kicked out of the group. On a few occasions when people expressed doubt about the Resistance and I asked why they didn't tell Reginaldo or even discuss it with other members, they were astonished at the suggestion. As one young man explained, "If Padre Constante said he'd respect us and our ways, I'd return [to the Morro church] and defend that we go back. But if I said this, people would say, 'You see? He's turning against us.'"[2]

Fear of being ostracized extended to fear of questioning Reginaldo's decisions or attitudes, and the reality of ostracism was felt beyond the community. In October 1991, at a meeting of nearby parishes that supported Reginaldo, he revealed a complex set of prayers and rituals that he and a few other Resistance members had designed for a novena (nine-day festa prelude) to parallel the official festa novena, which was to start at the end of the following month. He was explaining each night's theme enthusiastically when Gonçalo, a priest from another parish and a long-time friend of Reginaldo's, interrupted and asked who else had agreed that this was the right thing to do. Gonçalo said he didn't remember any discussion about it and that he was troubled. He asked if a better course wouldn't be working toward reconciliation, rather than holding a hard line, and asked if Reginaldo had met with the Morro priest, meaning Constante, or with Dom José recently.

Reginaldo grew very still. "There is no priest on the Morro," he said quietly. "Constante is on the Morro," replied Gonçalo, puzzled. "There is no priest on the Morro," Reginaldo repeated. "I do not recognize Constante as priest of the Morro. He does not exist. Constante does not exist." Later that evening, Morro residents who had been at the meeting harshly criticized Gonçalo for questioning Reginaldo, and said simply, "He is no longer on our side."

The traditionalists, too, threatened to ostracize people within their ranks, and they had an extra weapon: they could go to the bishop to warn him when someone seemed to be falling under Reginaldo's sway. One young Morro resident with Resistance sympathies who felt called to the priesthood was threatened with expulsion from seminary if he continued attending Reginaldo's worship services (though he became a loyal Morro traditionalist, he was expelled from seminary anyway a few years later).

Gossip and skillfully spread rumor made up another set of tactics both sides had in common. They were used against opponents, but like the threat of ostracism, gossip also functioned to intimidate those within the group who might have adopted a softer line. Among the Resistance, such sentiments were strongly discouraged through stories told to prove the evil of those who now control the church building. Reginaldo's people often referred to specific Constante followers as devils and accused some of following the practices of umbanda or another Afro-Brazilian religion — an ironic charge, since there were Resistance members who turned to the skills of an umbandista or *mae-de-santo* once in a while.

Gossip among traditionalists about Resistance people often concerned money and their disapproval of the material capital the other side was attracting. It was thought that Zé João, for instance, received money for his home and got his job through backdoor connections. Traditionalists wondered why Dona Luisa had a telephone (still a luxury for most Brazilians) and what one young woman in the community had done to get four months of tuition at a school in Bahia, a state south of Pernambuco. And where, asked traditionalists, did Reginaldo's group get the money for those loudspeakers, the ones they used on Sunday mornings to *atrapalhar* (confuse, disrupt) the Morro with their noise? Traditionalists added again that when Reginaldo was kicked out of the church and parish house, his followers stole many things — the chalice, Bibles, altar linens, the parish telephone, and office supplies.

Resistance members did not deny that their cause attracted material capital, though they vehemently denied stealing. They pointed out that Reginaldo always had an international network of support and that material succor for some Resistance needs, including special tuition costs for a few designated community representatives, came from those overseas funds. That was also the source of money for the loudspeakers. They lobbed counter-accusations against the traditionalists, claiming they were in cahoots with conservative politicians and that through these connections they earned special preference for jobs and other favors. They wondered where Constante found the money to buy the parish not just a telephone but also a brand-new car that they said he used more for himself than for parish business.

Both sides singled out individuals for special contempt. The more public a person, the more likely he or she was to be maligned. Dona Luisa was regularly discussed with great scorn by many of the traditionalists, as was Zé João. Because she had lived on the Morro most of her life, Dona Luisa earned special contempt, as she disproved the theory that only newcomers to the Morro were attracted by Reginaldo. Some Resistance members literally spat in disgust when they heard the names Nilton or Rui. Padre Constante once offered a residents' council member a ride up the Hill; she recounted this incredulously many times, asking rhetorically how the man could have been so stupid as to think she would actually ride in a car with him. But among Resistance members, there was no greater target of disdain than Dona Bene. She, too, had lived on the Morro for most of her life, thus robbing Resistance members of their claim that only outsiders liked Constante. It is a tradition in some parts of Brazil that an especially despised community member is deemed the local Judas and secretly hung in effigy in a conspicuous place on Good Friday eve. Doninha proposed hanging effigies of Dona Bene and Padre Constante from the church doors. It took some time to dissuade her from the impulse.

COMMUNITY DYNAMICS REMADE

The similarities between traditionalists and Resistance members that shaped their tactics within the church conflict pointed to very different understandings of the political role and behavior they supported. Until Reginaldo lived there, the Morro's movers and shakers were not interested in working with neighbors to figure out how to claim resources and improvements from the city. That style of political activism probably had never occurred to anyone, since at the time there were few models for it. Rather, Morro residents who engaged in political work followed an older, more established style that focused on individual politicians who promised to serve Morro interests, especially if a block of residents could be convinced to vote for them in upcoming elections. This approach was used with mayors, city council members, and state and federal legislators, and everyone involved understood exactly how it worked.

A candidate for city council, for example, might appear at the Morro São João festivities in June, give a pitch for his campaign, and promise that if elected, the Morro would get better street lighting, or a Morro builder would win a city contract. Behind the scenes, the candidate would work with Morro organizers to insure that residents actually voted for him. Insurance usually came in the form of money: people were, in essence, paid for their votes, though rewards could vary from mere T-shirts to the promise of jobs or the promise of better housing. If the man in question won the election, he would be expected to make good on at least some of his promises. While politicians the world over make grand promises in the effort to win elections, in northeast Brazil those promises are very specific and are made to individuals as much as to communities.

This network has its roots in the *coronel* system of the rural northeast. Coroneis controlled their political fortunes by delivering votes *en masse* on election day. Workers and others dependent on a coronel's good will were bussed to polling places. Often they received half of a currency note, with the other half delivered when the votes were counted and the results satisfactory to the coronel. Another reward easy to split this way was shoes — half a pair given before the vote, the other after. There were stories on the Morro that politicians used to go door to door, offering people a sum for their vote and giving half on the spot and half if they won. Many older residents grumbled that despite election victories, the money-doling politicians rarely reappeared to give out the second half of their promise. They also commented on neighbors who they said would promise their votes for next to nothing — for a bottle of rum or a few beers. And there were those who promised their vote to any politician who asked for it, reaping many short-term material rewards. These folks were supposedly found out over time and dropped from all pols' rolls.

This system required and reinforced a paternalistic subservience on the part of people who lived in communities like the Morro — low income, with a low political profile — that many resented even as they recognized its seemingly unshakable place within the region's political structure. The notion that there might be another way came slowly; on the Morro and in many other places, it started with the church. When

Padre Geraldo Leite, Reginaldo's predecessor, urged the parish to build itself a church, Morro residents saw a tangible and vitally important result of their united efforts. They applied their insight to the festa, forming its first organizational divisions. Reginaldo took this further when he encouraged the Encontro de Irmãos groups to become the genesis of base communities within the Morro parish, then encouraged them to form the community residents' council.

Both the CEBs and the council date their founding to 1980, the year that the nuclei of those two groups mounted their campaign for water. Morro residents wrote letters to the state water utility, to their city councilmen, to the press. They scheduled meetings with the utility. Finally, they demonstrated in front of city hall, banging pots and pans in a demand for running water. The older women led the charge, and they made a vivid image in the local papers and on the television news. One particularly vocal activist, the silver-haired Dona Hilda, told the story of men who came to her from the city and said they would install water pipes on her street if that would make her quiet down. She indignantly replied that she would not stop making a fuss until the entire Morro had water, and they couldn't buy her off by giving her and her immediate neighbors water but ignoring everyone else.

The Hill saw water installed that year, and it runs at least three or four days a week — a marked improvement over the shared well residents had used, trudging back and forth with buckets for decades. Despite the effort's success, however, many Morro traditionalists point to the water drive as the beginning of troubled times. "They embarrassed us at city hall," explained Alexandre the Gatekeeper's mother, "and then they never stopped embarrassing us with everything else they did."[3] She referred to the tactics that residents' council members employed in pressing city government for services; it often resembled those used to secure water.

Activism on the Morro coincided with events in other parts of the country that were opening space for protest against the government. During the 1970s, through policies of import substitution industrialization, Brazil's gross domestic product grew at a rate of 6.1 percent. While a remarkable figure, it was achieved at a high social cost. The economic model that produced such results depended on income concentration that excluded most citizens from the consumption market and that simultaneously created a huge reserve of labor, factors that intensified already stark social stratifications (Sader and Silverstein 1991:33). In 1978, strikes by metalworkers outside São Paulo quickly spread throughout the state, focusing national attention on laborers' discontent with the government's economic policies. These strikes were the first genuine cracks in the military's previously monolithic power.

Starting in 1979, partly inspired by the strength of the strikes and demonstrations the previous year, the dictatorship proclaimed a time of transition to democratic rule through a process called the *abertura* (opening). The two-party system mandated in 1965 was abolished, and additional parties were allowed, though with bureaucratic hurdles so difficult that many potential coalitions found it impossible to register themselves as parties. The official party of the state, ARENA (*Aliança Renovação Nacional*), was renamed the PDS (*Partido Democrático Social*), while the only previously legal opposition party, the PMDB (*Partido do Movimento Democrático Brasileiro*), now had company as another opposition party came into existence: *O Partido dos Trabalhadores* — the PT, or Workers' Party. The PT grew out of the leadership that had guided the metalworkers' strikes the year before. From modest beginnings, over the next decade it became a national, broad-based political organization that drew leftists of many stripes, from intellectuals and orthodox (though underground) Marxists to priests and bishops. It was all the more remarkable because the roots of the PT are in organized labor, never a persistent political voice in Brazil.

The abertura moved slowly. Direct elections were scheduled in gradations, starting with local and legislative contests in 1982, an indirect presidential election in 1984, more local elections in 1986, and finally direct presidential elections in 1989. At first relieved that the military was willing to consider alternative governance structures, Brazilians quickly grew impatient. A nationwide series of demonstrations demanding direct presidential elections surprised the military in 1982. The *Direitas Já!* campaign drew hundreds of thousands of protestors to the square outside São Paulo's cathedral. It was the largest demonstration in the history of the country, and rallies in the streets that drew thousands more and brought cities to a standstill were repeated around the country.

In this climate of increased protest and the gradual release of military control, the Morro residents' council came into being, one of the earliest effective councils in Recife. A tradition, started with the first meetings and continuing today, involves continual "auto-critique" of the council's decision-making processes. Virtually every meeting concludes with a formal discussion of how the meeting went. This can sometimes drag a meeting on for many hours, as the dynamics of what happened become the center of debate, and the original meeting purpose is lost in the criticism of one person's tone or another's alleged rudeness. While sometimes tedious, it does keep meetings remarkably inclusive; in the auto-critique, people who did not yet speak are often explicitly asked to contribute.

The residents' council changed the political dynamic of the Hill by altering the relationship between the community and the city agencies responsible for various community resources. Rather than kowtow or make nice to individual politicians in hopes that eventually a needed retaining wall would be built, or garbage collection would take place, or streets would be paved, the residents' council organized signature drives, visited individual city officials in charge of various services, wrote letters to the local papers, and held demonstrations. The council eventually divided itself into several *equipes*, or teams, responsible for various aspects of Morro life. Working collectively, they mapped out strategies to put pressure on, for instance, the city's department of transportation to get more buses added to the Morro route. Individual residents' council members took on specific responsibilities, like collecting information about bus frequency in other, similar neighborhoods. Sometimes these campaigns took months or even years, but after a decade, the council could point to an impressive list of accomplishments that directly benefited the community as a whole, and to an array of equipes dedicated to specific concerns. Today there are equipes organized around health, land and home ownership, women, breastfeeding, day care for children, day care for home-bound elderly, literacy, music, education, children with mental disabilities, security, retaining walls, sanitation, and communication, among others.

The political focus of the Hill before Reginaldo's time was mostly outward, away from the Morro itself, as individuals or groups from the community tried to form coalitions with city or state political powers and particular candidates. There was no tradition of answering community needs by relying on the skills and efforts of those who lived in the community itself. This changed with the residents' council. Instead of an atomized, outward-looking stance, political engagement first turned inward to neighbors and to family, then turned outward with a newly discovered collective and organized strength. Reginaldo did not govern this transformation, but he did start it by working with parishioners to found the council in the first place. There were even some within the council who learned the art of grant writing and who successfully won money from Oxfam, Caritas, and similiar organizations. The Morro's center for children with mental disabilities, which schools and feeds more than two dozen children, was established with Oxfam funds.

The council's successes did not deter criticism from those who disliked their methods or their officers. Since the council was formed by people originally inspired by Reginaldo, it will be a while before traditionalists on the Hill will sponsor a successful slate of candidates for council positions. Not that they don't try. Dona Bene and Nilton have put together slates over several election cycles, with themselves and other like-minded residents running for president, vice president, secretary, and treasurer, but traditionalists don't vote in council elections in large enough numbers to get the slate even close to victory. For a while, though, Dona Bene and Nilton were determined to take the council out of the hands of the allegedly corrupt people who they said had held its leadership positions for much too long, and they ran a slate of candidates every election season for several years.

While the council was organizing and defining itself and its roles, the Morro's CEBs were similarly engaged. When Reginaldo was parish priest, the CEBs were meant to bring the church into people's daily lives. Catechism classes took place in each of the six CEBs (there was a CEB base in each of the six neighborhoods that comprise the Morro parish), as did baptism preparation classes, festa planning, and events focused on the church calendar. Participants in each of the six CEBs took turns organizing the twice-weekly masses in the church, and leaders from each took part in workshops, retreats, and even theological trainings at seminaries in Recife and in other cities.

After Reginaldo was suspended, CEB members — calling themselves The Resistance — orchestrated negotiations with the bishop and strategized ways to get Reginaldo reinstated. When the bishop called out the troops and broke open the fight for the world, CEB members planned media campaigns, protest demonstrations, and calls for solidarity from sympathetic parishes in Recife and far beyond. Because the bishop had used a force outside the official realm of the church to get what he wanted, Reginaldo urged the CEBs to create the possibility of meeting him on similar ground. The CEBs would never be able to command riot police, but they decided to create a civic identity for themselves. They applied to the city for the same recognition granted residents' councils and other neighborhood civic organizations, thus allowing themselves a role in civic and political life that their status as a church organization denied them. When the approval came through in March of 1991, it was the first time in Brazil that CEBs won official state recognition as a secular entity. The move disturbed many clerics within the popular church. They wondered if it meant that the Morro CEBs intended to form their own church. Reginaldo assured them it did not, and explained that the new civic status didn't replace the CEBs' original religious status or intention; it merely broadened the groups' potential spheres of activity.

The CEBs on the Morro and elsewhere throughout Brazil became important bases for networking and organizing among members of the Workers' Party (PT) in the early 1980s. Many CEB members were attracted to the PT's optimism and to its imitation of CEB meeting and inclusion practices. The PT's rise from unlikely beginnings into national prominence in less than a decade made it even more appealing to people only recently used to their own political power. The first PT victories were modest: 3.3 percent of the vote in 1982 regional elections. By 1985, when capital city mayors were elected, the PT won a city hall. In 1988, sixteen PT mayors took office, and in 1989, the PT presidential candidate came within six points of winning the country's first free presidential election in nearly thirty years.

As the PT grew, and especially as its early successes were proven to be real and not just anomalies, CEB members in many parts of the country — including Recife — took up electoral politics with enthusiasm. The first significant church-affiliated organization to be affected by this were Encontro de Irmãos groups. By the mid-1980s, many previously active Encontro members were involved in city-level political efforts, deserting their weekly Encontro meetings to become dedicated *Petistas* — participants in the PT. By the time I lived in Recife, many Encontro members felt the organization's better days were gone because so many people, and especially younger people, had stopped paying much attention to their church involvement when their political commitments found outlets through the PT. Analysts of the PT claim that without the organizational structure of CEBs and groups like the Encontro de Irmãos, the party's early successes would not have been possible.

The bond between CEB members, Resistance members (the two groups were virtually the same after the police raid), and the PT brought special scorn from Morro traditionalists, who claimed that church involvement was nothing more than masked political ambition for Reginaldo and his closest associates. Since its inception, the residents' council by-laws had forbidden it to be officially affiliated with, or to endorse, any political party, but almost all the council leadership was active in Recife's PT. Zé João, who had first learned something of his own voice through the Center for Reading and Information that Reginaldo formed on the Morro in the late 1970s, came into greater confidence through his role with the Morro CEBs, and then in a job with CUT (*Centro Único dos Trabalhadores*), the PT-affiliated labor union that claims a larger membership than any other in Brazil. From that he ran for city council, after many months of exploratory discussions with Morro residents' council members.[4]

FROM PADRE TO FATHER

A few years have passed since the police invaded the Morro and installed Constante. The conflict on the Hill continues, though its harshness has become muted. Several changes have taken place that have refocused the energies of the Resistance. Some of the changes were complete surprises; others were years in the making. The traditionalists, too, have felt a shift and have also moved their attention away from the hectic day-to-day involvement of community discord.

The biggest single change is Reginaldo's status. In September of 1993 he announced his engagement to a woman from the Resistance, a dedicated activist thirty years his junior. He had courted her quietly in the previous several months. His followers in the Resistance were stunned. Many, particularly the older women, had believed firmly that Reginaldo wanted to be returned to his full rights as a priest. They had understood the Resistance fight to be about that goal, and had been willing to wait until Dom José dropped dead or was transferred, even if it took many years, so that Reginaldo's suspension could be lifted. When he went through with the wedding in April of 1994, officiated by Dona Luisa and Zé João, many of this Resistance cohort felt betrayed. Suddenly the previous years of stubborn struggle seemed meaningless if Reginaldo was going to ditch the entire effort for a girl and for a wedding.

Reginaldo countered that he did not intend to give up the fight nor give up resisting the bishop. He would now join a growing contingent of priests in the Recife area who had married but who still wanted to be considered full priests of the church.[5] This was too much for some of the Resistance members, who decided that Reginaldo's real goal in life was not to restore himself — and, by extension, them — to full relations with the church proper, but to fight with Dom José about anything at all. The birth of Reginaldo's son in May of 1995 confirmed that he was not going back, even if he could. Many of the most prominent members of the Resistance, the older women who had lived on the Morro for years and who had always sworn loyalty to Reginaldo and his cause, turned their backs on him. Most did not then go to Constante's church but instead joined parishes off the Hill — or stopped going to church completely.[6] The Resistance celebrations continued, but their numbers were considerably dwindled. Either Reginaldo coordinated them or they were directed by a core of loyalists. His wife and son did not come often; though remaining Resistance members attended the events because they were fond of Reginaldo as a person and were less invested in his role as priest, there were still enough stares, head-shaking, and whispers to make her uncomfortable.

Constante alienated a number of his congregants, too, though not as dramatically. Some of the traditionalists who were most upset about Reginaldo and the Resistance are now disillusioned with Constante, who seems content to run his parish without paying much attention to what's left of the Resistance. There are rumors from several sources that he's taken to drinking hard and often, but the parish continues to draw capacity crowds to the new church on Sundays, and the fence allows people from other parts of the city to drive to the Hill and to park inside the praça without fear of the neighborhood children. Dona Bene, the woman named as traitor by the Resistance, is particularly upset with Constante for not being more involved in getting Reginaldo off the Hill or at least shutting down the Resistance, but Constante calls her a fanatic and will have nothing to do with her. When last I spoke with her, Dona Bene was thinking about joining a Pentecostal church a short walk from the Morro.

WHITHER LIBERATION THEOLOGY?

It is possible to imagine a version of liberation theology that would not alienate as many people as it attracted, but the particular conditions in which it came to prominence did not foster a slowly developed set of rituals and doctrines that might, over time, replace older Latin American Catholic traditions. In fact, much of the practice of liberation theology stumbled because it did not allow room for vital and deeply held beliefs about how God, Jesus, Mary, and the church were understood to work in people's lives. In Brazil, the movement that coalesced around liberationist Catholicism was an aberration of church union in an otherwise fractious history. The church in Brazil did not speak as a unified entity before the dictatorship. It gave the impression of harmony during military rule because it had a large and clear enemy. But with the military gone, the church in Brazil once again speaks with many disparate, disagreeing voices. And it faces significant pressure from Rome to heed the spiritual responsibilities that the Vatican claims were neglected during liberation theology's heyday.

Vatican censure has focused on Latin American liberation theologians' use of Marxism as a tool for social analysis, claiming that it is difficult to take some of Marx's teachings without taking too much, and arguing that within Marxism it becomes too easy to attribute all worldly ills to oppressive social and economic structures. The Congregation for the Doctrine of the Faith, the pope's powerful doctrinal watchdog group, issued a statement about liberation theology in 1984 condemning, as one analyst phrased it, "false liberationism" that "gives a predominantly political interpretation to the Scriptures."

> As political goals become the supreme criterion of truth and morality, the whole of life is unduly politicized. [False liberationism] divides the church against itself on the basis of social and economic class. . . . One may rightly acknowledge the fact of severe social conflict, but one must not glorify

class conflict as the path to the classless society of the future.
(quoted in Dulles 1984:139)

The problem, I believe, was not liberationism's political emphasis, but that advocates of liberation theology tried to substitute political rhetoric and focus for religious practices that had been integral to the majority of Brazil's Catholics for centuries. Devout Brazilians of many traditions are willing to work to change social structures that oppress them, but not by neglecting the rituals, mysteries, and histories that inform their religious practice. Many who believed in and followed the teachings of liberation theology felt that the movement focused too much on political activism at the expense of religious expression, thus halving the arsenal available for any struggle. "It's important to have neighbors working together, to have a strategy, to be organized," said one thirty-two-year-old Recife woman who has spent most of her life around liberation-minded nuns and priests, "but it's also important to know that God is with us by remembering our prayers — and not just prayers for strikes or land reform."[7]

There were other dilemmas. Class differences between those bringing and those receiving the liberation message were often stark. Even people whose class of origin was not so different from those living in poor neighborhoods had often spent years acquiring a thorough education in seminary, and their ability to read, write, and analyze anything from Bible passages to federal economic policies was often intimidating to those they tried to serve. While liberation theology was supposedly a grassroots movement, there is little evidence of base communities that started or flourished without the presence of a pastoral agent — a nun, priest, seminarian or ex-seminarian. Most of the writings about liberation theology have come from university– or seminary–trained scholars. And most of them were men.

There were serious gender discrepancies in the movement. The membership of the Roman Catholic church is mostly female, while the leadership is male. Despite the stated goal to make women full participants (without taking on the issue of women's ordination), liberationism mostly replicated the old model. Again and again in Recife, I saw women doing the daily work of the community, the CEBs, the household, the residents' councils — and men going to the regional meetings or taking the prominent places in front of groups that were allegedly meant to be inclusive. Many of the nuns I knew in Recife noted the irony of their situations versus that of some of their more celebrated male colleagues. Many felt that they had been doing the community-level work essential to liberationism for many years, but that it only received attention when the Boff brothers — monk Clodovis and priest Leonardo — "discovered" it and made it the focus of their writings. The Boffs are recognized as two of the most famous and prolific liberation theologians in Latin America. "We do the work," remarked more than one sister, "and they get the credit!"

For roughly twenty years, from the late 1960s until the late 1980s, liberation theology offered new tools to people who found themselves ready to take on specific social struggles in an era when that was first dangerous, then increasingly possible, and today common among dozens of *movimentos populares* — popular movements — throughout the country. For many, this allowed them to answer the nagging insecurities of Brazilian life by meeting them head on and by learning the strength of collective initiative. But liberation theology often neglected the older church habits of giving comfort, sustenance, and guidance. The movement's secular emphases seemed to neglect this more familiar church role without offering anything similarly satisfying in its place. In promising to bring about the Kingdom of God, liberationists forgot to keep God in the picture, according to some critics. When this played out on a community level, especially in a poor neighborhood like the Morro da Conceição, the church became a foreign place to many who had known it all their lives. For them, the already often overwhelming insecurities and uncertainties of daily life were exacerbated because one well-used method for coping with them — turning them over to the Virgin, or to a saint, or to Jesus — was no longer emphasized.

Because of these discrepancies — differing uses of liturgy, class imbalances, gender gaps, heightened insecurity — the leaders of liberation theology, including Reginaldo, did not create a movement strong enough to contain and answer the needs of its followers. Liberationist Catholics tried replacing ancient definitions of the sacred with new symbols and rites, rather than expanding existing definitions to include the old and the new. But that doesn't mean the movement itself failed. The political direction that many former liberationists have now taken indicates an unusual future for Brazil's still-young left. Many people who today work to establish non-governmental organizations, to create political reform, to found women's health cooperatives, or to run for local and even state or federal offices had their start in base communities and in liberationist Catholicism.[8] The needs that the movement did meet in the 1970s and 1980s are now met by a host of other groups and initiatives. There is a new vibrance in Brazil today among popular movements, and many owe their genesis to liberation theology. The spread of base communities may have waned, and the rhetoric of liberationist sermons and songs may fill fewer and fewer chapels, but in many cases the individuals who were marked and changed by those sermons and songs continue to work toward the goals that liberationism espoused. And in the meanwhile, the Morro continues to host the annual festa, the Resistance celebrations, Constante's masses, residents' council meetings, and the countless doings of the daily lives of 20,000 people.

Liberation theology itself was transformed in many places around the world as clergy in various religious traditions adopted its approaches. Class issues were not as important to South African liberation theologians, for example, as were concerns about race. Across the African continent, many liberationists worked to change the persistent degradations of postcolonial economic policies. Asian liberation theologians focused on finding common ground between Christianity and more indigenous Asian traditions like Buddhism. There were advocates of Jewish liberation theology (see Ellis 1991) and Palestinian liberation theology (the latter is based on a Christian perspective; see Ateek 1989).[9] African Americans in the United States also took up themes of racism, even advocating a separatist Christianity that reclaims a genuine African heritage (see Cone 1970). Women in the United States and in other parts of the world used liberationist techniques to push for greater gender equality within their religious traditions, while gays and lesbians in many European and North American "mainstream" churches advocated queer liberationism in their struggles to end the religious condemnation that many face (see Heyward 1989).

I mention these expressions of liberation theology in the past tense because I believe the movement is waning, in Latin America and elsewhere. At the same time, I also believe that the momentum that drove it has merely slowed and that the central concerns that animated it are not answered — thus something like liberation theology will occur again within the Roman Catholic church. The movement, and its expressions of controversy like the conflict on the Morro, resembled dissension that has marked the church since its earliest days. At its most fundamental level, the struggle was between contrasting models of — as the Resistance phrased it — how to "be" church. Resistance activists pressed for an acceptance of new sources of theology and for a broader sense of sanctity, elements key to their definition of "church." For a tradition as integral to daily life as popular Catholicism in Brazil, however, parts of this definition touched on essential and very basic understandings of the way the world is supposed to work, or not to work, threatening some Catholics even as it galvanized others.

Roman Catholicism has tried to remain true to its definition of itself as the earthly incarnation of Jesus Christ while traversing the centuries ever more heavily draped with institutional pomp, legalistic doctrines, and bureaucracy. Since its inception (and even the precise founding of what became the Roman Catholic church is disputed among liberationists and traditionalists),[10] what is called Catholicism has had to heed those who want to alter the tradition's teachings and rituals. Across nearly two millennia, the changes have been so numerous and thorough that it is unlikely a first-century Christian would recognize today's church, despite the endurance of the eucharistic rites. The conflict in Recife will fade, but its themes are still urgent, and even as Morro residents grow weary of pressing that urgency, other voices take it up.

The often irksome presence of groups like the Morro Resistance is integral to the future and vitality of any institution as venerable, historically layered, and long-lived as the Roman church, particularly given the church's centralized power structure and the bureaucratic reach that structure has. To put it another way, those who control the church's narrative of itself cannot ignore those who insist on influencing that narrative. No institution as widespread as Catholicism can disregard clamoring demands for greater inclusion, even from unlikely corners of the world. No institution can hold itself changeless and survive.

Some in Recife and elsewhere urged the Morro Resistance activists to form their own church, to follow Martin Luther in establishing a new

Christian tradition. Resistance activists could not do that; it would have meant quick obscurity and easy dismissal by the church, much as the married Reginaldo is now dismissed by local church authorities in Recife as a powerless figure. The strength and justification of the Resistance came from its cry that the church must change from within. The Morro struggle will certainly end; in many people's eyes, it ended when Reginaldo wed, weekly Resistance celebrations notwithstanding. But at a broader level it will never end, precisely because it has been argued in different guises since before the community even existed — and it will continue to be argued as long as institutionalized religious expression endures.

CHRONOLOGY OF A CRISIS

A group of priests in Recife and Olinda anonymously compiled this chronology, which lists the more graphic changes instituted by Dom José Cardoso in his first few years as head of the archdiocese. It outlines the swift and resounding changes that one church leader may make in a short time, and provides an x-ray of the kinds of alterations faced by dioceses and parishes around Latin America when a liberationist model of church is dismantled. One of the authors, a priest who lives near the Morro da Conceição, gave me this document in September 1991, and I translate it here. Explanatory comments are in parentheses.

1988

April   The archbishop of Olinda and Recife, Dom José Cardoso, also the president of the Northeast Region II of the National Brazilian Bishops Conference (CNBB-RNII), which includes the states of Pernambuco, Paraíba, Alagoas, and Rio Grande do Norte, fires Padre H. The priest was executive secretary of the CNBB-RNII. He is replaced by Padre G., who is connected with the Folklorino Movement (a conservative movement of clergy, of which Dom José is a member).

August   A priest and three lay people who formed the Rural Pastoral Committee of the Northeast Region II are fired by Dom José under allegations of insubordination, unauthorized use of funds, and excessive independence in their pastoral activities. The Rural Pastoral is a northeastern version of the national Pastoral Land Commission. Representatives of fifteen offices within the CNBB-RNII sign a document repudiating the "calumnious" accusations of Dom Cardoso and protesting the dismissals. The document is also signed by nearly 200 pastoral agents.

September   Dom José closes the Documentation and Popular Information Service (SEDIPO, or *Serviço de Documentação e Informação Popular*), which functioned through the CNBB-RNII. The coordinator of SEDIPO is dismissed along with three other employees. The archivist is dismissed because she refuses to stop publishing the bulletin "Actuality," which gave news about the crisis in the church.

October   Claiming that it displeases him, Dom José suspends the local mass transmitted on Sundays over Recife's Rede Globo affiliate (Rede Globo is a national television network). The station instead broadcasts a mass produced in Rio de Janeiro.

December   Dom José closes the Center for Defense of Human Rights in the Northeast, an organization also connected with the Northeast Region II of the CNBB. The coordinator of the center is dismissed.

1989

May   A Scottish priest, Padre T., is expelled from the diocese. He had worked in a parish near Iguarassu (on the northern fringe of the diocese) with rural laborers and sugarcane cutters. Dozens of workers protest his removal by traveling to the Palace of the Manguinhos, the bishop's residence and offices, to talk with him. They are kept out by a contingent of armed military police, which guards the Palace gates.

July   Dom José refuses to allow Padre Reginaldo Veloso, priest of the Morro da Conceição, to participate in the CNBB's regional Presbytery Council, though the priest is a founding member.

August   For the second time the archbishop calls on the military police to prevent peasants from entering the grounds of the Palace of the Manguinhos. They again want to ask for the return of Padre T.

Seven priests receive letters of warning from the bishop. All have pastoral work in poorer neighborhoods.

A decree from the archbishop forbids the Justice and Peace Commission to use the name or the stationery of the archdiocese, limiting its actions to only juridical help.

Padre R., assistant to the Youth of the Poor Neighborhoods Pastoral and a priest in the diocese for 19 years, is informed by letter that he is fired from his job with the Pastoral. He is then expelled from the diocese.

September   The Vatican decides to close the Theological Institute of Recife (ITER) and the Seminary of the Northeast Region II (SERENE II), institutions that for more than 20 years taught priests, members of religious orders, and laity about the theology of liberation. Dom José is the executor of this measure. More than 1,000 people — priests, religious, seminarians, and laity — gather in front of the church of Our Lady of Carmo, in downtown Recife, to protest in a day of fasting and prayer.

Dom Hélder Câmara, archbishop emeritus of Olinda and Recife, is prohibited to discuss the crisis in the diocese. Dom João Evangelista Terra, auxiliary bishop, phones Dom Hélder to ask that he refrain from making statements about decisions of the archdiocese.

Almost 40 religious and civic organizations publish in the principal newspapers of the city a letter of support for the Justice and Peace Commission.

October   Some professors and religious return to protest the closing of ITER and SERENE II with a vigil of songs and prayers in front of the Church of St. Anthony in downtown Recife.

Northeastern bishops meeting in Arapiracá, Alagoas (south of Recife), write a letter supporting Dom José Cardoso. The letter is questioned for its strange unanimity when it is well known that several bishops hold positions against Dom José.

November   SERENE II is closed as directed, and the students coordinate a mass of thanksgiving for the many years of its functioning. The ceremony is presided over by several bishops.

December   Three members of the Justice and Peace Commission are dismissed.

Brother A., a Franciscan monk for 23 of his 49 years, is expelled from the archdiocese despite a demonstration in his favor by residents of the favela where he had worked for 12 years. The Franciscans protest Dom José's decision to Rome.

Padre Reginaldo Veloso, a priest for 29 of his 53 years, is dismissed from the parish of the Morro da Conceição and is suspended from his sacerdotal duties. More than 2,000 people take to the streets of Recife in a demonstration demanding that Dom José leave the archdiocese.

Eighty-two priests of the archdiocese of Olinda and Recife, all with pastoral responsibilities, publish in the principal newspapers of the city a letter disapproving of the archbishop.

1990

January   Residents of the Morro da Conceição begin a vigil in front of the church of St. Anthony in downtown Recife, asking for the return of Padre Reginaldo. Another demonstration of support occurs on the Morro, organized by parishioners.

An act of support for the archbishop unites 500 people at the Palace of the Manguinhos. At Dom José's side is State Deputy Severino Cavalcanti, who in 1980 requested the expulsion from Brazil of Padre Vitor Mircapillo, priest in the [northeastern] diocese of Palmares. (Padre Vitor, an Italian, was deported from Brazil; Reginaldo wrote a song supporting him and was thrown in jail).

March   The Official Bulletin of the Archdiocese of Olinda and Recife publishes a letter to all clergy elaborating the necessity for obedience.

April   More than 80 priests boycott the Mass of the Blessing of the Oils celebrated on Maundy Thursday at the Cathedral of the Sé in Olinda. The priests stay away for reasons of conscience. (Maundy Thursday, or Holy Thursday, is an occasion for a bishop to say mass with all his clergy, and to bless the oils that each priest will use in the coming year for baptisms and confirmations. The Cathedral of the Sé was the original cathedral of the diocese, until Olinda and Recife were joined.)

Two more priests are fired by Dom José: the priest of Macaxeira and of Guabiraba, poor parishes on the outskirts of Recife. Eighty priests take part in the going-away mass for their two colleagues.

September   Residents of the Morro da Conceição resist the take-over of the neighborhood's church, a move attempted by the Curia and the police. The parish has been under the direction of the Parish Council and the parishioners since December of 1989.

October The population of the Morro da Conceição is surprised by the appearance of 40 military police, a shock battalion used to protect the installation of a new parish priest, Padre Constante, and to secure the take-over of the parish by the archdiocese. The community resists while the new priest accompanies the police as they break open the doors of the church and the parish house.

While the military police are storming the Morro, the archbishop celebrates a mass for the armed forces in Nobrega College, with participation from the Army, Marines, and Air Force.

Fifty-seven priests sign a document condemning the use of police force to resolve a pastoral problem. The priests declare themselves ashamed by the authoritarian attitude of the diocese.

A march brings 3,000 people to downtown Recife. They protest the bishop's decision to use police force to take back the Morro church.

The military police remain at the door of the Morro church. There are daily demonstrations protesting the presence of Padre Constante and the intervention of the police.

November Twenty-six diocesan priests seek out the archbishop to have a conversation about the upcoming festa of Our Lady of the Immaculate Conception on the Morro. The archbishop refuses to see them.

Dom José brings the Capuchin monk Frei Damião to be part of the novena that leads to the festa on the Morro.

A group of young people protest during a deaconal ordination by Dom José at St. Luke's church in Olinda.

Police on the Morro prevent residents from carrying out a protest prayer service.

December The community of Alto José Bonifácio, part of the Morro parish, prevents Padre Constante from taking over their chapel.

1991

January Dom José tries to close the Salesian Institute of Philosophy. The Salesian Order in Recife protests to Rome, and the Institute stays open.

March Once again priests of the diocese stay away from the Mass for the Blessing of the Oils, celebrated on Maundy Thursday at the Cathedral of the Sé in Olinda. Of the 211 priests of the diocese, only 50 appear at the mass.

April   Dom José fires the Salesian Padre E., priest of Jaboatão, a parish on the outskirts of the diocese.

Dom José is quoted in the *Jornal do Comércio* as saying "the popular [base] church is nothing but a dangerous ideology."

Dom Marcelo Carvalheira, bishop of Guarabira and a progressive, is elected president of the CNBB-RNII, replacing Dom José.

Dom José wants the headquarters of the CNBB-RNII moved out of Recife.

June   The bishops of the CNBB-RNII, meeting in Caruarú, decide that the headquarters will remain in Recife.

July   Dom José dismisses Padre L., former dean of SERENE-II and priest of Boa Viagem parish.

August   No representative of the archdiocese, including Dom José or his two auxiliary bishops, attends the mass commemorating 60 years of the priesthood of Dom Hélder Câmara, archbishop emeritus of Olinda and Recife.

Almost 70 priests celebrate jointly with Dom Hélder, who receives warm homage. Several bishops from the CNBB-RNII are present.

A diocesan-wide Meeting of the Clergy, convened by Dom José after two years of no meetings, draws only 25 of the diocese's 211 priests.

1
Consecrated Politics and Activist Religion

1. The momentum that became the civil rights movement in the U.S. would not have been possible without decades of groundwork laid by African American churches, particularly those in the south (cf. Cone 1970; Lincoln and Mamiya 1990:199–215; Thurman 1949; Wilmore 1983. Genovese 1976:255–284 argues against this position).

2. Using this highway, the BR-101, as a dumping site made it a strategic symbol. It is a federal resource under centralized control, surrounds Recife, and is the region's principle link to north and south. A body left there suggested that the dictatorship likewise surrounded the city and controlled its relations with the rest of the country. It said that the military was everywhere — which, indeed, it was.

3. Peruvian priest Gustavo Gutierrez is credited with inventing the phrase. One of the best-known and most prolific liberation theologians in Latin America, he was on a plane headed to Europe for an international conference on the "theology of development." Supposedly he was not content with such a tepid phrase and coined "theology of liberation" as a more evocative replacement.

4. While there are many parallels between King's civil rights struggles and the work of liberationist Catholics in Latin America, there are also many differences. The Latin Americans always couched their critique of economic and political trends in analyses of global patterns of development, exploitation, and profit. They also paid close attention to class tensions inherent in much of Latin American culture. Race was only sporadically a central concern, as was gender.

5. Since my initial frustrated search in the mid-1980s, there have been several notable works that give just such a picture. See especially Burdick 1993, Canin 1994, W. Hewitt 1991, Ireland 1991, and Mariz 1994.

6. Different factions in Recife have very strong beliefs about the church's origins, and these beliefs play an important part in helping each faction define itself against the other.

7. An example is seen in Gregory I, a bishop of Rome who died in 604 and

whose leadership helped shape the early church. He directed Augustine, the missionary and famous church father, to "adapt both pagan temples and pagan holy days to Christian usage" (Pelikan 1971:66).

8. Areas like *favelas* have been a part of urban Brazil for decades. In 1916 a governor of Pernambuco, the state of which Recife is the capital, protested the "innumerable houses inhabited by an enormous population of poor people who live there and proliferate, creating a generation that is weak from the beginning, condemned to death by the environment into which it is born" (quoted in Denslow 1987:141).

9. The First Vatican Council took place in 1869 and 1870. Its most famous accomplishment was establishing the doctrine of papal infallibility, which teaches that the pope does not err in matters of faith or morals when speaking *ex cathedra.*

10. One vivid symbol of this was the shift in the mass. After nearly two millennia with the priest turned away from the congregation to consecrate bread and wine during the ritual of the eucharist (also called communion), the altar was pushed closer to the people, the priest faced them when performing this previously mysterious rite, and most important, all the proceedings of the mass were said in local vernaculars, not Latin.

11. There are many sources for these figures, among them Adriance 1986:16; Bruneau 1980:225; 1986:107; Della Cava 1989:144; Lernoux 1989:122; Mainwaring 1986:126; 1989:151; Mainwaring and Levine 1989:241; Pottenger 1989:2. None, however, indicates his or her source. Azevedo (1987:11) cautions that the numbers are far from certain. In June, 1991, Cecilia Mariz, a sociologist who has written about base communities and religion in Brazil (1994), told me a story that circulates among researchers in the area who focus on religion. The numbers, so the story goes, were created by a northeastern bishop who was being interviewed by a North American social scientist. The scholar asked the bishop how many CEBs there are in Brazil; the bishop said he didn't know and that because of the many understandings of exactly what a CEB is, it would be impossible to say. The scholar insisted that the bishop quote at least a ballpark number; when pressed, he offered the figures cited above.

12. This is often translated as "consciousness-raising," but Freire made a distinction between that and conscientization. The former, he argued, tends to be about self-reflective concerns especially as it was used in the United States, while the latter requires individuals to experience an explicitly political awakening for it to be complete.

13. The organizational skills that many of the schools' coordinators learned

during those five years were put to good use in forming CEBs, which became the heart of liberation theology on the local level.

14. This conclusion was based on Marxist interpretations of economics and on Andre Gunder Frank's world-systems theory of development (cf. Frank 1969).

15. There is controversy about the definition of CEBs. Many church leaders who oppose liberation theology support the idea of CEBs, so long as the groups are not politically active. Liberationists counter that without a political element, such a group is not a CEB but merely a Bible-reading collective.

16. The church provides a lectionary that lists readings for every Sunday and for each day of the week. The lectionary covers the entire Bible in a three-year cycle. Every church with a Catholic heritage — Episcopal, Lutheran, Methodist, and of course Roman — follows almost identical lectionaries all over the world.

17. The northeast encompasses nine states: Maranhão, Piauí, Ceará, Rio Grande do Norte, Paraíba, Pernambuco, Alagoas, Sergipe, and Bahia. The region is huge, so the church divides it administratively into Regions I and II. Recife is the administrative home of Region II.

18. The motto is also a rallying cry for CEBs in other parts of Latin America (D. Levine 1992:146–47).

19. Interview, 10 May 1991.

20. Interview, 20 September 1991. A *promessa* is a kind of contract made between a person and a saint or a deity. In exchange for some action on the part of the person — lighting a candle, giving alms, walking a long distance, walking backwards, crawling, or several other choices — it is hoped that the saint or deity will answer the person's particular needs. I choose to translate promessa as "pledge" rather than the more common "promise" because it almost always involves an action.

21. Interview, 3 June 1991.

22. Interview, 30 June 1991.

23. Residents' Council meeting, 12 January 1991.

24. I distinguish between *coronelismo* and patron/client relations. The former serves as local and unappealable law, and anyone wishing to find a means of survival within the jurisdiction of a particular *coronel* must find it from him. Patron/client relations are usually more benign, and the client will establish different relationships with several patrons, to answer different sets of needs. A classic patron/client tie is that between godparents and the parents of a baptized or confirmed child. In exchange for support that can include sponsoring a

confirmation party, buying the children appropriate baptismal clothes, and various responsibilities over the child's lifetime, the godparents understand that the parents are now obligated to them for as long as they want the favors to be extended.

25. Interview, 28 June 1991.

26. Interview, 6 April 1991.

27. The word "marginal" in Brazilian Portuguese has the connotation of "low-life" or "worthless." In news accounts of crimes or of deaths involving men from neighborhoods like the Morro, they are not usually referred to by name or as anything other than a "marginal." The word accurately describes their class status, but in common usage reads as a description of their quality as human beings.

28. Interview, 3 February 1991.

29. The Morro is 95 percent Roman Catholic, average education is to the fourth grade, and the average income is one and a half minimum salaries. This information came out of a questionnaire administered to approximately 400 households, representing around 2,500 individuals, between January and June of 1991. There was an error margin of plus or minus four points. I co-authored the survey with Cecíla Mariz, who was teaching at the time at the Universidade Federal de Pernambuco; she and I and a dozen of her students carried it out.

2
Portrait of the Northeast

1. Interview, 13 September 1991.

2. The homes were technically squats. The residents did not own the land on which they built, a detail that would haunt them years later. In 1945, two local families of sugar wealth formed Pernambucan Real Estate, claiming ownership of the entire northern zone of Recife and collecting rent from thousands of families for several decades. People living in the northern zone, including those on the Morro, faced a constant threat of eviction if they were unable to meet a single payment. Many families eventually paid more cumulative rent than the worth of their land and home combined.

3. Poverty is not limited to the northeast. Of 62 million economically active adults, 20 million are unemployed or underemployed, earning less than one minimum salary a month. With dependents taken into account, this means that between 70 million and 80 million Brazilians — roughly half the country's population — are too poor to give their children basic necessities. Thirty-two million

of these people suffer chronic malnutrition (Branford and Kucinski 1995:21).

4. See *Diário de Pernambuco* and *Jornal do Comércio,* 20 November, 1990. The study measured homicide rates, habitable space, access to public services, infant mortality, education, air quality, traffic congestion, water quality, health facilities, and cost of food, among other variables.

5. In Brazil, minimum salary is figured monthly, not hourly. Its fluctuates with the country's sometimes drastic, sometimes calm inflation rate. In late 1990, one minimum salary was roughly equivalent to sixty U.S. dollars. As of late 1996, it was approximately one hundred U.S. dollars.

6. The Portuguese word for sugar, "açucar," derives directly from the Arabic "as-sukkar," which in turn comes from the Sanskrit "çarkara."

7. While sugar was the first export profitable on a grand scale, it was not the first export taken from Brazil. Between 1500 and 1530, brazilwood was harvested and sent to Portugal, where the blood-red dye that the wood produced became as popular as indigo. The word *brasa* means burning coal or ember, and *pau–brasil* — brazilwood — is thought to be the source of the country's name.

8. One peça de escravo equaled one healthy young man. Children, women, and older people equaled less than one peça, so 120 peças meant more than 120 individuals (Cardoso 1983:77n).

9. Fugitive slaves founded settlements called *quilombos.* Most were discovered and destroyed in time, but some flourished for many years. One of the most famous and long-lived quilombos was the northeast's Palmares, founded by Zumbí, Brazil's best-known renegade slave (Andrade 1980:47). The word "zumbí," with African origins, meant a ghostly being who wanders at night (Freyre 1963:140n); Zumbí of Palmares earned the name because of his ability to elude capture. Palmares was like a small republic: it covered sixty square leagues, was made up of several towns, and was home to more than 20,000 people at its height in the late seventeenth century. A strict system of governance kept it peaceful, and its residents lived well by hunting, fishing, gathering, and farming. The settlement supported masons, tin-smiths, carpenters, and weavers. Palmares was finally destroyed after eighteen Dutch and Portuguese expeditions tried to rout it (for a more thorough discussion of this and other quilombos, see Dean 1995:103–05, Freyre 1963:285–86 and Mattoso 1986:139–42).

10. For more details about the Forte Real do Bom Jesus, see the *Anais Pernambucanos* Vol. 2:281, 568; Vol. 3:12–15, 37; Vol. 4:228; and Vol. 9:227.

11. Portuguese and Spanish disagreements about trade routes and land

claims almost led them to war. The pope intervened, and on July 7, 1494, the two nations agreed to divide the world between them along a line that ran from pole to pole 370 leagues west of the Cape Verde Islands. The Portuguese were granted control of the lands east of the line, and the Spanish had lands to the west. When Portuguese explorer Pedro Cabral landed on the east coast of South America in 1500, in keeping with the treaty, he was entitled to claim the whole coast for Portugal (see Burns 1980:15–19).

12. Closer scrutiny suggests that they would not have overthrown the existing social order, nor did they ever intend to do so. They were not "Robin Hoods" and they did not have anything resembling the nascent political organization that Hobsbawm (1959:14–29) argues is necessary to transform Robin Hood criminality into effective social protest (see also Burns 1980:349–50 and R. Levine 1978:46).

13. It is said that Lampião came to Padre Cícero to receive the priest's blessing. The cleric, after some reflection, refused to give it. Lampião was enraged, and his exploits from that point forward were marked by a more thorough and gruesome violence than he had previously shown. When recounting this story, people speculate that if the priest had been more generous, Lampião would have changed his ways and turned his attention to doing good rather than harm.

14. Journalist Euclydes da Cunha's eyewitness account of the settlement's demise is recorded in his classic *Os Sertões*, translated in English as *Rebellion in the Backlands* (1945). A more contemporary treatment is found in Mario Vargas Llosa's 1984 novel, *Guerra del fin del mundo* (*War of the End of the World*), while an especially thorough assessment is in R. Levine 1995.

15. Monks and other clergy who swore allegiance to foreign superiors were not trusted by those advocating a new Brazilian nationalism. Many clergy were known to be corrupt, ignoring requirements of celibacy and poverty. In the 1860s, Pope Pius IX rankled many Latin American governments, including Brazil's, when he declared that only the pope, not local monarchs, could name bishops; in one decision he changed an arrangement that had worked for the previous 300 years. Finally, a scandal erupted when the same pope issued an edict condemning Masonry. Since Brazil's emperor, prime minister, and many clergy were Masons, most churchmen chose to ignore the pope's decree. Two bishops who didn't, however, were convicted of treason and sentenced to several years' hard labor. They were rescued by Princess Isabella, heir to the Brazilian throne, but by then both the church and key secular factions of Brazilian society wanted the two institutions separated (see Bruneau 1974 and

Mainwaring 1986 for more details).

16. Like other subjects of Catholic veneration, Our Lady was often a stand-in for spirits and deities of African-based religions that had grown up throughout the Americas during slavery and colonialism. In *candomblé,* for instance, a tradition found in many parts of Brazil, Our Lady of the Immaculate Conception is also Iemanjá, the *orixá* or spirit-being who is among the most powerful in the candomblé pantheon. On December 8th in Recife, there is always a strong contingent of candomblé adherents who make at least some moments of the Morro's festa their own (see Bastide 1978 and especially Brown 1986 for more details about Afro-centric religions in Brazil).

17. *Diário de Pernambuco*, 8 December 1967; this and other newspaper accounts are my translations.

18. *Jornal Pequeno*, 2 November 1904.

19. Textile workers struck peacefully for higher wages in the 1890s, among the first in the area to do so. In 1900 they formed a workers' protective association, and started a socialist newspaper (R. Levine 1978:148). Dr. Carlos could have been working to avert unrest at his own factory with his organizational efforts, or to placate workers with at least outward indications of support.

20. *Jornal Pequeno*, 25 November 1904.

21. *Diário de Pernambuco,* 10 December 1904.

22. *Jornal do Recife*, 8 November 1904.

23. *Jornal Pequeno*, 30 November 1904.

24. *Jornal Pequeno*, 7 December 1904.

25. The history of the Great Western Railway demonstrates a peculiar but doomed collusion of Brazilian and British interests. It was established by the British in 1872; construction started in 1879 and lines were completed three years later, "just in time to take advantage of the re-newed optimism caused by the establishment of the first central sugar factories," the *usinas* (Graham 1968:70). The firm's eighty-three kilometers of track traversed most of northwestern Pernambuco. Always ineptly managed, Great Western suffered losses almost from the beginning, and relations between the English owners and the Brazilian employees were strained. Management even let local police infiltrate employee union meetings (R. Levine 1978:39–45). When workers struck for higher wages in the 1920s, they met violent reprisals. This practice backfired, notes Robert Levine, "when the opposition press began to attack foreign firms with a xenophobic fervor that raised some local sympathy for the strikers" (148–49). Once the railway fell, it was replaced with the Rede Ferroviaria do Nordeste, a wholly Brazilian-run enterprise, but no railroads in Brazil were

successful, and today there are virtually none.

26. *Jornal do Recife*, 7 December 1904.

27. *Jornal Pequeno*; 9 December 1904.

28. Ibid.

29. Ibid.

30. Recife was growing at a rate of 6.8 percent a year in this period, as opposed to a national growth rate of only 2.2 percent (Schneider 1991:69).

31. *Diário de Pernamabuco*, 6 December 1921.

32. Some sources say men on Galiléia started organizing around the desire to insure a decent burial for each other, but the stakes of the cause became too high to reflect merely that single issue. See Mallon 1978 for an elaboration of the version I recount here; see also Callado 1984: 86–88, 167.

33. For further discussion of demanding promessas, often paid through exhausting and physically damaging pilgrimages, see Dahlberg 1991, de Beauvoir 1974:743–53 and Eade and Sallnow 1991:21.

34. *Diário de Pernambuco*, 10 December 1952

35. *Diário de Pernambuco*, 6 December 1954.

36. *Diário de Pernambuco*, 10 December 1959.

37. This attracted the attention of the United States Agency for International Development, which spent two years channeling $131 million directly into church union efforts through Kennedy's Alliance for Progress. SORPE salaries were paid in part through monies funneled from the C. I. A. into the Cooperative League of the USA; "whether knowingly or not, the church entered an alliance with U.S. security efforts to blunt the class edge of the rural movement." When the military took power in 1964, League organizers, along with many others, were especially persecuted, but SORPE priests were not touched (Mallon 1978: 58–66).

38. *O povo* here means "the people" as something like an organized body, not merely as "many persons."

39. *Diário de Pernamabuco*, 8 December 1967.

40. Ibid.

41. Ibid.

3
The Politics of Theology

1. José Comblin, a Belgian theologian who has lived in northeast Brazil off and on for thirty years, noted that Catholics refer to older, more established

Protestant churches of the middle and upper classes as "churches," while they use "sect" to mean newer churches that draw the poor (lecture, Faculdade de Filosofia do Recife, 10 April 1991).

2. Ibid.

3. Charismatic Roman Catholicism is growing more and more popular in Brazil, a response to the attraction of charismatic Protestant traditions that are pulling members away from the Catholic church. Estimates of conversion rates from Catholicism to Protestantism are as high as 650,000 people a year just in Brazil.

4. Interview, 22 January 1991.

5. Interview, 27 September 1991.

6. Interview, 28 May 1991. Jorge gave up the idea of becoming a priest after Dom José told him he would have to take again many of the courses he'd already had at ITER. Even then, Dom José told Jorge, he might not consider him for ordination because he felt the young man's vision of the church was too different from his own.

7. Interview, 19 March 1991.

8. Interview, 5 June 1991.

9. Interview, 29 September 1991.

10. Interview, 15 January 1991.

11. Ibid.

12. Interview, 22 January 1991.

13. Ibid.

14. Interview, 15 January 1991.

15. Ibid.

16. At the continent-wide bishops' meeting in Puebla, Mexico, in 1979, the phrase "preferential option for the poor" was adopted as a necessary position for the church.

17. Interview, 22 January 1991.

18. Ibid.

19. Ibid.

20. This marks the senior Veloso as a staunch opponent of Getúlio Vargas, Brazil's populist dictator from 1930 until 1945. The UDN — National Democratic Union — was founded by a disparate collection of Vargas's adversaries around the country and was marked by its conservatism, or, as one source says, its "elite liberalism" (Mettenheim 1995: 80–81).

21. Interview, 5 April 1991.

22. Interview, 29 August 1991.

23. Veloso, n.d.

24. Ibid.

25. Ibid.

26. Interview, 29 August 1991.

27. Interview, 19 May 1991.

28. Ibid.

29. Caiaphas is depicted in the Bible as the Jewish high priest before whom Jesus was tried. Pontius Pilate was governor of Judea between the years 26 and 36; he sentenced Jesus to death.

30. Interview, 29 August 1991.

31. These other groups included the *Pastoral da Terra,* or Rural Land Pastoral, which was instrumental in mediating land disputes and vital to the PT's electoral victories in rural areas in the late 1980s. Members of the church's *Commisão Justiça e Paz,* or Justice and Peace Commission, also participated in PT initiatives, as did people in many other church-based organizations throughout the country.

32. Interview, 21 March 1991.

33. Interview, 5 April 1991.

34. This and the next quote are from The Revised English Bible.

35. Veloso, n.d.

36. Interview, 14 March 1991.

37. Interview, 20 March 1991.

38. Interview, 20 August 1991.

39. Interviews, 23 September 1991

40. In 1980 Italian priest Vito Miracapillo, head of a Pernambucan parish, refused to celebrate a mass on Independence Day, saying that under the dictatorship, there was no independence. The country's Supreme Tribunal accused Padre Vito of violating the National Security Law and ordered him out of Brazil. The case was well publicized and inspired many protests, including a song by Reginaldo that called the Supreme Tribunal a "national shame" and that said the judges "trample on justice while celebrating evil" (See Miracapillo 1985 for more details.)

41. Interview, 28 August 1991.

42. Interview, 3 September 1991.

43. Interview, 3 September 1991.

44. Interview, 15 September 1991.

45. Interview, 2 April 1991.

46. See Pang 1973–74 for a more detailed discussion of the political role of

the Roman Catholic church in Brazil from the empire through the rise of the 1964 military regime.

47. Interview, 6 May 1991.

48. From videotaped coverage of the event.

49. It was actually a man who claimed to despise Reginaldo, calling him a tyrant and a lunatic; he would never explain why he provided such a crucial and potentially dangerous service to the Resistance. Had the bishop found out, there could have been serious consequences.

50. Some sources could not resist describing the situation as a "holy war" or a "religious war." See, for instance, Aragão 1990, Ferreira 1990, Guerra 1991, Hoornaert 1990, and Lucia 1990.

51. Interview, 5 June 1991.

52. Interview, 14 January 1991. The song reads, in part, "We don't give up the key because the people are the builders of this church, in her is our blood and our suffering; our key is not of iron but of love; it opens the community but rejects oppression."

53. Interview, 6 May 1991.

54. Interview, 22 January 1991.

55. In early 1989 Dom José accused a popular foreign-born priest in an outlying parish of lax liturgical practices and of disobeying the vow of celibacy. He did not suspend the priest, but had him replaced with a less charismatic man. The parishioners protested, and several dozen went in person to meet with the bishop at his residence. He refused to see them, but they refused to leave, settling in on the steps. Dom José called in the troops to have them taken off the premises. His action met with harsh criticism.

56. The other, Brasília Teimosa, is the subject of a book by Willem Assies (1991) about popular political movements.

57. *Diário de Pernambuco*, 24 November 1989; 26 November 1989; 6 December 1989; *Folha de São Paulo*, 6 November 1989.

58. Interview, 14 March 1991.

59. Veloso et al. 1990.

60. Interview, 19 August 1991.

4
The Danger of Stories

1. Crites suggests that "such stories, and the symbolic worlds they project, are not like monuments that men behold, but like dwelling–places. People live

in them" (1971:295).

2. The church intends to do this through a massive television and satellite effort called Lumen 2000. See Della Cava 1991 for more details.

3. When I tested the validity of these composite stories by telling them to those represented in them, each side agreed with the rendition offered here, and scoffed at the one that represented their enemies. I took their reaction as verification that these stories do indeed accurately reflect their tellers' points of view.

4. Interview, 3 October 1991.

5
Ritualizing Dissension

1. Prayer can be disconnected from institutional religion and even from well-defined religious belief. In the late 1960s, a survey in (then) West Germany revealed that while 68 percent of the respondents believed in God, 86 percent admitted praying. This implies that "the effectiveness of the act of praying does not entirely depend on whether or not someone is listening" (Berger 1970).

2. This brings to mind the helpful observation by Hubert and Mauss that "religious ideas, because they are believed, exist; they exist as objectively as social fact" (1964:101), an assertion elaborated well by Klass (1995:1–7).

3. This was probably as much an act of political expedience as religious conviction (Herr 1985:65). The Roman Empire was struggling to maintain unity, and Christianity was already proving a strong cohesive force among disparate and geographically distant groups.

4. A diocese can be thought of as a county, and the bishop is like a county-level magistrate, responsible to the cardinal, his regional superior. Parishes within a diocese are like villages within a county, with priests like mayors. The bishop, however, has more power over his priests than a county magistrate has over mayors. Bishops are appointed; they in turn appoint priests. They can also replace and suspend priests.

5. According to Ratzinger, the "Mosaic event" is "the covenant event at Sinai and the cultic ritual that seals it — the ritual that perdured throughout the history of Israel" (1966:71–72).

6. There were those among the Resistance who believed in the symbolic representation and those who believed in the literal. The split seemed to run along generational lines. Older people believed that the bread truly had been

transubstantiated into the flesh of Christ, while younger people, particularly some former seminarians, were much more skeptical. Among the traditionalists I asked, no one ever expressed a doubt to me that the transformation was literal. One pointed out that since it is church teaching, how could it be doubted?

7. Reginaldo's suspension is only valid within the diocese of Olinda and Recife. He may perform priestly tasks in other dioceses with permission of that bishop.

8. This echoes the divisions between holiness and pollution, also understood as divisions between order and chaos, that are so fundamental to many religious traditions as to be a partial definition of religion itself. See Douglas (1984) for a particularly interesting discussion.

9. Scheper-Hughes recounted the irony of a liberationist priest who came to the town in rural northeast Brazil where she was doing fieldwork, an area with exceptionally high infant mortality. The priest refused to baptize dead infants before burying them, explaining to their distraught mothers that there was no need because Jesus already accepted them into heaven. This contradicted generations of faith-lore. The young cleric's "modernized" understanding of the processes of death, forgiveness, and entrance into heaven left the mothers angry and deeply worried for the souls of their dead children.

10. Interview, 19 September 1991.

11. An early and still seminal work on the godparent relationship in Latin America is found in Wolf and Mintz (1950).

6
What It Becomes

1. São João takes place every June and has its roots in a harvest celebration. The center of the festival is corn, freshly ripe and abundant. Originally a rural event, migrants to cities brought São João with them, and today it is enthusiastically marked in urban as well as rural areas. Participants dress like *matutos* — country folk — and dance the *Quadrilha*. This resembles a square dance but tells a story and lasts for hours.

2. Interview, 19 August 1991.

3. Interview, 8 April 1991.

4. Zé João has run twice and not yet won. He has not ruled out the possibility of future attempts.

5. The group named itself after Padre Antônio Henrique, Dom Hélder's

associate assassinated in 1969. The married clerics felt that Padre Antônio was a fitting symbol because he had lost his life supporting a church that was unpopular with secular powers of the day, just as they were now pushing a version of the church unpopular with churchly powers. Padre Antônio's views on celibacy, however, are not known.

6. Many had already stepped away from their earlier involvement with the residents' council. Though it was the Morro's older residents who started the council, younger members staged something like a coup in the early 1980s, and insults traded at a particularly contentious meeting were never retracted. Thus many former Resistance members were without any political outlet on the Hill once they left Reginaldo.

7. Interview, 3 December 1990.

8. A clear example of this was seen in the administration of Recife's leftist Jarbas Vasconcelos, mayor from 1992 until 1996. A large number of the people who worked for him started their engagement with social issues in base church work during their teens and early twenties.

9. For a survey of liberation theology in Asia, Africa, and Latin America, see Ferme 1986.

10. Dom José told me in an interview (22 January 1991) that the Catholic church was founded at the moment a Roman soldier pierced Jesus's side with a sword and blood and water gushed forth. Morro traditionalists said it was founded when Jesus chose his twelve apostles. The Resistance said it was founded when Jesus instructed Peter to carry on his work and gave Peter the metaphoric keys to do so.

❧ GLOSSARY ❧

abertura (*f.*) – opening

açucar (*m.*) – sugar

agreste (*m.*) – temperate climate land in Brazil that runs between the coastal rainforest and the interior desert

ARENA – for Aliança Renovação Nacional, the political party in power during most of Brazil's dictatorship

arraial or arrayal (*m.*) – hamlet, small village

atrapalhar (*v.t.*) – to confuse, disturb, interrupt

bairro da periferia – neighborhood on the outskirts

batismo (*m.*) – baptism

bobagem (*f.*) – nonsense, foolishness, drivel, silliness

brasa (*f.*) – ember, glowing coal

cabeça (*f.*) – head

cafezinho (*m.*) – a demi-tasse of coffee

candomblé (*m.*) – an African-Brazilian religion

carinho (*m.*) – affection, tenderness

CNBB – Conferência Nacional dos Bispos do Brasil

comentário (*m.*) – commentary

Comissão Justiça e Paz – Justice and Peace Commission

comunidades eclesiais de base – base ecclesial communities, called CEBs

coronel (pl. coroneis), coronelismo (*m.*) – rural landowners with extensive political power

cotidiano (*m.*) – daily, day to day

crente (*adj.*) – faithful; (*m.*) a Protestant

CUT – Centro Único dos Trabalhadores, the biggest labor union in Brazil; affiliated with the Workers' Party

direitas (*f.*) – rights

duro/a (*adj.*) – hard, difficult

ele/ela (*pron.*) – he/she

engenho (*m.*) – sugar plantation

envergonhado/a (*adj.*) – embarrassed, ashamed

equipe (*f.*) – committee, team, group organized around a specific task

escravo/a (*m./f.*) – slave

festa (*f.*) – festival, party

fita, fitinha (*f.*) – tape; also ribbon

frei (*m.*) – monk, brother (of a religious order)

gente (*f.*) – persons, people, humankind, folks

igreja (*f.*) – church

ITER – Instituto de Teologia do Recife

já (*adv.*) – now

jangada (*f.*) – a simple fishing boat common in the northeast; essentially a masted raft jeito (*m.*) – way, style, skill

latifundiário/a (*m./f.*) – landowner

lembrança (*f.*) – remembrance, souvenir

luta (*f.*) – struggle, conflict, fight

maconha (*f.*) – marijuana

maldade (*f.*) – wickedness, malice

marginal (pl. marginais) (*adj.*, or *m.*) – literally marginal, but taken to mean low-life, riff-raff, someone up to no good

matuto/a (*m./f.*) – country bumpkin, hick

menino/a (*m./f.*) – child

movimento (*m.*) – movement

nordestino/a (*m./f.*) – north-easterner

o lado de lá, o lado de cá – that side (over) there (the other side), this side here

orixá (*m.*) – a spirit or deity of candomblé

outeiro (*m.*) – hill

outro/a (*adj.*) – other

padre (*m.*) – father, as in the title used to address a priest

pae- or mae-de-santo — father or mother of the saint; a term in some African-Brazilian religions

Partido dos Trabalhadores – PT, Workers' Party

Pastoral da Terra – Land Pastoral

pau-brasil (*m.*) – brazilwood

PDS – Partido Democrático Social

peça (*f.*) – piece

peregrino/a (*m./f.*) – pilgrim

Petista (*f.*) – a member of the PT

PMDB – Partido Movimento Democrático Brasiliero

praça (*f.*) – square

promessa (*f.*) – pledge made to a saint or other spiritual entity

quilombo (*m.*) – fugitive slave settlement

rebelde (*adj.*) – rebellious; (*m.*) a rebel

reflexão (*f.*) – reflection

santa (*f.*) – saint

saúva (*f.*) – leaf-cutting ant

seita (*f.*) – sect

SERENE II – Seminário Regional do Nordeste II

sertão (*m.*) – the interior of the northeast, a desert-like region

sexta-feira (*f.*) – Friday

terreiro (*m.*) – a place of worship in African-Brazilian religious traditions

traidor/dora (*m./f.*) – traitor

UDN – União Democrática Nacional, a political party that opposed dictator Getúlio Vargas

usina (*f.*) – sugar processing plant

veja (*v.t., v.i.*) – present subjunctive form of the verb 'to look;' also the name of Brazil's largest weekly news magazine

verdade (*f.*) – truth

virar (*v.t.*) – to turn

você (*pron.*) – you (third-person singular)

voz (*f.*) – voice

zelador/a (*m./f.*) – one who tends to or takes responsibility for a locale; like a janitor

∽ BIBLIOGRAPHY ∽

Adriance, Marilyn

   1986. *Opting for the Poor: Brazilian Catholicism in Transition.* Kansas City: Sheed & Ward.

Andrade, Manuel Correia de

   1980. *The Land and People of Northeast Brazil.* Dennis V. Johnson, trans. Albuquerque: University of New Mexico Press.

Aragão, Gilbraz

   1990. "No Morro, A Igrega é do Povo." *Mandacuru* (October/November):3.

Arns, Dom Paulo Evaristo, ed.

   1985. *Brasil: Nunca Mais.* Petrópolis: Vozes.

Assies, Willem

   1991. *To Get Out of the Mud: Neighborhood Associativism in Recife, 1964–1988.* Amsterdam: CEDLA.

Ateek, Naim

   1989. *Justice, and Only Justice: A Palestinian Liberation Theology.* Maryknoll, NY: Orbis.

Azevedo, S.J., Marcello de C.

   1987. *Basic Ecclesial Communities in Brazil: The Challenge of a New Way of Being Church.* Washington, DC: Georgetown University Press.

Barbe, Dominique

   1987. *Grace and Power: Base Communities and Non-violence in Brazil.* Maryknoll, NY: Orbis.

Bastide, Roger

   1978. *The African Religions in Brazil.* Baltimore: Johns Hopkins University Press.

Beeson, Trevor, and Jenny Pearce

   1984. *A Vision of Hope: The Churches and Change in Latin America.* Philadelphia: Fortress.

Berger, Peter

   1970. *A Rumor of Angels: Modern Society and the Rediscovery of the Supernatural.* Garden City, NY: Anchor.

Berryman, Philip

   1987. *Liberation Theology: The Essential Facts About the Revolutionary*

Movement in Latin America and Beyond. Oak Park, IL: Meyer Stone.

Bloch, Maurice

1986. *From Blessing to Violence: History and Ideology in the Circumcision Ritual of the Merina of Madagascar*. New York: Columbia University Press.

Boff, Clodovis

1989. *Como Trabalhar Com O Povo*, 9a edição. Petrópolis: Vozes.

Bourdieu, Pierre.

1977. *Outline of a Theory of Practice*. Cambridge: Cambridge University Press.

Bowman, Glenn

1991. "Christian Ideology and the Image of the Holy Land: The Place of Jerusalem Pilgrimage in the Various Christianities." In J. Eade and M. Sallnow, eds., *Contesting the Sacred: The Anthropology of Christian Pilgrimage*. London: Routledge.

Branford, Sue, and Bernardo Kucinski

1995. *Brazil: Carnival of the Oppressed*. London: Latin American Bureau.

Brooke, James

1989. "Two Archbishops, Old and New, Symbolize Conflict in the Brazilian Church." *New York Times*, November 12, p.14.

Brown, Diana

1986. *Umbanda: Religion and Politics in Urban Brazil*. Ann Arbor: UMI Research Press.

Bruneau, Thomas

1974. *The Political Transformation of the Brazilian Catholic Church*. Cambridge: Cambridge University Press.

1980. "Basic Christian Communities in Latin America: Their Nature and Significance (Especially in Brazil)." In D. Levine, ed., *Churches and Politics in Latin America*. Beverly Hills: Sage.

1986. "Brazil: The Catholic Church and Basic Christian Communities." In D. Levine, ed., *Religion and Political Conflict in Latin America*. Chapel Hill, NC: University of North Carolina Press.

Burdick, John Samuel

1993. *Looking for God in Brazil: The Progressive Catholic Church in Urban Brazil's Religious Arena*. Berkeley: University of California Press.

Burkert, Walter

1987. "Offerings in Perspective: Surrender, Distribution, and Exchange." In T. Linders and G. Nordquist, eds., *Gifts to the Gods: Proceedings of the Uppsala*

Symposium 1985, pp. 43–50. Stockholm: Civiltryckerie.

Burns, E. Bradford

1980. *A History of Brazil*, 2d ed. New York: Columbia University Press.

Cabal, Hugo Latorre

1978. *The Revolution of the Latin American Church*. Norman, OK: University of Oklahoma Press.

Callado, Antonio

1984. *Quarup*. Rio de Janeiro: Nova Fronteira.

Campbell-Jones, Suzanne

1980. "Ritual Performance and Interpretation: The Mass in a Convent Setting." In M. F. C. Bourdillon and M. Fortes, eds., *Sacrifice*. London: Academic.

Canin, Eric

1994. "Between Religion and Revolution." Ph.D. Dissertation, Columbia University, New York, NY.

Cardoso, Geraldo

1983. *Negro Slavery in the Sugar Plantations of Veracruz and Pernambuco, 1550–1680: A Comparative Study*. Washington DC: University Press of America.

Clark, Constance Joyce

1991. "Fome e Estratégias de Desenvolvimento: Impactos na População de Baixa Renda na Região Metropolitana do Recife, no Periodo de 1860 a 1980." In *Modernidade e Pobreza, Vol.II; Anais de Quinto Encontro de Ciencias Sociais do Nordeste*, pp. 181–203. Recife: Fundação Joaquim Nabuco.

Clothey, Fred W.

1988. "Toward a Comprehensive Interpretation of Ritual." *Journal of Ritual Studies* 2 (2): 147–161.

Comblín, José

1991. Public lecture, Faculdade de Filosofia do Recife, Pernambuco, Brasil; 10 April.

Cone, James

1970. *God of the Oppressed*. New York: Seabury.

Crites, Stephen

1971. "The Narrative Quality of Experience." *Journal of the American Academy of Religion* 3: 291–311.

da Cunha, Euclydes

1945. *Rebellion in the Backlands*. Chicago: University of Chicago Press.

Dahlberg, Andrea
    1991. "The Body as a Principle of Holism: Three Pilgrimages to Lourdes." In J. Eade and M. Sallnow, eds., *Contesting the Sacred: The Anthropology of Christian Pilgrimage*. London: Routledge.

de Beauvoir, Simone
    1974. *The Second Sex*. New York: Vintage.

de Castro, Jose.
    1969. *Death in the Northeast: Poverty and Revolution in the Northeast of Brazil*. New York: Vintage.

de Kadt, Emanuel
    1970. *Catholic Radicals in Brazil*. New York: Oxford University Press.

Dean, Warren
    1995. *With Broadax and Firebrand: A History of the Brazilian Atlantic Forest*. Berkeley: University of California Press.

Della Cava, Ralph
    1970. *Miracle at Joaseiro*. New York: Columbia University Press.
    1989. "The 'People's Church,' the Vatican, and Abertura." In A. Stepan, ed., *Democratizing Brazil: Problems of Transition and Consolidation*. New York: Oxford University Press.
    1990. "Vatican Policy, 1978–1990: An Overview." Columbia University Institute of Latin American and Iberian Studies, Paper No. 30.
    1991. . . . *É o Verbo se Faz Imagem: Igreja Católica e os Meios de Comunicação no Brasil, 1962–1989*. Petrópolis: Vozes.

Denslow, David
    1987. *Sugar Production in Northeast Brasil and Cuba, 1858–1908*. New York: Garland.

Dilthey, Wilhelm
    1976. *Selected Writings*. Cambridge: Cambridge University Press.

Dix, Gregory
    1954. *The Shape of the Liturgy*. Glasgow, UK: Maclehose.

do Passo Castro, Gustavo
    1987. *As Comunidades do Dom: Un Estudo de CEBs no Recife*. Recife: Massangana.

Douglas, Mary
    1970. *Natural Symbols: Explorations in Cosmology*. New York: Pantheon.
    1984. *Purity and Danger: An Analysis of the Concepts of Pollution and Taboo*. London: Ark.
    1992. *Risk and Blame: Essays in Cultural Theory*. London: Routledge.

Dulles, Avery

1984. "Liberation Theology: Contrasting Types." *America*, September 22: 138–139.

Eade, John, and Michael J. Sallnow, eds.

1991. *Contesting the Sacred: The Anthropology of Christian Pilgrimage.* London: Routledge.

Eisenberg, Peter L.

1979. *The Sugar Industry in Pernambuco: Modernization Without Change, 1840–1910.* Berkeley: University of California Press.

Ellis, Mark

1991. *Toward a Jewish Theology of Liberation: The Uprising and the Future.* Maryknoll, NY: Orbis.

Fallaize, E.N.

1919. "Prayer (Introductory and Primitive)." In *Encyclopedia of Religion and Ethics* 10: 154–158.

Ferme, Dean William

1986. *Third World Liberation Theologies.* Grand Rapids: Eerdmans.

Ferreira, Laurien

1990. "A Guerra Santa no Morro da Conceição." *Veja*, November 12.

Fonseca, Homero, Ricardo Noblat, and Salette Alievi

1977. "O Poder de Frei Damião." *Cadernos do Nordeste* 1(2)/October.

Forman, Sheperd

1975. *The Brazilian Peasantry.* New York: Columbia University Press.

Foroohar, Manzar

1986. "Liberation Theology: The Response of Latin American Catholics to Socioeconomic Problems." *Latin American Perspectives* Vol. 13, No. 3: p. 37–57.

Foucault, Michel

1980. *The History of Sexuality.* Vol. I. New York: Vintage.

Fragoso, Antonio

1982. *O Rosto de uma Igreja.* Sao Paulo: Loyola.

Frank, Andre Gunder

1969. *Capitalism and Underdevelopment in Latin America: Historical Studies of Chile and Brazil.* New York: Monthly Review Press.

Freire, Paulo

1970. *The Pedagogy of the Oppressed.* New York: Herder and Herder.

Freyre, Gilberto

1963. *The Mansions and the Shanties: The Making of Modern Brazil.* New York: Knopf.

Furtado, Celso

  1963. *The Economic Growth of Brazil: A Survey from Colonial to Modern Times*. Berkeley: University of California Press.

Galeano, Eduardo

  1975. *Open Veins of Latin America*. New York: Monthly Review Press.

Genovese, Eugene

  1976. *Roll, Jordan, Roll: The World the Slaves Made*. New York: Pantheon.

Graham, Richard

  1968. *Britain and the Onset of Modernization in Brazil, 1850–1914*. London: Cambridge University Press.

Gross, Daniel

  1971. "Ritual and Conformity: A Religious Pilgrimage to Northeastern Brazil." *Ethnology* 10 (April): 129–148.

Guerra, Lemuel

  1991. "A Reação Neo-Conservadora em Pernambuco." *Modernidade e Pobreza, Vol. I; Anais de Quinto Encontro de Ciencias Sociais do Nordeste*, p. 337–354. Recife: Fundação Joaquim Nabuco.

Gutiérrez, Gustavo

  1973. *The Theology of Liberation*. Maryknoll, NY: Orbis.

Hebblethwaite, Peter

  1989. "Hope, anguish of the people of our time." *National Catholic Reporter*, March 17: p. 15.

Hemming, John

  1978. *Red Gold: The Conquest of the Brazilian Indians*. London: Macmillan.

Herr, William

  1985. "This Our Church." Chicago: Thomas More Association.

Hewitt, Cynthia N.

  1980. "Brazil: The Peasant Movement of Pernambuco, 1961–1964." In H. Landsberger, ed., *Latin American Peasant Movements*. Ithaca: Cornell University Press.

Hewitt, William

  1991. *Base Christian Communities and Social Change in Brazil*. Lincoln: University of Nebraska Press.

Heyward, Carter

  1989. *Touching Our Strength: The Erotic as Power and the Love of God*. San Francisco: HarperCollins.

Hobsbawm, Eric

  1959. *Primitive Rebels: Studies in Archaic Forms of Social Movements in the*

19th and 20th Centuries. New York: W. W. Norton.

Hoornaert, Eduardo

1990. "O Caso de Recife." *Sem Fronteiras*, December: 13–17.

Hubert, Henri, and Marcel Mauss

1964. *Sacrifice: Its Nature and Function*. Chicago: University of Chicago Press.

Huizer, Gerrit

1972. *The Revolutionary Potential of Peasants in Latin America*. Lexington, MA: D.C. Heath.

Ireland, Rowan

1972. "The Catholic Church and Social Change in Brazil: An Evaluation." In R. Roett, ed., *Brazil in the 1960s*. Nashville TN: Vanderbilt University Press.

1991. *Kingdoms Come: Religion and Politics in Brazil*. Pittsburgh: University of Pittsburgh Press.

Keck, Margaret

1992. *The Workers' Party and Democratization in Brazil*. New Haven: Yale University Press

Kertzer, David I.

1988. *Ritual, Politics and Power*. New Haven: Yale University Press.

Klass, Morton

1995. *Ordered Universes: Approaches to the Anthropology of Religion*. Boulder, CO: Westview.

LADOC (Latin American Documentation Service)

1986. "Basic Christian Communities in Argentina." (16)18: March/April, p. 1–6.

Leach, E.R.

1976. *Culture and Communication*. Cambridge: Cambridge University Press.

Lelotte, Fernand.

1947. *Para Realiza a Ação Católica: Princípios e Métodos*. Rio de Janeiro: Agir.

Lernoux, Penny

1979. "Long Path to Puebla." In J. Eagleson and P. Scharper, eds., *Puebla and Beyond*. Maryknoll, NY: Orbis.

1986. *Cry of the People*. New York: Penguin.

1989. *People of God: The Struggle for World Catholicism*. New York: Viking.

Levenson, Jon D.

1991. "Liberation Theology and the Exodus." *Reflections* (Spring): p. 2–12.

Levine, Daniel

1979. "Church Elites in Venezuela and Colombia: Context, Background and Beliefs." *Latin American Research Review*. 14 (1): 51–79.

1992. *Popular Voices in Latin American Catholicism.* Princeton: Princeton University Press.

Levine, Robert

1978. *Pernambuco in the Brazilian Federation 1889–1937.* Stanford: Stanford University Press.

1995. *Vale of Tears: Revisiting the Canudos Massacre in Northeastern Brazil, 1893–1897.* Berkeley: University of California Press.

Lincoln, C. Eric, and Lawrence H. Mamiya

1990. *The Black Church in the African American Experience.* Durham, NC: Duke University Press.

Linger, Daniel

1992. *Dangerous Encounters: Meanings of Violence in a Brazilian City.* Stanford: Stanford University Press.

Lucia, Nara.

1990. "É a Guerra Santa da Igreja Católica." *Jornal do Comércio*, December 30, p. 3.

MacEoin, Gary

1980. *Puebla, A Church Being Born.* New York: Paulist Press.

Mainwaring, Scott

1986. *The Church and Politics in Brazil, 1916–1985.* Stanford: Stanford University Press.

1989. "Grassroots Catholic Groups and Politics in Brazil." In S. Mainwaring, ed., *The Progressive Church in Latin America.* Notre Dame, IN: University of Notre Dame Press.

Mainwaring, Scott, and Daniel Levine

1989. "Religion and Popular Protest in Latin America: Contrasting Experiences." In S. Eckstein, ed., *Power and Popular Protest.* Berkeley: University of California Press.

Mallon, Florencia

1978. "Peasants and Rural Laborers in Pernambuco, 1955–1964." *Latin American Perspectives* 5: 49–70.

Maraschin, Jaci

1988. "Latin American Models of Authority." Talk given at the Trinity Institute Conference, New York City, 21 January.

Mariz, Cecilia Loreto

1994. *Coping with Poverty: Pentecostals and Christian Base Communities in Brazil.* Philadelphia: Temple University Press.

Martin, David

1991. *Tongues of Fire: The Explosion of Protestantism in Latin America*. Oxford: Blackwell.

Mattoso, Katia M. de Queiros

1986. *To Be a Slave in Brazil, 1550–1888*. Rutgers, NJ: Rutgers University Press.

Mernissi, Fatima

1983. "Women, Saints, and Sanctuaries." In E. Abel, ed., *The Signs Reader: Women, Gender and Scholarship*. Chicago: University of Chicago Press.

Mesters, Carlos

1985. *Seis Dias Nos Porões da Humanidade*. Petropolis: Vozes.

Metcalf, Peter

1989. *Where Are You Spirits: Style and Theme in Berawan Prayer*. Washington, DC: Smithsonian Institution Press.

Mettenheim, Kurt von

1995. *The Brazilian Voter: Mass Politics in Democratic Transition, 1974– 1986*. Pittsburgh: University of Pittsburgh Press.

Meyendorff, John

1966. "Notes on the Orthodox Understanding of the Eucharist." In Hans Kung, ed., *The Sacraments: An Ecumenical Dilemma*. New York: Paulist Press.

Mink, Louis

1978. "Narrative Form as a Cognitive Instrument." In R. H. Canary and H. Kozicki, eds., *The Writing of History: Literary Form and Historical Understanding*. Madison: University of Wisconsin Press.

Mintz, Sidney

1985. *Sweetness and Power: The Place of Sugar in Modern History*. New York: Penguin.

Miracapillo, Vito

1985. *A Caso Miracapillo: Conflito Entre o Estado e a Igreja no Brasil*. Recife: Nordestal.

Mitchell, Simon, ed.

1981. *The Logic of Poverty: The Case of the Brazilian Northeast*. London: Routledge & Kegan Paul.

Murphy, John

1994. "Performing a Moral Vision: An Ethnography of Cavalo-Marinho, A Brazilian Musical Drama." Ph.D. dissertation, Columbia University, New York, NY.

Ostling, Richard N.
   1989. "Some Arns-Twisting in Brazil." *International Time Magazine,* June 12, p. 29.
Page, Joseph
   1972. *The Revolution That Never Was: Northeast Brazil 1955–1964.* New York: Grossman.
Palmeira, Moacir
   1978. "The Aftermath of Peasant Mobilization: Rural Conflicts in the Brazilian Northeast Since 1964." In N. Aguiar, ed., *The Structure of Brazilian Development.* New Brunswick, NJ: Transaction Books.
Pang, Eul-Soo
   1973–74. "The Changing Roles of Priets in the Politics of Northeast Brazil, 1889–1964." *The Americas* 30: 341–372.
Pelikan, Jaroslav
   1971. *The Christian Tradition: A History of the Development of Doctrine.* Vol. 1. Chicago: University of Chicago Press.
Porfiro Miranda, Jose
   1981. *Communism in the Bible.* Maryknoll, NY: Orbis.
Pottenger, John R.
   1989. *The Political Theory of Liberation Theology: Toward a Reconvergence of Social Values and Social Science.* Albany, NY: SUNY Press.
Ratzinger, Jospeh
   1966. "Is the Eucharist a Sacrifice?" In Hans Kung, ed., *The Sacraments: An Ecumenical Dilemma.* New York: Paulist Press.
Reis, Jaime
   1981. "Hunger in the Northeast: Some Historical Aspects." In S. Mitchell, ed., *The Logic of Poverty: The Case of the Brazilian Northeast.* London: Routledge & Kegan Paul.
Richter, Klemens
   1990. *The Meaning of the Sacramental Symbols.* Collegeville, MN: Liturgical Press.
Roett, Riordan
   1972. *Brazil in the Sixties.* Nashville TN: Vanderbilt University Press.
Rouillard, Phillipe
   1982. "From Human Meal to Christian Eucharist." In R.K. Seasoltz, ed., *Living Bread, Saving Cup: Readings on the Eucharist.* Collegeville, MN: Liturgical Press.

Sader, Emil and Ken Silverstein

1991. *Without Fear of Being Happy: Lula, the Workers' Party and Brazil*. London: Verso.

Salem, Helen, ed.

1981. *Brasil: A Igreja dos Oprimidos*. São Paulo: Brasil Debates.

Sanchis, Pierre

1983. "The Portuguese 'Romarias.'" In Steven Wilson, ed., *Saints and Their Cults: Studies in Religious Sociology*. Cambridge: Cambridge University Press.

Scheper-Hughes, Nancy

1989. "Death Without Weeping." *Natural History* (October): 8–12.

1990. "The Madness of Hunger." *New Internationalist* (July).

1992. *Death Without Weeping: The Violence of Everyday Life in Brazil*. Berkeley: University of California Press.

Schleiermacher, Friedrich

1988. *Brief Outline of Theology as a Field of Study*. Terrence N. Tice, trans. Lewiston, NY: E. Mellen Press.

Schneider, Ronald M.

1991. *Order and Progress: A Political History of Brazil*. Boulder, CO: Westview.

Shepherd, Massey H.

1965. *At All Times and in All Places*. New York: Seabury.

Slater, Candice

1984. "Representations of Power in Pilgrim Tales from the Brazilian Northeast." *Latin American Research Review* 2: 71–91.

Smith, Brian

1975. "Religion and Social Change: Classical Theories and New Formulations in the Context of Recent Developments in Latin America." *Latin American Research Review* 10 (2): 3–34.

Stein, Stanley, and Barbara H. Stein

1970. *The Colonial Heritage of Latin America: Essay on Economic Dependence in Perspective*. New York: Oxford University Press.

Stepan, Alfred

1988. *Democratizing Brazil: Problems of Transformation and Consolidation*. New York: Oxford University Press.

Thurman, Howard

1949. *Jesus and the Disinherited*. Nashville TN: Abingdon Press.

Turner, Victor

1957. *Schism and Continuity in Everyday Life: A Study of Ndembu Village Life*.

Manchester, England: Manchester University Press.

1978. *Image and Pilgrimage in Christian Culture*. New York: Columbia University Press.

Vallier, Ivan

1970. *Catholicism, Social Control and Modernization in Latin America*. Englewood Cliffs, NJ: Prentice-Hall.

Vargas Llosa, Mario

1984. *The War of the End of the World*. New York: Farrar, Straus & Giroux.

Veloso, Reginaldo

1991. Sermon, Morro da Conceição, 28 August.

n.d. Unpublished manuscript; Recife.

Veloso, Reginaldo, et al.

1990. *Festa do Morro–1990: porque estaremos ausentes*. . . Xeroxed sheet; Recife.

Webb, Kempton

1974. *The Changing Face of Northeast Brazil*. New York: Columbia University Press.

Whitefield, Teresa

1995. *Paying the Price: Ignacio Ellacuría and the Murdered Jesuits of El Salvador*. Philadelphia: Temple University Press.

Wilmore, Guyraud

1983. *Black Religion and Black Radicalism: An Intepretation of the Religious History of Afro-American People*. Maryknoll, NY: Orbis.

Wirpsa, Leslie

1990. "Bishops lack support in poor Colombia church." *National Catholic Reporter*, 27 July: p. 9.

Wolf, Eric and Sidney Mintz

1950. "An Analysis of Ritual Co-Parenthood (Compadrazgo). *Southwestern Journal of Anthropology*. (6)1: 341–68.

Other Sources

Anais Pernambucanos
Diário de Pernambuco
Jornal do Coméricio
Jornal do Recife
Jornal Pequeno

INDEX